New Mexico

Nancy Harbert
Photography by Paul Chesley, Michael Freeman, and Kerrick James

COMPASS AMERICAN GUIDES
An imprint of Fodor's Travel Publications

Compass American Guides: New Mexico

Editors: Kristin Moehlmann and John Morrone
Designer: Siobhan O'Hare
Compass Editorial Director: Daniel Mangin
Compass Senior Editor: Kristin Moehlmann
Compass Creative Director: Fabrizio La Rocca
Editorial Production: Linda Schmidt
Photo Editor and Archival Researcher: Melanie Marin
Map Design: Mark Stroud, Moon Street Cartography

Cover photo by Kerrick James: Gila Cliff Dwellings National Monument
Copyright © 2004 Fodors LLC
Maps copyright © 2004 Fodors LLC

The details in this book are based on information supplied to us at press time, but changes occur all the time, and the publisher cannot accept responsibility for facts that become outdated or for inadvertent errors or omissions.

Fifth Edition
ISBN 1–4000–1393–3

Compass American Guides, 1745 Broadway, New York, NY 10019
PRINTED IN CHINA
10 9 8 7 6 5 4 3 2 1

To Jessica and Jack Harbert.

C O N T E N T S

Maps

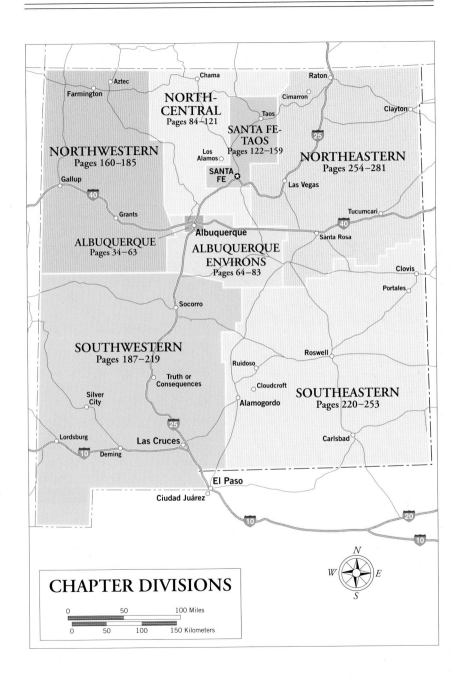

Chama

Raton

Aztec

Farmington

Cimarron

Clayton

NORTH-CENTRAL
Pages 84–121

Taos

SANTA FE-TAOS
Pages 122–159

25

NORTHWESTERN
Pages 160–185

Los Alamos

NORTHEASTERN
Pages 254–281

SANTA FE

Las Vegas

Gallup

40

Grants

Tucumcari

40

ALBUQUERQUE
Pages 34–63

Albuquerque

Santa Rosa

ALBUQUERQUE ENVIRONS
Pages 64–83

Clovis

Portales

Socorro

SOUTHWESTERN
Pages 187–219

Roswell

Ruidoso

Truth or Consequences

Silver City

Cloudcroft

SOUTHEASTERN
Pages 220–253

Alamogordo

25

Lordsburg

Las Cruces

Carlsbad

10

Deming

El Paso

Ciudad Juárez

10

20

10

N
W E
S

CHAPTER DIVISIONS

0   50   100 Miles

0   50   100   150 Kilometers

Topical Essays

Literary Excerpts

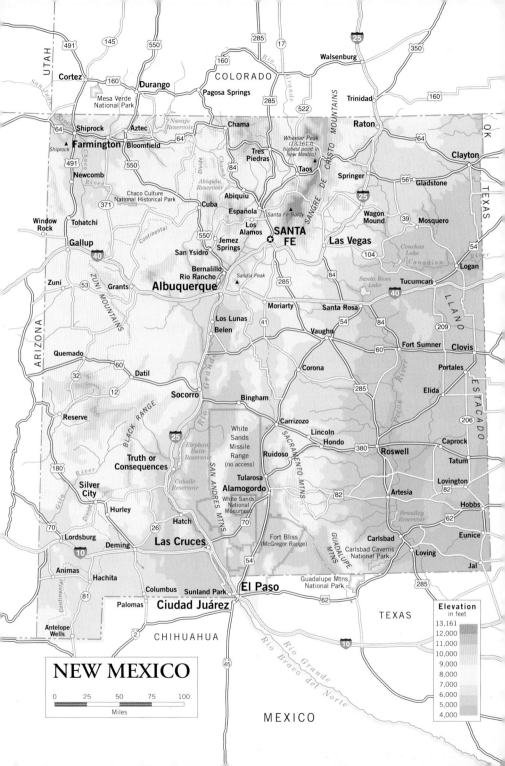

OVERVIEW

ALBUQUERQUE

New Mexico's largest city, **Albuquerque** flanks the Rio Grande, stretching between the petroglyph-etched boulders of the **Seven Sisters** and the tawny red slopes of the **Sandia Mountains.** Museums and galleries reflect the city's rich history and its long-established ethnic mix of Native American, Anglo, and Hispanic. In historic **Old Town,** 300-year-old adobe buildings line the narrow streets, and the smell of hot tortillas wafts from restaurants on the old Plaza.

NORTH-CENTRAL, SANTA FE, AND TAOS

Edged by the rugged **Sangre de Cristo** and **San Juan Mountains** and the softer **Jemez Range,** north-central New Mexico contains much that has made the state famous. **Santa Fe,** the capital city and birthplace of Southwestern style and cuisine, attracted painter Georgia O'Keeffe, who admired the brilliant light. She later immortalized the purplish brown sandstone cliffs at **Abiquiu,** as well as **Taos Pueblo,** a multistoried adobe structure occupied since 1350. The low-key, high-altitude town of **Taos** draws artists and skiers.

NORTHWESTERN NEW MEXICO

American Indian influence is greater here than anywhere in the state. About a thousand years ago, the Anasazi built massive rock and mortar buildings like **Pueblo Bonito** in **Chaco Canyon.** Today, much of the land belongs to the Navajo, Apache, and Pueblo peoples; the town of **Gallup** is the heart of American Indian country. The region's landscape of sandstone bluffs and meadows is punctuated by the **Bisti/De-na-zin Wilderness,** a dreamscape of mushroom-shaped stones, and **Shiprock,** a jagged, vertical shaft towering 7,000 feet above the desert.

SOUTHWESTERN NEW MEXICO

In this wild and beautiful corner of the state may be found cactus prairie, forested mountains, and, farther south, vast stretches of desolate desert basins. Old railroad towns like **Deming** line what is today Interstate 10; to the north, historic mining towns like **Silver City** lie in the foothills of the **Mogollon Mountains,** where centuries ago Indians built cliff dwellings. The **Rio Grande** divides the state's southwestern and southeastern regions.

SOUTHEASTERN NEW MEXICO

Most of southeastern New Mexico is made up of vast prairies and sandy desert—the latter notably at **White Sands National Monument. Lincoln National Forest,** with its pine-covered mountains and the resort town of **Ruidoso,** which hugs the Rio Ruidoso, stands out here. The area's major attraction, **Carlsbad Caverns,** is a 3-mile maze of vaulted rooms "furnished" with draperies and grand obelisks of stone.

NORTHEASTERN NEW MEXICO

Here in the high plains, windmills and ranch houses dot the grama grasslands, where cattle outnumber people. The otherwise flat landscape is interrupted by a

few ancient cinder cones, including **Capulin Volcano,** not far from the Colorado border. At the foot of the **Sangre de Cristo Mountains** is **Las Vegas,** a repository of Victorian architectural styles, thanks to a wave of high-minded 19th-century settlers.

INTRODUCTION

New Mexico's magic has intrigued visitors for centuries. Its natural beauty immediately captivates those who see it, and its elusive, indefinable character enriches those who take it to heart. Spacious skies and vistas, bewitching plays of light, and a sense of purity have attracted travelers, settlers, artists, and scientists, who have come in search of treasures tangible and intangible.

In prehistoric times, Native Americans hunted game in New Mexico's mountains and farmed along its riverbanks. Pueblo Indians expressed their reverential relationship with the land through flat-roofed earthen architecture, drawings on rock faces, and rhythmic chants and dances. Spanish explorers followed, first in search of gold, then souls. The two cultures clashed, often violently. Over time, however, they came to tolerate each other and even to share their traditions. Pueblo

The Rio Grande.

Indians passed on their innovative uses for chile, beans, and corn, the main ingredients of what has come to be known, somewhat ironically, as Mexican food. The Spanish passed on their skill at metalwork, which the Indians employed in the creation of intricate jewelry.

In the latter half of the 19th century, determined groups of "Anglo" settlers from the eastern United States began to arrive via the Santa Fe Trail, bringing to New Mexico a third culture—Victorian in much of its taste, and technologically emerging. In the early 20th century, a new wave of immigrants of Italian, Lebanese, German, Irish, and Russian descent—also "Anglos," in New Mexican parlance—came to set up shops or work in mines across the state. The Anglos may have been the last of the three main cultural groups to arrive, but they became the most influential. They mined the mountains for gold and precious metals, and uncovered vast deposits of coal, oil, and natural gas. They brought the railroad and the highway, and developed the atomic bomb. Some sought to capture New Mexico's fascination and appeal—on canvas, in photographs, in their souls.

White Sands National Monument.

The state's Spanish community, once made up mainly of descendants of the original settlers who came via Mexico, has expanded to include thousands of new immigrants from Central and South America. Through their longstanding traditions, today's Hispanics contribute a vitality and sensuality intrinsic to New Mexico's mystique. Religion still permeates this culture, and nearly every town honors its patron saint annually in an exuberant fiesta. The same sensibility carries through in the imperfect sloping walls of adobe buildings, hand-punched tinwork, and strains of melodic *corridas* (love songs) that waft from open doorways. Carved *bultos* and intricately painted *retablos* once adorned only church altars and walls, but now are found in gift shops, galleries, and artists' studios.

Today, New Mexico's Indians are apt to straddle two worlds: teaching math to fifth-graders or arguing First Amendment rights before a federal judge during the week, then returning to the reservation on weekends to exchange their buttoned-down clothes for body paint and moccasins and participate in traditional dances.

The state's landscape is as varied as its cultures. The Rio Grande is the lifeblood for much of this arid land, and serves as the natural east-west dividing line as it snakes through the mountainous north and provides the lifeline for the agricultural southwest before flowing into Texas at El Paso. Away from the river, pine and spruce forests blanket much of northern New Mexico. There you'll find pristine trout streams, bountiful hunting grounds, and world-class ski slopes. A small section of the vast Navajo Reservation covers the northwestern corner of the state and continues into neighboring Arizona. In the southwest is the 3.3-million-acre Gila National Forest, once the home of the Mimbres Indians, known for their distinctive black-on-white pottery. Southeast of the mountains lies the irrigated Mesilla Valley, with acres of green chiles, cotton, and onions.

On the vast plains of eastern New Mexico, lumbering herds of cattle and bands of sheep share windswept grasslands. Dryland farming has prospered in pockets of the Llano Estacado (Staked Plain), a western extension of the Great Plains that covers much of this part of the state. To the west rise the Sacramento Mountains, home to the Mescalero Apaches. Underground at Carlsbad Caverns, one of the world's greatest natural wonders is arrayed in a series of massive chambers beneath a limestone ridge.

New Mexico's cities are small, with the exception of Albuquerque, which holds one-third of the state's people and serves as its economic and educational center. A cursory glance might not distinguish it from any other sprawling Western metropolis, but most residents agree it's an unusually congenial place to live: traffic jams are few, winters are mild and summers dry, and friendly smiles abound.

Sixty miles north of Albuquerque, the state capital, Santa Fe, huddles in the shelter of the Sangre de Cristo Mountains. Here, narrow streets wind among adobe buildings that are centuries old, and dirt roads are considered assets in the city's nicer neighborhoods. Students of acupuncture, massage, and natural healing live among longtime Hispanic residents and Indian artisans. On the outskirts, a first-class opera company performs in an elegant, state-of-the-art theater.

It's not a coincidence that New Mexico is known as the Land of Enchantment. The spells it casts are many and varied. For those who haven't yet experienced it, all it takes is to step within its borders to enter New Mexico's magical embrace.

H I S T O R Y

The landscape we now call New Mexico has not always appeared as it does today; long before humans made their way to the area, it went through many changes. In the Paleozoic Era, some 570 million to 245 million years ago, shallow seas extended over the nearly 122,000 square miles covered by the present state. When the waters receded they left behind brachiopods, trilobites, corals, and crinoid stems, now found fossilized in limestone and shale. In southeastern New Mexico, the Capitan Reef grew to surround the 10,000-square-mile Delaware Basin. That sea, too, is long gone, but vast deposits of oil and gas remain, along with gypsum, potash, and salt. During this time volcanic explosions created mountain ranges and coated the earth with layers of lava that hardened into a jagged black landscape.

Some 80 million years ago, the Rocky Mountains jutted into existence, their southern end spilling into northern New Mexico. As the seas dried up, parts of the state assumed a lunar appearance defined by rugged peaks and vast plains covered with boulders and gravel. Warm-blooded species—camels, bears, large cats, and wild dogs—replaced the dinosaurs.

Then as now, two fault zones cut across New Mexico from north to south. About 25 million years ago, mounting tension between the faults caused a long sliver of the Earth's crust to drop down and create a chasm. This trough, known as the Rio Grande Rift, would eventually carry the waters of the Rio Grande from its headwaters in the Colorado Rockies 1,885 miles to the Gulf of Mexico. The western side of the rift, where the crust had been stretched thin, erupted with violent volcanic explosions, one of which created the Jemez Mountains, centered by the Valle Grande caldera, 12 miles in diameter. Volcanoes also erupted along fissures in other parts of the state, forming Capulin, a near-perfect cylindrical cinder cone east of Raton in northeastern New Mexico, and El Malpais (literally, "the Badlands"), miles of hardened lava flows south of Grants. Such widespread vulcanism left behind rich deposits of copper, lead, zinc, and other minerals throughout the region, as well as numerous geothermal pockets, some of which bubble to the surface as hot springs to this day.

El Malpais National Monument and Conservation Area.

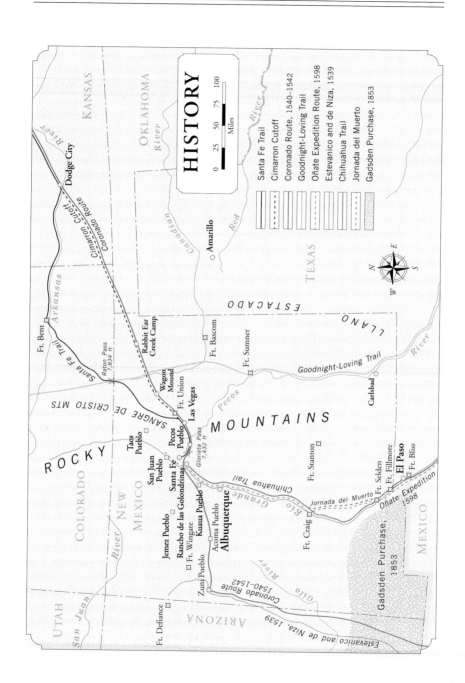

HISTORY

Miles
0   25   50   75   100

Santa Fe Trail
Cimarron Cutoff
Coronado Route, 1540-1542
Goodnight-Loving Trail
Oñate Expedition Route, 1598
Estevanico and de Niza, 1539
Chihuahua Trail
Jornada del Muerto
Gadsden Purchase, 1853

During the ice ages that began two million years ago, glaciers covered the state's highest mountains and spread as far south as present-day Sierra Blanca. Later, melting waters filled basins in closed valleys and created large lakes in southern and central New Mexico. One of these, Lake Lucero, evaporated, and winds blew its gypsum sediments into 50-foot drifts now known as White Sands. When the first human visitors arrived, as early as 20,000 years ago, it's probable that glaciers still shrouded the mountaintops and a few active volcanoes could be heard blowing their tops.

■ EARLY INHABITANTS

Grasslands and forests covered much of New Mexico when big-game hunters arrived tracking the mammoth, mastodon, sloth, bison, antelope, camel, and horse that had been driven south by the movement of ice-age glaciers across much of the continent. These early hunters chipped scrapers and spear points from flint, obsidian, jasper, and chert, then staked out their prey at watering holes.

About 12,000 years ago, the Clovis people routinely pursued the giant bison throughout southeastern New Mexico. Hundreds of miles away in the Sandia Mountains, the Sandia people, who historians say were unrelated to the Clovis, hunted the same animals. The Folsom people, who appeared in northeastern New Mexico a thousand years later, crafted spear points up to three inches long and more finely honed than those of the Clovis or Sandia cultures. Mysteriously, no bones of any of these early people have been found—only the skeletons of prey pierced with their weapons.

As the glaciers dissolved amid steadily rising temperatures, New Mexico dried out. Piñon and juniper forests thinned, drought-resistant grama grass replaced lush grasslands, and cactus, mesquite, and creosote bush prospered. Lakes near present-day Estancia and Lordsburg evaporated. Mastodons and mammoths died out, their extinction hastened perhaps by disease, lack of food, and overzealous hunters.

■ THE INDIANS

The big-game hunters moved on—most likely to the Great Plains, where smaller animals could be pursued for food—and were succeeded by the hunters of the Desert Culture, who spread across western New Mexico beginning in A.D. 900. Stalking elk, deer, antelope, turkey, and rodents, they also fished in streams and

gathered nuts, berries, seeds, and the thirst-quenching fruit of cactus. Noticing that seeds left in place grew into plants, these people soon added farming to their hunting and gathering. Later, because it was easier to care for crops by staying in one place, they established permanent settlements.

The Desert Culture spawned two primary groups. In southwestern New Mexico, the Mogollon gained agricultural skills from their neighbors to the south, in present-day Mexico, learning how to cultivate corn, squash, and beans, as well as how to fashion pottery. (One branch, the Mimbres Indians, developed exquisitely stylized black-on-white pottery designs, based on bird and animal shapes and meticulous geometric patterns.) The Mogollon's first homes were oval pits dug four feet into the earth, covered with timber and dirt roofs. Built close together, these pit houses formed villages.

In northwestern New Mexico, the Anasazi culture borrowed agricultural and pottery techniques from the Mogollon, but developed more slowly. At the society's peak, however, the Anasazi displayed a sophistication far beyond that of their predecessors. By A.D. 900–1000, they were living in stone dwellings cut into the sides of high cliffs and in freestanding, multistoried apartment complexes of finely fitting rock slabs held together with mud mortar. At Chaco Canyon, they designed a system of dams and ditches that directed the flow of water into fields, and built roads to connect far-flung pueblos. Men wore ornamental jewelry made of shell, turquoise, and other gemstones, and women wove textiles from cotton they grew in their fields. These ingenious people were the ancestors of today's Pueblo Indians.

Between A.D. 1000 and 1500, Athabascan-speaking tribes, including the Navajos and Apaches, began making their way down from Canada into the Southwest. Decidedly different from the sedentary, agrarian Pueblo Indians, the nomadic Navajos were adept traders, exchanging baskets, animal hides, and jerky with the Pueblos for corn, cotton cloth, and turquoise. Eventually, the Navajos learned from the Pueblo Indians how to grow corn, beans, squash, and melons; and after the Spanish introduced sheep and goats, they drove small herds across the countryside. Families lived in clustered hogans—circular mud-plastered dwellings—but villages as we think of them did not develop and the Navajos never completely gave up their wandering ways.

Voices from the past at Boca Negra Canyon in Petroglyph National Monument.

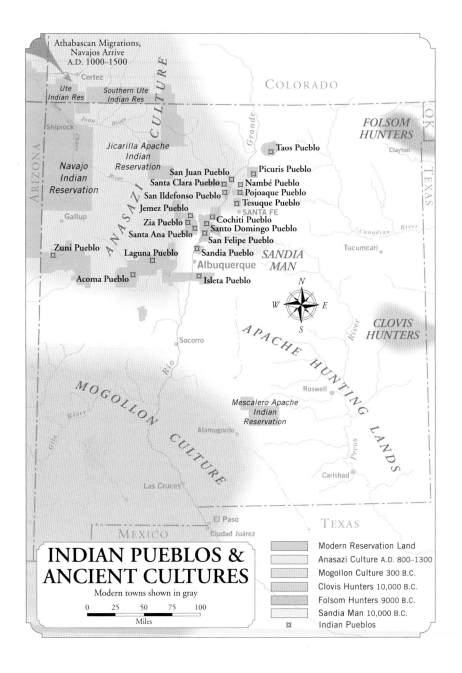

Athabascan Migrations,
Navajos Arrive
A.D. 1000–1500

Cortez

Ute
Indian Res

Southern Ute
Indian Res

COLORADO

ANASAZI CULTURE

FOLSOM
HUNTERS

Clayton

Shiprock

San Juan River

Chaco River

Grande

ARIZONA

Jicarilla Apache
Indian
Reservation

Navajo
Indian
Reservation

Taos Pueblo

Picuris Pueblo

San Juan Pueblo
Santa Clara Pueblo
San Ildefonso Pueblo
Jemez Pueblo

Nambé Pueblo
Pojoaque Pueblo
Tesuque Pueblo

SANTA FE

OK

TEXAS

Gallup

Zia Pueblo
Santa Ana Pueblo

Cochiti Pueblo
Santo Domingo Pueblo
San Felipe Pueblo

Canadian River

Tucumcari

Zuni Pueblo

Laguna Pueblo

Sandia Pueblo
Albuquerque

SANDIA
MAN

Acoma Pueblo

Isleta Pueblo

N
W   E
S

CLOVIS
HUNTERS

River

APACHE HUNTING LANDS

Socorro

MOGOLLON CULTURE

Rio

Roswell

Mescalero Apache
Indian
Reservation

River

Gila

Alamogordo

Pecos

Las Cruces

Carlsbad

El Paso

MEXICO

Ciudad Juárez

TEXAS

INDIAN PUEBLOS &
ANCIENT CULTURES

Modern towns shown in gray

0   25   50   75   100

Miles

Modern Reservation Land
Anasazi Culture A.D. 800–1300
Mogollon Culture 300 B.C.
Clovis Hunters 10,000 B.C.
Folsom Hunters 9000 B.C.
Sandia Man 10,000 B.C.
Indian Pueblos

The Apaches, who never considered themselves a single tribe, separated into bands upon their arrival and staked out their territory. The Mescalero Apaches remained within southeastern New Mexico; the Jicarilla Apaches wandered across northern New Mexico and southern Colorado; and the Chiricahuas, who were later renowned for their fighting skills, roamed throughout southwestern New Mexico and southeastern Arizona. Like the Navajos, the Apaches hunted bison and deer and gathered roots, nuts, and berries. Broad-faced with high cheekbones and a muscular physique, they lived in thatched wickiups and animal-skin tepees. The Mescalero women roasted the flesh of the mescal plant (an agave cactus also known as a century plant) and wove baskets from its fibers; they tanned buckskin and buffalo hides into silky smooth shirts and knee-high boots for the men and straight shifts decorated with beads for themselves.

Meanwhile, Pueblo culture was thriving, settled and sophisticated. The Spanish explorers who arrived in the 16th century found nearly 80 pueblos scattered along the Rio Grande and along adjacent streams to the west.

■ Spanish Explorers

It was the lure of gold and silver that initially drew Spanish explorers to New Mexico. In 1521, after they had conquered the great Aztec empire of Mexico, Spanish officials in New Spain, as Mexico then was called, heard rumors from the Aztecs about the existence of seven cities of gold in the uncharted lands to the north. The story wasn't too different from a familiar Spanish legend, dating from the 8th century, in which seven bishops, fleeing Spain after it was conquered by the Moors, sailed westward until they reached a land where each set up a church and each church became fabulously wealthy. The legend told of streets paved in gold, houses bedecked with sapphires and turquoise, and natives so weighted in diamonds and other valuable minerals they could hardly walk.

Such similarities between the Spanish and Aztec myths propelled the conquistadors northward, and in 1539 a party of adventurers went looking for the seven cities. They were led by Fray Marcos de Niza and an extraordinary Moorish slave named Estevanico (who had survived the wreck of a Spanish ship off the coast of Florida and made his way to Mexico by convincing hostile Indians he encountered that he was a god). Estevanico and a small band of associates went ahead of the de Niza party as an advance scout, with instructions to send back crosses to signal their discoveries—small ones representing insignificant finds and large ones for discoveries of value. Before the main party had entered New Mexico, a cross "as high as a man" returned via messengers to the friar. The expedition hurried ahead, only to learn that Estevanico had been killed upon entering Hawikuh, a Zuni village. Undaunted, de Niza proceeded, but was refused entry to the pueblo, forcing him to view it from afar. His account to Antonio de Mendoza, viceroy of New Spain, told of terraced stone houses in a settlement comprising seven villages, the total larger than Mexico City.

Within a year, on February 22, 1540, Francisco Vásquez de Coronado went forth from Compostela, New Spain, leading a slow-moving caravan of 336 horsemen (equipped with 559 horses), some of their wives and families, a few priests, and 100 Indians who tended small herds of cattle and sheep. Six months later, the entourage arrived at Hawikuh only to find small villages of mud huts. Hawikuh's reputation had been wildly exaggerated.

Disappointed but not discouraged, Coronado headed east and wintered at Alcanfor, known later as Kuaua, a pueblo on the Rio Grande near present-day Bernalillo. The following spring, he continued his eastward drive, this time in search of Quivira, described by a Pawnee slave as another rich land with gold-paved streets and golden water jugs. Coronado's journey took his party far afield: they ended up near Lyons, Kansas, at the grass huts of the Wichita Indians. A copper plate hung around the neck of the tribe's chief, and no gold was in sight. Furious with the Pawnee's deception, Coronado ordered him executed, then returned to Alcanfor across the plains of eastern New Mexico. After another winter there, the expedition returned empty-handed to New Spain, where Coronado stood trial for defrauding his country of immeasurable wealth and of abusing the natives. He was cleared, but never recovered his pride or his status, and died in 1556 a broken man.

■ SPANISH SETTLERS

Despite their curiosity about the lands north of New Spain, the Spanish made no attempt to settle New Mexico until the Juan de Oñate expedition in 1598. Oñate, the son of a wealthy Zacatecas miner, led a caravan consisting of 83 *carretas*, or oxcarts, 129 soldiers, 7,000 head of cattle, a handful of clergy, and 400 settlers, some with families. Following the Rio Grande northward, the weary travelers encountered one pueblo after another, receiving the wide-eyed stares and forced hospitality of Indians whose lives would forever be changed by these newcomers.

Coronado party arrives in New Mexico. Mural by Gerald Cassidy, 1921.

Six months after they left Mexico, the thirsty, ragged, and demoralized colonists came to an arable river valley near the confluence of the Rio Grande and Chama River. With the slate-blue Sangre de Cristo Mountains as a distant backdrop, construction began on San Gabriel, New Mexico's first capital. Nearby, residents of San Juan Pueblo guardedly observed the Spaniards, many of whom were disappointed to find no gold jewelry accenting the Indians' simple clothing.

Leaving the settlers behind, Oñate and his men fanned outward from San Gabriel, claiming the far reaches of the state for the Spanish Crown. But the gold-crazed colonists, instead of working the soil and planning for a future, spent their time searching for precious metals. They failed to find any, and returned to New Spain, having been unsuccessful as both farmers and miners. Even Oñate admitted defeat; on October 7, 1604, he, too, left.

Six years later, Pedro de Peralta led a second group of settlers into the area. With dreams of riches now tempered, he chose a high valley tucked into the shadows of the Sangre de Cristo Mountains alongside a narrow stream. De Peralta named the

Jornada del Muerto

There's a stretch of desert in southwestern New Mexico that most early explorers wished they'd never seen. This 90-mile-long expanse of sandy prairie strewn with spiny mesquite trees, black grama grass, and creosote bush starts north of Las Cruces and ends south of Socorro. It has earned its name, *Jornada del Muerto,* or "Journey of Death." Luckily today no one will double dare you to cross it, because a portion of it is within the confines of White Sands Missile Range, off limits to adventuresome travelers seeking to relive the horrors of the past.

But in the 17th century, Spanish expeditions regularly crossed this near-waterless portion of El Camino Real. They had the option of taking a more circuitous route, thick with deep arroyos and dense vegetation along the Rio Grande, but most opted for the Jornada, a shortcut that departed from the river at a certain point, to return to it later. It was more direct, easier on their wagons, and could save a few days' time. But it had its perils: in addition to the absence of water, temperatures ranged from daytime highs of 100 degrees Fahrenheit in summer to nighttime lows of 20 degrees below zero in winter. Then there were the Apaches. Unlike the Europeans, they knew the location of every water hole. They also knew when the travelers would be at their weariest and most susceptible to attack.

The first Spaniard to cross the Jornada was Juan de Oñate, when he set out in 1598 to colonize New Mexico. The day before he headed into the unknown desert, an ominous incident occurred—one of his men, Pedro Robledo, died and was buried at the base of a mountain that today bears his name. Undaunted, the explorer and his company left the Rio Grande Valley behind as scheduled, hoping to curve their way back to the river. They did make their way back, but not for many miles; they were kept from the Rio Grande by the Caballo and Fra Cristobal mountain ranges to the west, forcing a detour that proved to be lacking in water and deadly.

Within a day, water ran short and animals began to die. The party crept along, spread out for miles. On the evening of the second day, a resourceful dog in all likelihood saved the expedition when it returned to camp with mud on its paws and muzzle. Its paw prints in the sand led one soldier to a nearby spring, which he named *Los Charcos del Perrillo,* "the Pools of the Little Dog." This site became a regular stop on the trail for future travelers, and its name was shortened to Perrillo.

Refreshed, the settlers forged on, and after a few days they arrived—exhausted, dehydrated, and certainly dispirited—at present-day Socorro. Oñate spied the sun-dried adobe walls of Pilabo, a Piro pueblo, where he found long-haired men and women planting fields of corn, beans, and squash. They were probably startled at his unkempt appearance, but he nevertheless convinced them to provide corn and water for himself and the other hungry travelers.

After Santa Fe was settled in 1610, the Chihuahua Trail became a major trade route between Chihuahua, New Spain, and the New Mexico capital, but the Jornada remained certainly the most dreaded portion of the trip. Apaches, increasingly upset by the invasion of their territory, stepped up their attacks, and this godforsaken expanse claimed many lives. Even Oñate's family wasn't spared. During a return trip to Chihuahua, his son was killed in an Indian ambush.

After the Pueblo Revolt of 1680, an estimated 2,500 colonists fled from the Indians. On their trek across the Jornada del Muerto—unfortunately the escape route of choice—nearly 600 Spaniards died before help reached them a few miles north of Perrillo.

Throughout the centuries that followed, Indian raids continued to be the major hazard along the trail. In response, Fort Craig was built at its northern end in 1854 and Fort Selden at its southern end in 1865. After the railroad arrived in the early 1880s, paralleling the trail, nobody with any sense crossed the feared Jornada any other way.

---

new capital La Villa Real de la Santa Fé de San Francisco de Asís, ultimately shortened to Santa Fe (Holy Faith). An able administrator, de Peralta marked municipal boundaries, assigned house and garden lots to colonists, and supervised the construction of government offices using forced Indian labor.

As the capital took shape, church officials wasted no time imposing a theocracy, extolling the virtues of God and the Catholic church among their new neighbors. For the next 70 years, 250 Franciscan friars circulated among the pueblos, converting the Indians and compelling them to adopt a Spanish lifestyle. Indian men were required to wear pants and shirts and Indian women to wear skirts and blouses. Christian wedding ceremonies prevailed, and marriages became monogamous. Indians were forced to construct large mission churches, the men cutting and hauling logs for roof beams, the women and children laying adobe bricks, which they plastered with mud and whitewashed with gypsum. The Indians also labored in the missions' workshops, barns, vegetable gardens, and orchards.

By 1680, exasperated by the destruction of their culture, the Pueblo Indians moved to expel the Spanish intruders from their land. On August 10 they attacked settlers, burned mission churches, destroyed holy statues, and killed priests at their altars. Led by Popé, a medicine man from San Juan Pueblo, the angry Indians proved too much for the unprepared Spanish, who surrendered the capital 12 days later and marched—frightened and defeated—south to El Paso.

For the next 12 years, the Spanish shied away from New Mexico, reevaluating their position on the unruly province. Was it worth the cost? By 1692, they had decided it was, and chose Diego de Vargas to recapture it. After two attempts, the capital was reclaimed, never again to fall into Indian hands.

To ensure harmony, the Spanish made concessions to the Indians. They would no longer destroy their sacred objects or punish those who did not attend church. Throughout the 18th century, the Spanish and Pueblo Indians lived a cooperative existence, accepting their differences and even sharing farming, weaving, jewelry-making, and carving techniques. With the province secure, more colonists traveled by caravan north on the Camino Real, also known as the Chihuahua Trail, a 533-mile trade route that connected the Mexican city of Chihuahua with Santa Fe and was—because the Spanish Crown prohibited Santa Fe from trading with the United States—the only trade route out of New Mexico.

Lured by vast tracts of land, these homesteaders lived in small settlements and grew corn, wheat, beans, chiles, and cotton, and grazed cattle and sheep. The life was basic and the work was hard, made even more challenging by surprise attacks of Apache, Comanche, Navajo, and Ute Indians, who usually made off with live-stock and occasionally captured or killed settlers.

■ UNDER MEXICAN RULE

When Mexico gained its independence from Spain in 1821, it took New Mexico with it. Little changed, except that Mexican leaders allowed Santa Fe to trade with the United States. This new situation proved a lucky break for William Becknell, a famed Indian fighter who arrived in New Mexico amidst its independence celebra-tions, laden with the brightly colored cloth, kettles, knives, and looking glasses he hoped to exchange with Indians. Instead, the Missouri trader promptly sold his wares to Spanish settlers in Santa Fe and quickly returned to Missouri for more. From this beginning, the Santa Fe Trail was born.

At first, the trail was used by daring tradesmen, who hauled tools, cloth, shoes, and nails across the prairie. But once word spread of a new frontier, New Mexico became a new destination for Anglo settlers from the United States.

For 25 years, Mexico ruled the territory from afar. Although Mexican officials regarded Anglos with suspicion, they took a hands-off approach, for the most part allowing the New Mexico governor to run the show. In 1846, war broke out between Mexico and the United States, the culmination of a disagreement over the U.S. annexation of Texas the year before, which Mexico refused to recognize. Aggravating the situation was the growing expansionist movement in the United States led by the president, James Polk, who coveted New Mexico and California and was intent on acquiring them.

President Polk charged Gen. Stephen Watts Kearny with the task of seizing these areas, but he was warned not to frighten their residents. With the support of 1,600 troops, Kearny crossed the Santa Fe Trail's Mountain Branch, which wound into Colorado before dropping into New Mexico. He met no resistance at Las Vegas, where, on August 15, 1846, he announced from a rooftop that New Mexico was now part of the United States. On August 18, he peaceably claimed the capital, Santa Fe, for his homeland, promising its citizens that their property rights would be respected and that their new country would protect them from hostile Indians.

A month later, Kearny moved on to California, leaving behind a portion of his Army of the West to manage the transfer of authority to the Americans and appointing trader Charles Bent as New Mexico's first U.S. governor.

Not everyone in New Mexico wanted to be an American, however. In mid-January 1847, on a visit to his home in Taos, Governor Bent was scalped and killed by an angry mob of colonists and Indians. The insurgents were trapped swiftly inside a mission church at Taos Pueblo. A bloody battle ended with the rebels' capture, followed by speedy trials and executions of their leaders. Opposition to the new government was effectively quashed.

For the next year, New Mexicans lived by American rules, although they did not officially become part of the United States until 1848, when the signing of the Treaty of Guadalupe-Hidalgo ended the war. Even then, the southwestern corner of the state remained part of Mexico until the Gadsden Purchase in 1853 bought for the U.S. the fertile fields of the Mesilla Valley and the cactus-pocked desert west of the Rio Grande.

■ THE ANGLOS

Across the Santa Fe Trail they came, each with an agenda: German-Jewish merchants eager to take advantage of a wide-open market; a French bishop, Jean

Baptiste Lamy, prepared to lead the territory's Catholic church; and lawyers seeking to snatch up New Mexico's valuable land and gain a foothold in its fledgling political arena. Military officials erected forts across the territory, honoring Kearny's promise to protect its citizens. In addition to providing a refuge from marauding Apaches, Comanches, Navajos, and Utes, these army posts also helped to secure stagecoach routes through the Southwest. When the Civil War broke out in 1861, New Mexico found itself in the middle of the conflict: Mesilla Valley settlers identified with the Confederates, but northern residents sided with the Yankees. Officially, the territory remained affiliated with the Union.

In February 1862, Brig. Gen. Henry Sibley led a small Confederate army of 2,600 men up the Rio Grande. The soldiers met little resistance until they reached Valverde, a tree-shaded ford on the Rio Grande. Here, on February 21, Sibley was greeted by 3,800 Union troops led by the West Point pal who had served as best man at his wedding: Col. Edward Canby, commander of federal forces in New Mexico. Brandishing squirrel rifles, double-barrel shotguns, pistols, and Bowie knives, the rebels charged across the river, overrunning the inexperienced Union troops. By day's end, Canby's troops were retreating south toward Fort Craig. Sibley led his men northward and hoisted the Confederate flag above defenseless Albuquerque and Santa Fe. Both cities were devoid of troops, which had shifted north to join forces with Fort Union soldiers and a group of Colorado Volunteers.

A month later, at Glorieta Pass, a wide swath of grassland bordered at both ends by steep cliffs, Sibley's army was outsmarted. Maj. John Chivington and a group of Colorado Volunteers crept behind Confederate lines, destroyed ammunition supplies, burned 73 wagons, and killed 600 horses and mules. Often referred to as the Gettysburg of the West, this battle marked the beginning of New Mexico's expulsion of Confederate troops. Canby and his regrouped army gave chase to the retreating Sibley until the Confederates slipped out of the territory.

While Union and Confederate soldiers were preoccupied with the Civil War, New Mexico's Indians stepped up their raids on settlers, driving off their sheep and cattle. They met little resistance until Gen. James Carlton and his California Column arrived in 1862. After enlisting the help of Col. Kit Carson (who had been a federal Indian agent and spoke various Indian languages) to negotiate with the Navajos, the general rounded up 400 Mescalero Apaches in southern New Mexico and moved them to the new Bosque Redondo Reservation, which spread along the banks of the Pecos River near Fort Sumner, a new installation built to supervise the Indians' relocation. Carlton's misbegotten idea was that the Apaches—warriors and hunters whose nomadic way of life was integral to their identity—would somehow agreeably settle down to new lives as farmers.

Over in western New Mexico and eastern Arizona, Kit Carson was unable to make peace with the semi-nomadic Navajos. His response to their recalcitrance was to wage a campaign in which his men relentlessly burned hogans and butchered sheep, chopped down peach trees and destroyed cornfields. Weakened and demoralized, the Indians acquiesced finally in 1864 and agreed to relocate to Bosque Redondo. What followed was the "Long Walk," in which more than 8,000 Navajos trudged across 300 miles of desert covered with yucca, cholla cactus, and hardened lava beds. This brutal march so affected the Indians that they date historical events according to whether they occurred before or after the Long Walk.

Once on the reservation, the Navajos failed to mix well with the Apaches, their historic enemies. Both tribes resented their imprisonment. Disease ravaged their ranks, and parasites destroyed their crops. A few years later, General Carlton admitted failure. In 1868, the Navajos were given 3.5 million acres amid the red-rock canyons and piñon mesas of their home-land, and in 1873, the Mescaleros received 460,177 acres among the forested slopes of the Sacramento Mountains.

To reward the Pueblo Indians for their neutrality throughout the Civil War, President Lincoln in 1863 presented each of the 19 pueblos with a black ebony cane crowned with silver and inscribed with his signature. To this day, these canes, symbols of the pueblos' sovereignty, along with silver-tipped staffs given to the pueblos by the Spanish government in 1620, are brought out each January and ceremoniously conferred upon a new governor as he takes office.

Kit Carson.

Comanches and Kiowas remained a threat on New Mexico's eastern plains, raiding caravans and sometimes brutally murdering travelers on the Santa Fe Trail. Chiricahua Apaches attacked soldiers and looted settlements along the southern Rio Grande and in Arizona. The raids conducted by these nomadic Indians began diminishing not long after the completion of the Santa Fe Railroad, which reached Santa Fe in 1880, connecting the territory to the rest of the country. Because the Indians' horses couldn't keep up with the "iron horses," travelers inside the trains were safe. The Indians' lifestyle eroded, and it wasn't long before they were living on reservations.

With the Indian threat removed, settlers crowded onto trains bound for the vast Southwest, where they transformed railroad camps into thriving towns, established enormous sheep and cattle ranches, and irrigated acres of farmland with annual snowmelt and the water from small streams. Drovers escorted thousands of longhorn cattle up from Texas through the Pecos River Valley and on to Colorado, establishing the Goodnight-Loving Trail. Miners arrived to search for gold (though no longer expecting to find seven cities of the mineral) and to work in the coal mines near Gallup, Raton, and Madrid, as well as the silver and copper mines near Silver City.

Many of New Mexico's immigrant newcomers of the late 1800s were the sort who took the law into their own hands. In many towns, true to the depictions in countless Western films, saloons outnumbered churches, and the law of the smoking gun prevailed often over the authority of men with badges. Range wars erupted, accompanied by violent struggles for power. Cattle rustlers operated more or less freely, and Anglo lawyers who received their fees in property benefited the most in disputes over land-grant boundaries.

■ STATEHOOD

Soon after Stephen Kearny raised the stars and stripes above Santa Fe in 1846, debate began over whether or not New Mexico would be better off as a state or a territory. Eastern politicians feared the strong Hispanic influence and uncivilized character of the frontier; as a result, every time the motion for statehood reached the halls of Congress, it was defeated.

That attitude changed after 1898. Determined to demonstrate New Mexico's dedication to the Union during the Spanish-American War, Gov. Miguel Otero called for 340 cowboys to ride with the Rough Riders, the cavalry unit led by

Theodore Roosevelt. Never did these men, many of Spanish ancestry, hesitate as they struggled up San Juan Hill on foot after a lack of transport forced them to leave their horses behind.

Nevertheless, it took another 14 years, until 1912, for statehood to arrive. Immediately, New Mexico's powerful politicos jockeyed for seats in the new state legislature and vied for election to the U.S. Congress. But most of the newest state's nearly 300,000 citizens held onto their own well-rooted ways of life: Pueblo Indians maintained their intimate relationship with Mother Earth, dancing in thanks for their health and bountiful harvests, while learning the language and customs that would help them get along in an increasingly Anglo world. Hispanics devotedly filled Catholic churches and danced whenever they had cause to schedule a fiesta—weddings and saints' days did just fine.

In the 1920s, New Mexico's clear air and uncluttered landscape attracted a new wave of eastern Anglos—some of them sent by their doctors to recover from respiratory ailments such as tuberculosis, others by the military to establish air bases on the expansive prairie. Another group of Anglo settlers worked tirelessly to capture the soft red glow of the desert sunsets and the square jaws of New Mexico's native citizens in photographs, on canvas, and in the written word. Once exposed to the state's ever-changing skies, these artists rarely looked elsewhere for their subjects.

An isolated plateau at the edge of the Jemez Mountains, blanketed in volcanic ash and tall pines, in 1943 lured a small group of scientists who worked in secrecy for two years. They and their families lived in near-seclusion at what had been the Los Alamos Ranch School, a private boys' institution. In the early morning hours of July 16, 1945, before the parched earth heated up for the day, the result of the scientists' efforts burst spectacularly amid the cholla and yucca cactus of the Tularosa Basin in central New Mexico. The detonation of the world's first atomic bomb set the state on a direct path toward a nuclear future and was the beginning of its role as a setting for government-sponsored scientific research. Los Alamos National Laboratory, Sandia National Laboratories, and White Sands Missile Range were later created to fabricate and test this potent technology.

Regardless of the impact history has had on New Mexico's people, they remain rooted to tradition and the earth: adobe construction first used by the Pueblo Indians remains a status symbol; Spanish rolls off tongues in offices, schools, and playing fields; and the brilliant sunsets that bathe mountain slopes and tall-grass prairies in rosy light still evoke a sense of wonder from artist and scientist alike.

A L B U Q U E R Q U E

Once no more than a dusty frontier outpost of the Spanish colonial empire, an isolated enclave of rudimentary adobe homes hugging the banks of the Rio Grande, Albuquerque is today the most energetic city in New Mexico, spreading 12 miles east of the river to the foothills of the Sandia Mountains and 3.5 miles west to a rugged volcanic escarpment. A major center of high-technology and science industries, it drives the state's economy and serves as its education locus and transportation hub. With a population approaching 500,000, Albuquerque is a melting pot for the state's three primary cultures—Native American, Hispanic, and Anglo—to which may now be added an ever-growing Asian community.

The Rio Grande, shaded by leafy cottonwoods, cuts a north-south swath through the city, and five dormant volcanic cones, affectionately known as the Sleeping Sisters, mark its western edge, with a shrub-covered mesa spreading out under their shadow. Between this mesa and the cactus-covered foothills of the Sandia and Manzano Mountains, Albuquerque stretches forth—a shimmering sea of asphalt and flat rooftops.

To early Spaniards, the Sandia ("watermelon") Mountains resembled a wedge of watermelon, especially at sunset, when they glowed a pinkish red. The Manzano ("apple") Mountains received their handle not because they resemble the fruit, but because an apple orchard was planted on their eastern flank in the 19th century.

Sandia Crest rises 10,678 feet from the valley floor, and its cool summit is within easy reach of Albuquerque by way of an 18-minute aerial tram ride. Looking out from the tramway, you're granted a breathtaking panorama of the city, the river, and mesas that extend toward 11,000-foot snow-capped Mount Taylor, 70 miles away. Looking up, you may see red-tail hawks and golden eagles, hot-air balloons and hang gliders, or fighter jets from Kirtland Air Force Base.

To someone merely driving through or flying overhead, the city might seem at a glance just one more homogeneous, sprawling, western metropolis, with streets laid out in a grid, shopping centers at nearly every major intersection. Those more liberal with their time, however, will find much to discover. Because Albuquerque is not a congested city, it's easy to take a leisurely drive through its neighborhoods. At the original town site, a restored area known as Old Town, tourists and locals alike may enjoy watching a Sunday afternoon gunfight (a dramatic reenactment, naturally). In the mostly Hispanic, rural South Valley, which follows the river south of Old Town, advertising billboards promise "El Sabor Rico y Suave" rather than "A Mild, Rich Flavor"; come autumn, newly harvested green chiles roasting outside fruit and vegetable stands saturate the air with a nose-tingling aroma. Northeast Heights and Southeast Heights are made up of new developments and a heavy proportion of the city's businesses. In the North Valley, tall grass grows along Rio Grande Boulevard as it winds past horse farms and orchards.

Even though the city contains a third of the state's residents and is New Mexico's most significant urban center, Albuquerque retains the informality of a small town. Among shopkeepers and folks on the street, friendly smiles come naturally. Albuquerque doesn't tolerate pretensions, and its citizens aren't much concerned with desert visions, astral planes, or other elements of Southwest-styled New Age spirituality so popular with their neighbors to the north in Santa Fe. Residents are down to earth and readily accept, and even thrive on, their city's normalcy.

Twilight view over the city from Sandia Crest.

ALBUQUERQUE: CITY WITHOUT AIRS

All the reasons why people choose Albuquerque come down to one; they like it. It is a pleasant and comfortable place to live; not a town for getting rich, one gets along all right. Few fortunes have been made in Albuquerque. Now and again a big money-maker blows in and high-pressures everybody. But such people pass like a tornado, leaving the town shaken and littered with the trash of the grandiosity, but glad to settle back into quiet ways while the rest of the world gets rich. Sometimes the high-pressure gentleman comes a bit sheepishly back to admit that he too "just likes it."

—Erna Fergusson, *Albuquerque,* 1947

■ HISTORY

The first people to scale the granite outcroppings of the Sandia Mountains and gaze over the future site of Albuquerque probably arrived at the end of the last ice age, about 12,000 years ago. They came in quest of mammoths, mastodons, bison, and antelope. Over the course of their time in the valley, they left behind spear points and scrapers in Sandia Cave, a deep opening on the northeastern flank of the mountains. Accordingly, they are referred to as Sandia Man.

Thousands of years after these primitive hunters moved on, the ancestors of today's Pueblo Indians began living along the Rio Grande in settlements that date from A.D. 500. By about 1300 they were cultivating beans, maize, and squash, coiling pottery, and living in four-story pueblos built of *terrones*—sod squares composed of twigs, grass, dirt, and water. When a man wished to marry, he wove a blanket and placed it in front of the woman of his choice, and if she wished to accept him, she did so by wrapping the blanket around herself, thereby becoming his wife.

This was the culture that Spanish conquistador Francisco Vásquez de Coronado stumbled upon when he arrived in the autumn of 1540 at the Kuaua Pueblo (called Alcanfor by the Spanish), 17 miles north of present-day Albuquerque. Needing a place to winter his entourage, he ended up staying for two winters and one summer, while searching ceaselessly for gold. In 1542, he returned to New Spain empty-handed.

Despite subsequent Spanish expeditions into New Mexico and a settlement in Santa Fe to the north, the area around Albuquerque remained largely free of European influence until the end of the 16th century. By then the Pueblo Indians were more or less subdued (although not the Apaches), and with increasing numbers of Spanish settlers arriving in the New World, the Spanish crown began to issue land grants for areas at the far northern reaches of its empire.

Typically, a land grant was a small plot near a water supply. On it, settlers could build a rustic home and grow corn, wheat, beans, chile, and fruits. They cultivated cotton for cloth, wove fabric, and sewed their own clothes. Cattle and sheep were grazed on *ejidos*—larger parcels of common land shared by grantees. Life on the

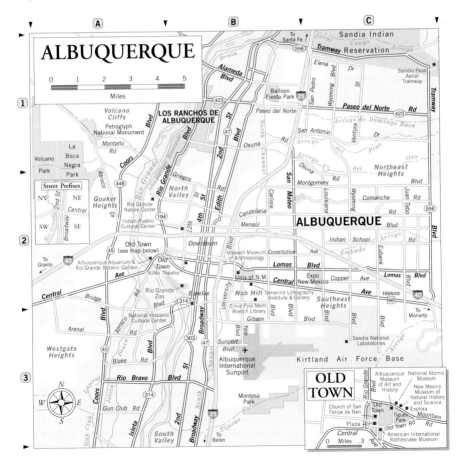

The carreta *was the most common vehicle of transport in Spanish colonial New Mexico. This one was photographed at Tesuque Pueblo, north of Santa Fe, in 1890.*

rancho was grueling and very basic, but the settlers believed they were investing in a provident future.

These individuals were a hardy lot. Women helped with the planting, spent long hours grinding corn on well-worn *metates,* fashioned brooms from meadow grass, and bore and raised many children. Men braved blinding windstorms and cold winters to herd cattle and sheep, and felled tall ponderosa pines to fabricate furniture. Because metal was scarce, they designed wooden plows, hoes, and shovels, as well as *carretas*—the two-wheeled, wooden oxen-drawn carts that were the only vehicles used in the state during the 18th and early 19th centuries.

The entire family worked the land, breaking the soil, planting seeds, pulling weeds, and harvesting crops. Irrigation was a necessity, and the men dug and maintained ditches, called *acequías*, that transferred water from the Rio Grande to fields in the Albuquerque area. (These *acequías* were so wide that small bridges were built across them.) Homes were constructed of handmade adobe bricks, each of them five inches thick and weighing 50 pounds. For insulation, thick mud was plastered in between the bricks. At the more isolated ranchos, which were frequent targets for Apache attacks, defensive *torreones* were built—round, rock-walled towers equipped with a few small windows.

In 1706, Francisco Cuervo y Valdés, provisional governor of New Mexico, moved 30 families from the trading center of Bernalillo (where a number of haciendas flourished adjacent to Kuaua) to a spot 17 miles south, in the middle Rio Grande Valley, which boasted steady water, good soil, grassland, and timber. To flatter the Duke of Alburquerque, then viceroy of New Spain, Valdés named the new community after him (the first "r" was later dropped). Settlers cleared the land, cut the timber, and baked bricks, building their squat mud houses and a small adobe church around a central plaza in the area known today as Old Town. Ten soldiers were assigned to protect the new settlement from Indian attacks. No walls or fortifications were constructed around it, although as Indian raids increased, homes were built closer together and closer to the plaza.

The settlers' earliest residences weren't much to look at, but their adobe construction provided natural insulation: relief from a glaring summer sun, and warmth during winter. By day, they looked dreary. But as the sun set on the West Mesa, the rosy and golden glow that bathed the nearby mountains also fell across the town of "Alburquerque," giving it the appearance, however fleeting, of a prosperous village.

■ The Railroad Arrives

For the sake of protection, Albuquerque remained huddled around its plaza for more than 170 years—until the arrival in April 1880 of the Santa Fe Railroad. Built across the desert two miles east of the original settlement, the railroad soon caused a second community—New Albuquerque—to sprout along its tracks. Because many in this new wave of residents came from east of the Mississippi River, their gabled wooden homes reflected the favored architecture of the Midwest. These two-story, pitched-roof houses proved to be far less amenable to life in the desert than those of naturally insulating adobe bricks built low to the ground, however, and later construction followed the stuccoed, flat-roofed adobe style. The early two-story homes were left to deteriorate until the late 20th century, when homeowners dedicated to historic preservation moved in and restored them to their original beauty. Today, a walk through the Huning-Highland neighborhood evokes an Albuquerque often forgotten.

This period also brought Albuquerque its first African-American residents, who came west to work for the railroad. Today, the South Broadway neighborhood remains a center of black cultural life, and the books and other materials in the public library branch there reflect a broad range of African-American interests.

With the arrival of the railroad, Albuquerque's population skyrocketed, as did its vitality. The city's first entrepreneur was Peter "Shorty" Parker, who opened a saloon by staking out space in a vacant lot and erecting a bar that consisted of a board placed across two upended barrels. Pretty soon, 14 new saloons (with roofs) and gambling houses sprang up between First and Third Streets on Railroad (now Central) Avenue. Men stood along the wooden bars, paying 15 cents for a shot of whiskey. Respectable women listened from afar to songs played on an accordion or honky-tonk piano. The White Elephant, whose solid mahogany bar could accommodate 50 men at one time and whose glassware was imported from Belgium, served the town nabobs. One block away, the no-frills Bucket of Blood catered to the railroad workers; even if a man drank away his paycheck during the course of a weekend, owners John and Mary Boyle made sure he sobered up in time to report to work on Monday morning. Another early tavern, the Silver Dollar, embedded its namesake in the floor.

Street fights, murders, and hangings were commonplace, as were stories like this one: In 1881 someone fired a shot into the air at the same time a railroad carpenter by the name of Charles Campbell was crossing First Street. A bystander said it was the carpenter who had fired the shot, so the town's marshal, Milt Yarberry, and his friend, Monte Frank Boyd, pumped 12 bullets into Campbell to teach him a lesson. Two years later, Marshal Yarberry was hanged for murder in front of 100 people, some of whom had paid a dollar to witness the event. One newspaper related that the marshal had been "jerked to Jesus."

The era's showpiece was the Huning Castle, which had wood-veneered sod walls no less than five feet thick, a flat roof trimmed with ornamental grillwork, and a tower decorated with balconies. Such details gave the two-story home the look of a castle, and that's what owner Franz Huning—a German immigrant and one of Albuquerque's prominent Anglo merchants—called it. (By 1955, the architectural novelty was considered an embarrassment by the community and was torn down.)

The railroad may have ushered in a certain amount of mayhem and debauchery, but education arrived at the same time—public schools in 1884 and parochial schools the following year. In 1889, the University of New Mexico was founded a mile east of the railroad tracks on a sandy, yucca-filled tableland. The university's third president, William Tight, was responsible for transforming this part of the desert into a shady oasis. Under his watch, hundreds of trees and native plants were transplanted from the nearby mountains, and a well was dug to water them. He

(top) Original Victorian-style Hodgin Hall at the University of New Mexico, and Hodgin Hall redone in the Pueblo Revival style (bottom).

even imported squirrels from his previous home in Ohio. It is, presumably, the descendants of these squirrels that romp among the trees today.

President Tight was so impressed by the surviving Pueblo Indian culture that he envisioned a campus that would reflect their unique architecture. He quickly saw to the construction of flat-roofed adobe buildings with portals and vigas—giant roof beams made from the trunks of ponderosa pines—and went so far as to remove the gables from the Victorian-style Hodgin Hall and to plaster over the walls with adobe. Public outcry over Tight's attachment to "primitive" architecture soon grew so loud that the public removed him from office. (In later years, however, Tight's vision returned to favor and was manifested in the work of famed Santa Fe architect John Gaw Meem, a major proponent of Spanish pueblo style. As the university's architect of choice for 25 years, Meem designed many of the campus's finest examples of the style, including Zimmerman Library and Scholes Hall.)

As the 19th century became the 20th, the high desert city of Albuquerque was becoming a haven for tuberculosis patients. Seventeen tuberculosis centers were built, including Lovelace Clinic, founded by a patient, William Randolph Lovelace. Today a branch of the full-service medical facility carries out cutting-edge medical research.

In 1926, Route 66, the much ballyhooed national highway that linked Chicago with the West Coast, passed through Albuquerque's central business district. As a result, a highway culture of tourist courts, diners, and storefronts blossomed on Central Avenue. Eight decades later many of these establishments retain a down-home ambiance—as well as vintage architecture and some dazzling neon signs.

Up-and-coming financier Conrad Hilton made his home state the focus of his attention in 1939. A native of San Antonio, a rural hamlet 86 miles south of Albuquerque, Hilton was convinced that Albuquerque was ripe for growth. On the lot of the former Trimble Livery Stable, he set about building the 10-story Albuquerque Hilton, accenting its airy two-story lobby with carved corbels, a Mexican tiled floor, and whitewashed arches. The hotelier himself spent a few nights there, in 1942, with new bride Zsa Zsa Gabor, after their wedding in Santa Fe. The hotel escaped the ravages of 1960s urban renewal and underwent a restoration in the 1980s, but is no longer a Hilton; today, it operates as La Posada de Albuquerque (125 Second Street NW; 505-242-9090).

■ MILITARY, AVIATION, AND BALLOONING

Few things suit an airplane pilot better than clear sky, and because Albuquerque enjoys an abundance of it, the United States Army Air Corps designated the city as a service station for military planes in 1940. The following year, as the nation seemed about to become embroiled in war, the Air Corps Advance Flying School was established on land adjacent to the municipal airport. The school was soon expanded, and in 1942 became Kirtland Field, a major defense installation.

With the end of World War II and the outset of the Cold War, Kirtland Field, now named **Kirtland Air Force Base**, took on a new role: it housed Sandia National Laboratories, which had been established in wartime as part of the Los Alamos atomic bomb project and in 1948 became a separate entity. Today, the base and the labs are Albuquerque's largest employers, with more than 19,000 workers between them. Among these are some of the world's foremost experts in nuclear technology, their science servicing the needs of military weapons development as well as more life-enhancing applications. From technology initially created to assess how chemical explosives in nuclear warheads can age over time, for instance, Sandia's scientists developed a noninvasive infrared technology now used to measure glucose levels in the blood of diabetics painlessly and with great accuracy. For years, Kirtland housed the National Atomic Museum, but security and other concerns have caused it to be relocated elsewhere (see "Museums and Galleries," page 49).

Hot-air ballooning is another type of flight that has captured the imagination of Albuquerqueans. In the early 1970s, pioneer balloonists Sid Cutter, Maxie Anderson, and Ben Abruzzo first fired up propane burners and injected heated gas into 60-foot-high nylon balloons attached to wicker baskets. Soon they were gracefully lifted upward, flying thousands of feet above a silent sweep of desert. In 1972, Cutter established the **Albuquerque International Balloon Fiesta,** which today is the largest balloon gathering in the world, attracting more than 800 balloons for nine days every October. *Balloon Fiesta Park: I-25, Exit 234 (Tramway Boulevard); 505-821-1000.*

Anderson and Abruzzo, meanwhile, pursued adventure. The two pilots, along with Larry Newman of Phoenix, Arizona, won worldwide fame in 1978 when they completed the first helium balloon flight across the Atlantic. Using helium instead

(following pages) The annual Albuquerque International Balloon Fiesta is the largest such event in the world.

of propane allowed them to fly at higher elevations and for longer periods. Later, Abruzzo and Anderson participated in the first trans-Pacific helium balloon flight. Sadly, both died in flight accidents: Anderson in 1983 at a balloon race in West Germany and Abruzzo two years later in the crash of a private plane. To honor these intrepid balloonists, the Anderson-Abruzzo International Balloon Museum will open in 2005 at the southern end of Balloon Fiesta Park.

■ OLD TOWN *map page 37, C-3*

Old Town offers a refuge from the sameness of Albuquerque's modern-day strip shopping centers. All it takes is a few steps down Romero Street to become surrounded in an aura of the past. Ambling along the narrow streets of the city's original town site, you'll pass adobe buildings whitewashed or tinted in colors from beige to chocolate brown. Wooden doorways and windowsills are livelier—painted in magenta, turquoise, and navy blue.

The original **San Felipe de Neri Church** was begun in 1706, but disintegrated after years of weathering and neglect. Its 1793 replacement, by contrast, is impeccably cared for. Outside, flower beds are tidy and bright; inside, a pressed tin ceiling contrasts with wooden arches and dark wooden paneling and pews. No stained glass graces San Felipe's windows, but flickering lights from votive candles contribute to an atmosphere of reverence.

The church overlooks the **central plaza**, once a dirt-covered square familiar to settlers and adventurers as well as to soldiers preparing to fight the Indians. Later, Confederate and Union armies alternated possession of the outpost, and today two Civil War cannons are on permanent display. A whitewashed wood-and-cement gazebo now serves as a bandstand for musicians and dancers, and tall, broad-leafed cottonwood trees provide shade for picnickers and shoppers.

The original homes that face the plaza have long since been transformed into shops, galleries, and restaurants. An example is **La Placita Dining Rooms**, built in 1706 as the Armijo family home. Today, the smell of *sopaipillas* (deep-fried bread dough) and tortillas frying in hot oil wafts through the old house, and its meandering rooms are alive with the chatter of restaurant guests. Out front, local artisans line the brick sidewalk with blankets upon which they display handmade jewelry and weavings. *208 San Felipe Street NW; 505-247-2204.*

Farther from the plaza, narrow back streets weave among adobe buildings nearly 300 years old. If time is limited and you want to know where to find authentic Navajo rugs, Acoma pottery, and cookie cutters in the shape of hot air balloons, pick up a map at the visitors center at the plaza's northwest corner. And to gain some insider knowledge about Old Town, take one of the **guided walking tours** that leave from the Albuquerque Museum at 11 A.M. daily, except Monday, from March through November. *2000 Mountain Road NW; 505-243-7255.*

Old Town receives most of its visitors during the warm summer months, but those willing to brave the brisk temperatures of a chilly Christmas Eve will find it transformed into an expanse of shimmering light. In traditional Hispanic style, neighborhood residents set out more than 500,000 *luminarias* (votive candles nestled in a handful of dirt in a small brown paper bag—called *farolitos* in other parts of New Mexico) along sidewalks, adobe walls, and rooftops as a sign of rejoicing and festivity.

Luminarias decorate the plaza in front of Albuquerque's San Felipe de Neri Church at Christmas.

■ Museums and Galleries

Albuquerque's museums reflect the region's unique heritage and rich history, natural or not. Let's start with several in or near Old Town, and then fan out.

New Mexico Museum of Natural History and Science *map page 37, C-3*
Spike the Pentaceratops and Alberta the Albertosaurus stand guard at the entrance. Inside, a Quetzalcoatlus hovers in midair over a Camarasaurus, an Allosaurus, and a life-size model of Coelophysis—the New Mexico state fossil, so small you can look him straight in the eye. A walk through 4.6 billion years of New Mexico's geologically tumultuous past immerses you in a tropical seacoast environment complete with fossils of dinosaurs found only in New Mexico, and leads you inside a simulation of an active volcano. An "evolator," which looks suspiciously like an elevator, whisks you through 39 million years of evolutionary progress in no time. Also inside the museum is the **LodeStar Astronomy Center** (505-841-5955), which offers visitors a ride on a virtual science mission (with seats moving in six directions) and a look at the stars in a highly sophisticated planetarium. *1801 Mountain Road NW; 505-841-2800.*

National Atomic Museum *map page 37, C-3*
Although its location has moved from Kirtland Air Force Base to temporary quarters (while awaiting its transformation into the National Museum of Nuclear Science and History, to be built in 2006 at Balloon Fiesta Park), this museum continues to trace the history of the top-secret Manhattan Project, once centered at Los Alamos. Along with a copy of a letter Albert Einstein wrote to President Franklin D. Roosevelt encouraging him to develop the atomic bomb, the museum mounts detailed exhibits on the development of nuclear weapons and the peaceful uses of nuclear energy. *1905 Mountain Road NW; 505-245-2137.*

Albuquerque Museum of Art and History *map page 37, C-3*
This huge, city-owned museum documents 400 years of the state's history and provides an excellent introduction to the history of Albuquerque. Through the years, it has amassed a fabulous collection of works by New Mexico artists, and these pieces are often on exhibit. Regularly changing shows in the main gallery are usually well worth a visit as well, and listening and dancing to local salsa bands and jazz combos in the museum's sculpture garden is a wonderful way to spend a summer evening. *2000 Mountain Road NW; 505-242-4600.*

Doing business in Old Town Albuquerque: Indians sell their crafts on the plaza.

American International Rattlesnake Museum *map page 37, C-3*

Let the squeamish beware. This museum houses the world's largest collection of poisonous snakes. Slithering about in natural settings—and all safely behind glass—they can most often be seen resting indolently, coiled beneath a piece of petrified wood. With your fears addressed, you might even discover a fascination for the legless creatures and find that you can't live without a rattlesnake license plate to adorn your car. *202 San Felipe Street NW; 505-242-6569.*

Explora Science Center and Children's Museum of Albuquerque
map page 37, A/B-2

When children ask Why? and you don't know the answer, this place may supply one. In fabulous new digs that opened in December 2003, youngsters of all ages can test their centers of gravity, learn about balance atop a high-wire bicycle that runs across a cable suspended 20 feet above the ground, operate a giant 40-foot-long lever to rescue a car dangling from the edge of a deck, and learn how light creates shadows, how to conduct edible experiments, or how to make wearable art. *1803 Mountain Road NW; 505-224-8300.*

National Hispanic Cultural Center *map page 37, B-2*

This sprawling campus opened in 2000 in the heart of Albuquerque's traditional Hispanic core. Still a work in progress, it aspires to become a major center for Hispanic arts and culture. Changing exhibits in its three art galleries provide glimpses of works by emerging artists along with the historical perspective of antique *retablos* (depictions of saints painted on wood) and traditional tinwork. A state-of-the-art theater complex is scheduled for completion in late 2004; in the meantime, you can catch a salsa dance competition or flamenco performance at the outdoor plaza, or a poetry reading in the center's small theater. *1701 Fourth Street SW; 505-246-2261.*

University Museums *map page 37, B-2*

Several museums on the campus of the University of New Mexico are devoted to the state's history and culture. The **Maxwell Museum of Anthropology** invites you to walk through four million years of human evolution. Do so, and you'll see a a life-size (3-foot-7-inch) reconstruction of an average woman of three million years ago; facing her in a glass case are primate jawbones (complete with teeth) charting the slow transition from chimpanzee to human. The artwork of our more recent ancestors is reproduced in a cave with red-and-black wall paintings of horses, bison, and wolves resembling those found at Lascaux, France. A two-story gallery shows off items from the museum's permanent collection of Mimbres and Pueblo pottery, Navajo weavings and textiles, American Indian basketry, kachina dolls, and jewelry. Think it's easy to grind corn the Indian way? Try your skill by using a *mano* (hand stone) in a *metate* (stone bowl). *Redondo Road near intersection of Dr. Martin Luther King Jr. Street; 505-277-4404.*

Also on campus are the **Geology and Meteoritic Museum** *(Northrup Hall, Room 106; 505-277-4204)*, with meteorites and a variety of rocks; the **University Art Museum** *(Popejoy Hall; 505-277-4001)*, with exhibits of contemporary regional work; and the **Jonson Gallery** *(1909 Las Lomas Road NE; 505-277-4967)*, which houses works by the late modernist painter Raymond Jonson.

Tamarind Lithography Institute and Gallery   *map page 37, B-2*
South of the campus, this is affiliated with the university's College of Fine Arts and was founded in 1970. Some of the world's foremost modern artists—Sam Francis, Jasper Johns, Roy Lichtenstein, Robert Motherwell, Claes Oldenburg, and Frank Stella, among others—have processed prints of their work here. The work of artists in residence is displayed in the gallery in changing shows. On the first Friday of the month you can sign up for a tour, which includes a video on the lithography process and a printing demonstration. *108–110 Cornell Drive SE; 505-277-3901.*

Ernie Pyle Memorial Branch Library   *map page 37, B-2*
Before the days of "embedded" war correspondents, there was Ernie Pyle—a World War II correspondent who became famous for dispatches that told the story of the war from the GI's point of view. The Pyle Library is not an official museum, but this shady bungalow was Pyle's last home; in addition to library books, it contains memorabilia from the war correspondent's life, including his typewriter and a pair of glasses. *900 Girard Boulevard SE; 505-256-2065.*

Indian Pueblo Cultural Center   *map page 37, B-2*
New Mexico's Pueblo Indians—so-called by the early Spanish explorers because they lived in communities surrounding a central plaza (*pueblo* in Spanish means town)—are the subjects of this enterprise. It is operated by the All-Indian Pueblo Council, a coalition of the governors of the state's 19 pueblos, each of which is its own sovereign nation and has its own government.

(following page) Dancer at the National Hispanic Cultural Center.

Don't miss the museum on the lower level, with its exhibits on native languages and lifestyles. You'll learn, for example, that men and children used to wear little in summer other than sandals woven from yucca fibers, while women wore miniskirts made of string. In the winter, they all wrapped themselves in soft robes of tanned deerskin or rabbit fur. Men's hair was kept long, but women cut theirs to make cords and ropes. Also of interest are instructions on how to bake bread in an *horno* and a video screening in which the late Maria Martinez, famed San Ildefonso Pueblo potter, demonstrates the process by which she achieved her distinctive black-on-black glaze. Each pueblo has its own display case: Sandia Pueblo exhibits red clay pots and buckskin moccasins; San Felipe its heishi necklaces, made from semi-precious and precious stones; and Isleta its clay storyteller sculptures. Upstairs, Indian crafts are for sale, and a restaurant serves a selection of Indian staples, including frybread, tamales, and buffalo burgers. On most weekends and holidays, Indians don traditional dress and dance to rhythms beat out on animal-skin drums in the center's courtyard. *2401 12th Street NW; 505-843-7270.*

■ ALBUQUERQUE PARKS

Albuquerque Biological Park *map page 37, A/B-2*

Among the 200 or so parks breaking up the city's sprawl, this complex is well worth a visit. The **Rio Grande Zoo,** set in a grove of ancient cottonwood trees about a mile south of downtown, houses more than 1,200 exotic animals from around the world. A bleached-white polar bear splashes in a giant pool that only he can make appear small, and a lanky cheetah wanders silently amid sandstone cliffs and outcroppings. In the reptile house, iguanas, skinks, and crocodiles enjoy a cozy simulation of their natural environments; special controls vary temperatures and seasonal day lengths for each species. *903 10th Street SW; 505-764-6200.*

At the **Albuquerque Aquarium,** located along the river about 2 miles north of the zoo, you can imagine what life is like in the Gulf of Mexico. Exhibits take visitors through salt marshes all the way to coral reefs and the open ocean, where moray eels 6 feet long swim with scores of colorful butterfly fish—all watched closely by a variety of sharks, who clearly are in charge. Reflecting an environment closer to home for Albuquerqueans is a simulated mountain stream where Rio Grande cutthroat trout swim safely, certain that no fisherman will catch them for dinner. Next door, at the **Rio Grande Botanic Garden,** visitors can learn about native plants. *2601 Central Avenue NW; 505-764-6200.*

The Shark Reef Cafe at the Albuquerque Aquarium.

Rio Grande Nature Center *map page 37, A-2*

Because the visitors center here is built partially underground, its unobtrusive design enables visitors to observe bird life both above and below the surface of a 3-acre pond. During the migration months of May and October, Canada and snow geese, along with sandhill cranes, stop at the center to rest. Two miles of trails lead hikers through a riparian environment or bosque (woodland) that also attracts pheasants, roadrunners, toads, skunks, and beavers. Free guided walks along these trails are conducted every weekend. *2901 Candelaria Road NW, near Rio Grande Boulevard; 505-344-7240.*

Petroglyph National Monument *map page 37, A-1*

Across the Rio Grande on the West Mesa, along a boulder-strewn volcanic escarpment beneath the five Sleeping Sisters, are at least 15,000 petroglyphs, some dating as far back as A.D. 1300. An excursion among the craggy boulders of this national monument, created to protect the mystical rock art from encroaching housing developments, takes you past depictions of long-legged birds, animated dancers, snakes, and shields etched in dark basalt. Standing in front of any of these draw-

Hiking past petroglyphs at Boca Negra Canyon, Petroglyph National Monument.

ings, it's hard not to wonder about the world these artists inhabited. Most scholars agree that the designs were symbolic and not meant to represent actual events, but all the same, what were the artists trying to say?

Start at the visitors center, at Unser Boulevard and Western Trail, and go 2 miles north to Boca Negra Canyon. Three short paved trails lead to a concentration of petroglyphs. Rangers conduct guided tours during the summer. For the best viewing and to minimize your exposure to the intense summer sun, schedule your visit into the park's canyons in the morning or late afternoon. *6001 Unser Boulevard NW; 505-899-0205.*

■ ALBUQUERQUE EATS

Because Albuquerqueans are cowboys at heart and expect to get their money's worth, food almost spills over the edges of plates at most city restaurants. But if quantity—and not necessarily originality—has long characterized the city's cooking, today's chefs are experimenting with new versions of local favorites. Cooks find countless uses for the state vegetable, chile, using it in soups and sandwiches,

Chile versus Chili

In New Mexico, when folks believe in something, you'd best believe it too. Take, for example, the spelling of "chile." A small matter, you might say, but not for New Mexicans, who refuse to accept the way the rest of the country spells it—"chili." Chile, the Spanish spelling, is found on menus, in stores, and in newspapers throughout the state. New Mexicans are so adamant about the spelling that in 1983 they directed their senior U.S. legislator, Sen. Pete Domenici, to enter into the Congressional Record the state's stand on chile and its preferred spelling:

"New Mexicans consume mass quantities of this magical and life-giving fruit from birth, and labels on chile products, descriptions of dishes at New Mexican restaurants and billboards and advertisements all reinforce the fact that chile is spelled with an 'e' and not an 'i.' A naiveté exists among native New Mexicans who wrongly assume that everyone spells it with an 'e.'

"Even the dictionary makes the error, stating that chili is defined as the pod of any species of capsicum, especially *Capsicum frutescens.* Chili is the preferred spelling and chile is only mentioned as an alternate spelling. Knowing that criticizing the dictionary is akin to criticizing the Bible, I nevertheless stand here before the full Senate and with the backing of my New Mexico constituents state unequivocally that the dictionary is wrong.

"Native New Mexicans are extremely sensitive about this spelling, for the *Capsicum frutescens,* commonly known as green chile, and when dried in the autumn sun in great strings called *ristras,* becoming red chile, is New Mexico's most famous agricultural product. Though the chile can be grown in other parts of the country, it is known worldwide that the New Mexico soil produces a chile pod with a mouth-watering flavor that none can even brag about coming close to.

"New Mexicans know that 'chili' is the inedible mixture of watery tomato soup, dried gristle, half-cooked kidney beans, and a myriad of silly ingredients that is passed off as food in Texas and Oklahoma. The different tabascos and jalapeño sauces added to the mixture do little good and in most cases simply cause a casual visitor to suffer great gastrointestinal distress.

"Contrast this to New Mexico, where ordering a bowl of chile is a delightful experience. Hospitable as we are to all visitors, we have chile that is mild enough to make a baby coo in delight, or hot enough to make even the strongest constitutions perspire in a sensual experience of both pleasure and pain.

"I could go on and on about the wonders of red and green chile, but in reality, all I wanted to do was inform Congress on the correct way to spell the word."

The state's loyalty to chile didn't stop with Senator Domenici's speech. In 1999, the state legislature approved an official state question: "Red or Green?" It's the standard question asked in restaurants when you place an order for New Mexican food—do you prefer red or green chile atop your enchiladas or burritos? (Some diners ask for "Christmas," which indicates they want both.)

Cornucopia of chiles.

as well as in pizza and cornbread. Piñon nuts are popular in ice cream, tarts, and muffins; at **Scalo** (3500 Central Avenue NE; 505-255-8781), green chile is added to a honey glaze on chicken wings. At **Jennifer James Contemporary Cuisine** (2813 San Mateo Boulevard NE; 505-884-3665), chipotle chiles might be found brightening up a butternut squash soup, or red chiles firing up a sauce blanketing polenta cakes.

Ethnic restaurants have brought international tastes to this frontier town, and there is now no lack of Thai, East Indian, Vietnamese, Chinese, and Mediterranean cooking. By no means, however, has Albuquerque stopped dishing up classic New Mexican food. At **Sadie's Dining Room** (6230 Fourth Street NW; 505-345-5339), in the North Valley, check out the *papitas fritas con frijoles* (fried potatoes with beans) or chicken tacos with guacamole—just *try* to finish a dinner plate here! At **El Patio de Albuquerque** (142 Harvard Drive SE; 505-268-4245), across from the university, the green chile chicken enchilada plate is a favorite and the honey *sopaipillas* are tops. Downtown, the **M&J Sanitary Tortilla Factory** (403 Second Street SW; 505-242-4890) is an institution where students, lawyers, artists, and the occasional visiting Hollywood celebrity vie for mismatched vinyl booths. The food is excellent, the atmosphere even better. Walls are covered with local artwork and letters of appreciation to the friendly owners, who bustle about making sure you have enough fresh salsa and iced tea.

At daybreak, Albuquerque has more percolating than cowboy coffee and a pot of mush for breakfast. You can easily find first-rate cappuccino, croissants, and bagels, but if you find yourself craving chile first thing in the morning, try a breakfast burrito—a flour tortilla wrapped around scrambled eggs, bacon or chorizo (spicy sausage), cheese, home fries, and chile, then topped with more cheese and chile. That same combination is offered as a "Pile-up" at the **66 Diner** (1405 Central Avenue NE; 505-247-1421), a 1950s-style eatery serving 21st-century food. Wipe your plate clean and you won't need to eat for the rest of the day.

■ NIGHTLIFE

Albuquerque's nightclub circuit runs the usual gamut of musical tastes: rock and roll, rhythm and blues, jazz, Latin, acoustic, piano bar, and, of course, country and western. Most of the country bars offer free dance lessons on weeknights, when you'll see men with their names engraved into their leather belts exert magnetic

At the 66 Diner, you can listen to golden oldies on the jukebox while waiting for your green chile cheese dog, tall stack of pancakes, or trademark Pile-up.

attraction on the full-skirted women heading toward them, determined to learn the two-step, polka, waltz, jitterbug, and cotton-eyed joe.

If you're a gallery hopper and your visit to Albuquerque falls on the third Friday of the month, consider joining **ArtsCrawl,** a free self-guided tour of galleries that concentrates on a different part of town each month. From 5 to 9 P.M., gallery owners offer beverages, hors d'oeuvres, and a look at their current exhibits, while patrons check out the art—and each other. To find out where the next ArtsCrawl will take place, contact the Albuquerque Art Business Association (505-244-0362).

A drive along old Route 66, these days known less romantically as Central Avenue, takes you past the city's colorful spectacle of neon signage. Some of it dates to the 1930s, when the highway bustled with transcontinental traffic. Central Avenue is marked by two stainless steel, tile, and neon arches that bookend Nob Hill, largely a shopping district by day, but one of the city's most active gathering places after sunset. Restaurants with outdoor seating quickly fill up, and coffeehouses serving powerful java buzz with conversation. Window shopping is a great way to walk off the food. Stop by **Flying Star Cafe** (3416 Central Avenue; 505-255-6633) for a late-night piece of pie and the best people-watching in the area.

Similarly, Albuquerque's downtown, which centers around Central Avenue, is the province of suits from 9 to 5, but gives itself over to a jauntier, less serious crowd come nightfall. Local bands play everything from jazz to hard-driving rock at the numerous bars and restaurants, making this one of the city's liveliest nocturnal neighborhoods, especially for the younger set. At the heart of downtown sits the ornate KiMo Theatre, a former picture palace where some variety of live performance is on offer nearly every weekend.

■ **KiMo Theatre** *map page 37, B-2*
Electric eyes beam from garlanded, horned buffalo skulls, installed as sconce lights. Indian shields made of plaster of paris decorate inside and outside walls. Wrought-iron balusters resembling stylized waterfowl grace stairways leading to the balcony. Ceiling beams are textured to look like wooden vigas and painted with thunderbirds, butterflies, and geometrical designs. Chandeliers are shaped like war drums, and air vents are disguised as Navajo rugs. Everywhere you turn are visions that could only be described by an exotic vocabulary.

The KiMo (the name means "mountain lion" in Pueblo dialect) was given to the community by Oreste Bachechi, an Italian immigrant who had become a success-

Inside the KiMo Theatre.

ful liquor and grocery dealer. Wishing to build a movie theater worthy of the city that had fulfilled his American dream—but uninterested in the Moorish or Chinese fantasias popular among the era's grandest cinemas—Bachechi hired Carl Boller, a Hollywood architect, to design a theater that would reflect the arts and culture of New Mexico and the American Indian. After traveling throughout the state, researching and scouting styles, Boller fused traditional Indian designs, Spanish mission styles, and certain other flamboyant motifs of the day into a new—if short-lived—architectural style called Pueblo deco. He took months choosing colors and ensuring that Native American interpretations were properly represented in minute detail. For example, red portrays the life-giving sun; white, the approaching morning; yellow, the setting sun of the west; and black, the darkening clouds from the north.

Bachechi spent $150,000 building the magnificent theater, which opened in 1927. He spent an additional $18,000 to install its elaborate Wurlitzer organ, which was played during each silent film showing.

The KiMo also served as a venue for live theater. Albuquerque resident Vivian Vance, who gained fame as *I Love Lucy*'s Ethel Mertz, performed here, and so did

The Sandias form a backdrop to downtown Albuquerque.

Hollywood actresses Gloria Swanson and Ginger Rogers, the burlesque queen Sally Rand, and the western movie hero Tom Mix.

The KiMo suffered several alterations over the years, and its stage was destroyed in a 1963 fire; it was serving as office space when the city purchased it in the late 1970s, renovated it, and reopened it as a performance space. The restoration included the murals in the lobby, painted by Albuquerque artist Carl von Hassler, who was a member of the ashcan school of art in Greenwich Village before he moved to New Mexico in 1922. Although one of his larger murals had been destroyed, the six still extant depict panoramic *trompe l'oeil* views of low mountains, cloud-filled skies, and peaceful pueblos. Painted into one scene is a fetching detail—a striped Navajo blanket draped over the wall separating spectator from the landscape. The KiMo can be seen in all its splendor most weekends, when it presents attractions ranging from Opera Southwest and Ballet Folklorico de Albuquerque productions to children's theater and touring stage shows. *423 Central Avenue NW; 505-768-3522.*

■ SANDIA CREST *map page 37, C-1*

In just 18 minutes, one of two cars at the **Sandia Peak Aerial Tramway** whisks passengers nearly 4,000 feet to the top of Sandia Crest. On its silent 2.7-mile journey, the tram quickly leaves behind clusters of cholla cactus and ascends above jagged granite outcroppings until it reaches the windy, pine-covered summit of the Sandia Mountains. From there, the city and surrounding desert stretch to the horizon, sliced by the winding greenbelt of the Rio Grande. In summer, hikers and backpackers embark along forested trails to enjoy cool relief. In winter, skiers glide along cross-country trails or schuss the groomed slopes of **Sandia Peak Ski Area,** carved from the forest on the mountain's eastern flank. On select days in summer and fall, one of the ski area's chairlifts carries sightseers over grassy slopes where deer and rabbits dart for cover in nearby stands of pines. The ride is especially enjoyable in fall, when the aspens' green leaves turn golden and shimmer in the sunlight. Dusk is the most dramatic time to find oneself atop the 10,678-foot peak. When the sun disappears behind the West Mesa, it casts a glow across the city, which gradually becomes a sea of twinkling lights.

At the summit of Sandia Crest, the **High Finance Restaurant** (40 Tramway Road; 505-243-9742) serves steaks and hot chocolate and provides luxurious shelter from gusty winds that often buffet the mountaintop. A one-mile trail along the edge of the ridge leads to Sandia Crest House, a small gift shop and snack bar. The tram operates daily; hours vary. *Sandia Peak Aerial Tramway, 10 Tramway Loop NE; 505-856-7325.*

ALBUQUERQUE
ENVIRONS

In the immediate area outside the bustle of Albuquerque lie ancient Indian pueblos, the site of Francisco Coronado's first winter encampment in New Mexico, lovely countryside, and the Turquoise Trail. Visiting these sights can make for a day or two of pleasurable meandering.

Bernalillo, one of the earliest towns in the United States to be settled by the Spanish, lies 15 miles north of Albuquerque. Heading north out of Albuquerque on Fourth Street (NM 313, or old U.S. 85), you'll come first to the sleepy village of **Alameda**, once a Tiwa Pueblo. After the 1680 Pueblo Revolt, it was abandoned for 15 years, at which time a small group of Spanish colonists moved in. You'll know you're in Alameda when you see the adobe church that fronts the street.

North of Alameda, NM 313 slices through the Sandia Indian Reservation, paralleling railroad tracks and irrigation ditches. If you turn west onto Alameda Boulevard, cross the Rio Grande, then turn north onto NM 448, you'll find your-

Heavy winter snowfall is common in the mountains of northern New Mexico.

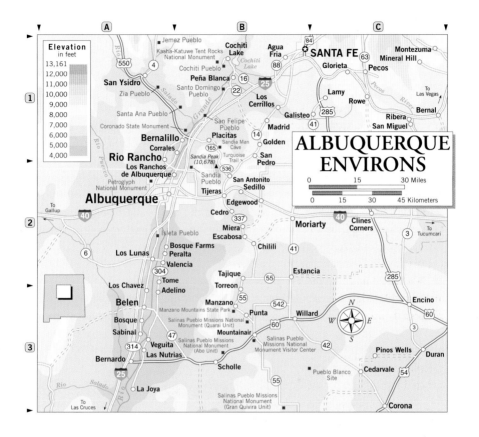

Elevation in feet
13,161
12,000
11,000
10,000
9,000
8,000
7,000
6,000
5,000
4,000

ALBUQUERQUE ENVIRONS

0   15   30 Miles
0   15   30   45 Kilometers

self in the quiet village of **Corrales,** where the pace is slow and police are quick to enforce the speed limit (25 mph). In addition to a few shops and cafés, the village holds a prize acquisition of the Albuquerque Museum, **Casa San Ysidro.** This 18th-century rancho was carefully restored over the course of 40 years by its former owners, Ward Alan and Shirley Minge. These days, you can see it only on a guided tour, and entering the house is like taking a walk back in time. The 18th-century furnishings include a print of San Ysidro Labrador, the casa's patron saint, set in a frame made of tin cans, and a leather-seated chair they acquired from Taos Pueblo. Wooden lanterns with mica window panes hang from beams in the courtyard, but are just for show; their flammable materials were the cause of many fires before tin lanterns came along. *973 Old Church Road; 505-898-3915.*

■ To Bernalillo   *map page 65, A/B-1*

From Corrales, follow NM 448 north to NM 528 until it ends at U.S. 550, just north of Bernalillo, where Coronado wintered at Kuaua Pueblo in 1540. This 1,200-room Tiwa pueblo was the home of a group of Indians who had drifted down from Chaco Canyon around A.D. 1300. At the pueblo, built along the banks of the changeable Rio Grande, which flows muddy in the spring and deep green in the winter, these Indians grew beans, squash, and corn. They built several underground ceremonial kivas, which they entered by ladder through an opening in the roof. On the walls of one kiva they painted black fish, white rabbits, white clouds, seed and corn, white-tipped red arrows, and masked kachinas dressed in yellow shirts with black skirts and white sashes. Near the end of the 17th century, the Indians abandoned the pueblo, probably moving south, and sands drifted over Kuaua's mud walls, burying it for the next 250 years.

■ Coronado State Monument   *map page 65, B-1*

When archaeologists excavated Kuaua in 1935, they discovered 85 layers of adobe plaster inside the kiva, 17 of which contained painted symbols of the Indians' complex relationship with the earth and the heavens. After the monument was created in 1940 to preserve the pueblo ruins, some of these original murals were encased in glass inside the visitors center. Reproductions of others line the walls of a reconstructed kiva, which can be entered by climbing down a solid wooden ladder into the cool subterranean interior.

Outside, tumbleweeds wedge themselves into corners of the crumbling rock walls of the pueblo. A trail winds alongside the low, eroding walls that divide the pueblo's rooms, passing cholla cactus, four-wing saltbush, and clumps of grass. In the distance, the craggy ridges of the pale-green Sandia Mountains loom against the eastern sky; closer in, ducks float atop the gently flowing Rio Grande, which passes by rust-colored reeds and sweet-smelling Russian olive trees in front of the pueblo. *NM 550, 1 mile west of town; 505-867-5351.*

Even though Coronado was unimpressed by Bernalillo's fertile greenbelt, other Spaniards recognized its value and made their homes along the river there in the late 16th century. Unlike most pioneers to the north, who built simple homes and tended their own small farms or ranches, these upper-class colonists received large land grants. Families like the Montoyas, Bacas, Castillos, and Pereas hired *paisanos* to tend the new crops they introduced, such as grapes, Castilian wheat, plums, and peaches, and to look after their vast herds of cattle and sheep. The Gonzales-Bernal family owned the largest spread, and the town took its name from theirs.

These *hacendados,* or wealthy land barons, lived in 40-room houses and protected their privacy by erecting high adobe walls around the immaculately kept grounds. Inside their houses were finely carved tables and tall cupboards, hauled up from Mexico over the Chihuahua Trail. They ate with silver knives and forks, sometimes off silver plates. Men trimmed their clothes with silver buttons, silk sashes, and silver buckles, and women adorned bright skirts with ribbons, silk, lace, and velvet. Their field workers and servants and their families lived in Las Cocinitas (Little Kitchens)—a barrio of squat adobe houses whose ruins can be seen today at the south end of Bernalillo.

Diego de Vargas spent a night at the settlement during his reconquest of New Mexico after the Pueblo Revolt and founded Bernalillo officially three years later, in 1695. He died there nine years later, while on a campaign against Indians, probably from wounds received in a skirmish. From the beginning, Bernalillo flourished as a trading center; local hacienda owners exchanged vegetables, wool, and meat for iron tools, shoes, paper, and sugar from caravans heading north on the Chihuahua Trail.

In 1871, Nathan Bibo, who already had stores in the lumber town of Porter and the gold-mining settlement of Bland, along with trading posts near Acoma and Laguna pueblos, opened the Bernalillo Mercantile Company. No item was too large or too unusual for Bibo to stock. He sold coffins, harnesses, overalls, tractors, Studebaker wagons, feathers, spittoons, loggers' hooks, blue cornmeal, and dolls. Customers could rent rooms at the "Merc" while they waited to have their wheat ground or to sell their sheep. Today, the refurbished building sells groceries under the name T&T Supermart.

Bernalillo's decline began in 1878, when five well-tailored men disembarked from a stagecoach to meet with José Leandro Perea, the leading *patron* of the day. The men had selected the town as the site of the main offices and chief division point of the Atchison, Topeka & Santa Fe Railroad, which soon would wend its way into the region. Perea, however, saw no need for the noise and clutter the operation would bring and intentionally overpriced the plots requested by the rail line. The men returned to their coach, headed instead to Albuquerque, and built

(following pages) Paddling on the Rio Grande near Bernalillo.

the main offices there, spurring the growth of what went on to become the state's largest city. Bernalillo received a red-painted frame depot, a railroad siding, and a grade crossing. As its southern neighbor grew, Bernalillo remained unchanged. Today, most of its streets have Spanish names. The single-story, tin-roofed adobe homes at the north end of town are the work of Abenicio Salazar, a local carpenter who built hundreds of adobe buildings in the early 1900s.

Every August, townsfolk spend weekends and evenings rehearsing for the **Fiesta de San Lorenzo.** During the three-day event, they share great spreads of chile, tortillas, bread, and desserts, and some of them turn into actors and perform Los Matachines, a dance-drama whose origins are traced to medieval Europe. The colorful dance reflects Spanish, Moorish, and Aztec influences and most likely has been performed every year since the 1600s.

The story pits good against evil as Montezuma, last emperor of the Aztec Empire, becomes a Christian during the dance. A young girl dressed in white to emphasize her goodness is said to be Doña Marina, an exiled Aztec princess who spoke both the Mayan and Aztec languages and served as interpreter and later mistress to Hernán Cortés. The Montezuma figure leads in dance other rulers dressed like himself in brightly colored shawls draped over street clothes. Red, pink, yellow, and blue ribbons cascade down their backs. They wear tall headgear, known as *coronas,* decorated with silver belt buckles and jewelry, striped brocade, beads, and Christmas ornaments. In one hand these men carry a gourd rattle, in the other a three-pronged wooden ornament known as a *palma.* Plaintive strains from fiddles and guitars create a somber mood. Providing comic relief are the *abuelos* (grandfathers) who serve as clowns, threatening the town's children with whips to keep them in line.

■ **INTO THE SANDIAS**   *map page 65, B-1*

Across I-25 east of Bernalillo, NM 165 traverses gently rolling hills covered with bushy piñon pines and junipers, passing through the tiny village of Placitas. Once home to 21 families, recipients of the 1745 San Antonio de las Huertas grant, Placitas has evolved from a rural hippie haven into an upscale Albuquerque subdivision. Overlooking the Rio Grande Valley are expensive multilevel adobe homes built on spacious lots, with walls of windows, high viga-and-*latilla* ceilings, and indoor hot tubs. The slate-blue Jemez Mountains rise to the west and the majestic Sandias form a closer backdrop to the south.

Once past Placitas, NM 165 heads into the Sandias, following the tree-lined banks of Las Huertas Creek. The gravel road passes under tall pines, locusts, and elder trees and alongside granite outcroppings covered with orange lichen. A turnout marks **Sandia Man Cave,** where prehistoric spear points and scrapers were discovered in 1936 by Dr. Frank Hibben, then an anthropology student at the University of New Mexico. These tools were chipped by hunters who pursued bison and woolly mammoth throughout the middle Rio Grande Valley nearly 12,000 years ago. Known as Sandia Man, these early people were contemporaries of Clovis Man, another hunter who roamed southeastern New Mexico.

An easily maneuvered half-mile trail leads to the cave, but at the cave itself is a concrete staircase followed by a 12-foot spiral of metal steps scaling the sheer rock face up to the opening. Inside, the narrow shaft has been sealed off to protect would-be explorers from getting stuck while crawling on their bellies 300 feet to its end.

Back on NM 165, the narrow road weaves its way through scrub oaks, ponderosa pines, and aspen groves until it joins NM 536, a paved road that ascends the mountain's eastern flank. Because of deep snow and a scant shoulder, NM 165 is closed during winter months.

Corn Dance photographed at Santo Domingo Pueblo in 1913.

SPANISH COLONIAL LIFE: THE WEDDING FEAST

At last all was ready, and the engaged youth and maiden, who though under the same roof since their betrothal had kept away from one another, now met again and before the altar in the evening, accompanied by their godparents. They were married in candlelight, with the hand-shaped earthen walls of their family about them, and a burden upon them of solemn commitment. Tensions broke when the vows were done. All gathered in the sala for the wedding feast. Now a river house had put forth another reach of growth and promise of the future, all in proper observance of ways that were as old as memory. In her white silk wedding dress the bride went on the arm of her husband in his rich silver-braided suit and his lace-ruffled shirt. Everyone came past to embrace them, and then the feast began. Roast chickens basted in spiced wine and stuffed with meat; piñons and raisins; baked hams; ribs of beef; fresh bread of blue meal; cookies, cakes, sweets; beakers of chocolate and flasks of wine; bowls of hot chile; platters of tortillas, all stood upon extra tables draped to the floor with lace curtains. All feasted.

Then came music, and dark eyes fired up. The sala was cleared, while the musicians tuned up on two or three violins, a guitar and a guitarron, or bass guitar. Servants came to spread clean wheat straw on the earth floor to keep dust from rising, or stood by with jars of water from which to sprinkle the floor between dances. In the candlelight the faces of the woman, heavily powdered with Mexican white lead, looked an ashen violet, in which their eyes were dark caves deeply harboring the ardent emotion of the occasion. The orchestra struck up. They danced quadrilles and minuets, whose figures drew all dancers into fleeting touch with each other. There were paired dances, like la raspa, with its heel thunderings and its laughing fast walk.

While the dancing went on, the bride had an obligation to fulfill. Retiring from the floor in her wedding dress, she reappeared presently in another gown from her trousseau, and later in another, and another. Everyone was eager to see what she had been given. Politely and proudly she gratified them. They fingered her silks and examined the set of jewels given her by the groom—matching earrings, necklace, bracelets, combs, brooches, and gold inlaid with enamel, or seed pearls, rose diamonds, amethysts or garnets.

Before midnight the bride retired not to reappear. Her maiden friends and her godmother went with her. The groom drank with the men in whose company he now belonged, while boys watched and nudged. The dancing continued, and humor went around. The groom's father calling above the noise in the hot, hard-plastered room, urged everyone to keep right on enjoying themselves. Presently the groom managed to slip away. In the bridal chamber the ladies admitted him and left him with his bride. Across the patio the merriment continued. Voices were singing. Someone shouted a refrain. The violins jigged along in a remote monotonous sing, and the gulping throb of the guitarron was like a pulse of mindless life in the night.

—Paul Horgan,
Great River: The Rio Grande in North American History, 1954

■ ANCIENT PUEBLOS *map page 65, B-1*

North of Bernalillo, NM 313 passes the modern stuccoed homes of **Santa Ana Pueblo** before meeting up with I-25, which veers away from the Rio Grande as it heads north toward Santa Fe. Through this region, the river courses alongside three Keres-speaking pueblos: San Felipe, Santo Domingo, and Cochiti. While the three share a language, each has its own dialect and each is known for its own special tradition: San Felipe for its Christmas Eve dances; Santo Domingo for its Corn Dance; and Cochiti for its pottery. In recent years, San Felipe and Santa Ana have opened casinos, which operate 20 hours a day. Even with gambling nearby, San Felipe remains one of the most traditional pueblos, as does Santo Domingo; cameras and tape recorders are not allowed at either. Remember to ask permission at the governor's office before walking around the communities. Not to do so would be discourteous.

Though many of the ceremonies at **Santo Domingo Pueblo** are closed to the public, every August 4 visitors are welcome to view the elaborate Corn Dance. It begins mid-morning, when the comic Koshare appear, painted in black and gray stripes, to warn the pueblo of attackers approaching the village. Having issued their warning, the dancers pantomime the ensuing battle, in which the Indians defeat the invaders. A steady drumbeat announces the arrival of the singers: about 50 Pueblo men who slowly walk into the enormous dirt plaza, chanting rhythmically. As they arrange themselves along one side, a line of male and female dancers, the squash, or pumpkin, group, their bodies tinted orange-tan colors, emerges from a kiva to the south. With measured steps, they move gracefully to the drumbeat, shaking turtle and gourd rattles. This group then moves out and the turquoise group, dancers painted blue, enters the plaza. The men in both groups wear kilts adorned with a foxtail at the waist and skunk skins and bells around each ankle. Women wear one-shouldered black dresses and colorfully painted stiff boards (*tablitas*) atop their heads. After a break for midday feasting, the dancing continues until the sun sinks below the Jemez Mountains.

At **Cochiti Pueblo,** outsiders are always welcome to view the Church of San Buenaventura, whose interior displays tin candlesticks brought from Chihuahua and a larger-than-life painting of the patron saint on the center wall above the altar. The pueblo is also recognized for its pottery, especially red-and-black "storyteller" dolls that depict little children crawling and clinging to an open-mouthed grandmother or grandfather figure.

Clowns play an important role in the Corn Dance. These performed at San Juan Pueblo in 1935.

Just north of Cochiti Pueblo's water tanks (painted to look like animal-skin drums), the Rio Grande backs up behind Cochiti Dam, creating a swimming hole and a haven for windsurfers. Also near the water tanks, an otherworldly tableau of rock spires rises from the desert scrub. **Kasha-Katuwe Tent Rocks National Monument** is a maze of cone-shaped formations eroded long ago from volcanic debris. Trails, some only hip-wide, wind through this lunar landscape, offering one of the state's most unusual hiking outings. *505-761-8700.*

■ TURQUOISE TRAIL *map page 65, B-1/2*

More than a thousand years ago, Pueblo Indians in the Cerrillos Hills south of Santa Fe were using stone hammers to mine for turquoise—highly prized for its beauty as well as its purported ability to ensure good fortune and a long, healthy life. This stunning blue mineral found its way to Mexico, where, according to legend, Montezuma II, the powerful Aztec emperor, proudly displayed his pendants and necklaces of Cerrillos turquoise.

Later miners coaxed gold, coal, silver, lead, and zinc from the Ortiz and San Pedro Mountains, which extend south to Tijeras Canyon, a scissors-like passage (*tijeras* means "scissors") that bisects the Sandia and Manzano Mountains east of Albuquerque. Today NM 14, now called the Turquoise Trail, connects these long-dormant mining districts.

Tall yellow-green grasses mix with an occasional cholla cactus as the two-lane road leaves behind the bedroom communities of Cedar Crest and Sandia Park, which sprawl on the eastern edges of the Sandia Mountains. The air is scented with juniper berries and hills are dotted with piñons and junipers, a refreshing change from Albuquerque's gas stations, burger stands, and auto parts stores. As the road wends its way northward, the snowcapped peaks of the Sangre de Cristo Mountains appear behind corners.

Not much is going on anymore in **Golden,** once a bustling gold-mining district on the northern edge of the San Pedro Mountains. Piñons sprout from the ruins of the rock homes that proliferated in the mid-1800s, when the town was booming with 22 stores and 100 houses. Still, nobody got rich, because there wasn't enough water to wash the gold dust from the sand.

Golden's most impressive building is a little mission church atop a hill at the northern edge of town. Built in the late 1830s soon after the gold rush began, the adobe church honored St. Francis of Assisi. A hand-carved and carefully detailed figure of the church's patron saint, brought by *carreta* from Mexico in the early 1700s, was displayed inside for more than 130 years, until it was moved to the cathedral in Santa Fe. A newer St. Francis has replaced its predecessor, along with two other statues, one a five-foot rendering of St. Peter. Services are conducted at the simple church twice a year—on June 29 for the Feast of St. Peter and on October 4 for the Feast of St. Francis. Keep in mind that this is private property, so be sure to respect fences and closed gates.

The green slopes of the Sandia Mountains rise to the southwest; in the distance, the ski runs of Sandia Peak Ski Area, snow-covered in winter, appear in summer like fairways divided by the deeper green dark groves of pine trees. Pale-green lichen cover rock outcroppings as the road penetrates the Ortiz Mountains and descends into the once-thriving coal mining district of **Madrid**. Charcoal-gray and pinkish-red tailings pile up underneath bare slopes, reminders of an era that began in 1889, when the mines produced 500 tons of coal daily. Wooden cabins, two

Artist Edward Gilliam paints in his studio in Madrid.

stories high, once lined the main street, and white picket fences protected groomed lawns and well-tended flower gardens. Company-owned Madrid even boasted a 30-piece brass band that marched in a parade each Fourth of July.

In the 1930s, Madrid was so famous for its annual Christmas display that TWA pilots made detours to catch an aerial view of its 150,000 lights. Christmas decorations covered every inch of the main street, and the city ballpark was transformed into a giant toy-land, in which a miniature train carried children past the House that Jack Built and Peter the Pumpkin Eater. In recent years, Madrid residents have revived the Christmas light tradition.

During World War II, Madrid shipped 20,000 tons of coal to the secret mountain community of Los Alamos, where scientists were developing the world's first atomic bomb. By 1947, the demand for coal as heating fuel dwindled, and the mines were forced to close. In 1975, tired of waiting for another boom or a buyer for the entire town, owner Joe Huber sold Madrid piece by piece. It took 16 days. Artists, craftsmen, and back-to-the-earth characters purchased the 150 dilapidated buildings for between $1,500 and $7,500 each. Today, many of the miners' cabins and hillside adobe homes sport new roofs and windowpanes, and new galleries and gift shops face NM 14. Mexican folk art, custom clothing and toys, jewelry made by Santo Domingo Pueblo craftsmen, and locally crafted pottery line the shelves of the quaint shops. You can still descend into an old mine shaft at the Old Coal Mine Museum.

A few more bends in the road and **Los Cerrillos** appears beneath leafy cottonwoods. Its boom days also long over, this sleepy hamlet resembles a movie set, with a few faded storefronts, dirt streets, and rundown exteriors. In the late 1800s, when Los Cerrillos still offered lodging at hotels, and when the 21 saloons were filled with miners seeking their fortunes in gold, Thomas Edison paid a visit. He tried to extract gold from sand and gravel using static electricity, but he wasn't able to do it.

Today, the Casa Grande Trading Post sells souvenirs and gifts, and also features a turquoise mining museum and a homespun petting zoo in which goats, sheep, and burros await caresses—and handouts—from soft hands. The Clear Light Opera House is now a recording studio.

Detour west to the **Eaves Movie Ranch** and you'll be back in the days when frontier justice reigned—at least on the silver screen. Scores of westerns have been filmed on this movie set, including *Young Guns, Silverado,* and *The Cheyenne Social Club.* Movies continue to be filmed here; daily tours are available and the ranch can be reserved for your own private party. *Take NM 14 south of Santa Fe, turn west on NM 45 (Bonanza Creek Road); 505-474-3045.*

Farther west on NM 45 is the **Millennium Turquoise Mine**, where some of the world's highest-grade turquoise was first mined in A.D. 500. Known as the Tiffany-Cerrillos Mines when the Tiffany Company of New York was part-owner, the site no longer is open to the public. But you can stand at the fence along this lightly traveled road, gaze at the distant Jemez and Ortiz Mountains on either side of you, and imagine those ancient Indian miners cracking the rocks with their crude picks.

■ East and South of Albuquerque

East of Albuquerque, I-40 bisects the Sandia and Manzano mountain ranges as it follows Tijeras Canyon en route to the eastern plains. One of the state's more interesting drives curves along the eastern foothills of the Manzano Mountains on NM 337. Leaving the canyon, the road climbs and dips, at times hugging granite outcroppings covered with lichens and at others crossing wide-open meadows of yellow wildflowers. Along this route are villages with such musical-sounding names as Chilili, Tajique, and Torreon, created through 19th-century land grants.

In 1829, at the mountain range's southern end, Spanish settlers built a small fort for protection from Apache attacks and named their community **Manzano**, after an apple orchard established there probably in the 1600s. Still bearing fruit today, this orchard is the oldest in the country. Manzano remains a sleepy town of tin-roofed adobe homes, some with horses in the yard, and a stuccoed adobe church. A gravel road winds away from town to Capilla Peak. Another leads to a shady campground at the base of Manzano State Park—the starting point for hikers who wish to scale the mountains on foot. *505-847-2820.*

South of Manzano, the rolling slopes of junipers and piñons give way to the meadows of the Estancia Basin, traveled by nomadic hunters who camped on the shores of a huge lake that filled the basin 12,000 years ago. In the 10th century, Mogollon Indians established villages alongside streams and fresh springs they could depend on to water their corn, beans, and squash; they also hunted antelope and deer, gathered piñon nuts and wild berries in nearby hills, and fashioned simple red or brown clay pottery. Their homes were pit houses, which later were replaced by *jacales,* or log-and-mud huts.

Nearly 200 years later, the Anasazi arrived, bringing with them their stone-and-mortar architecture and multilevel homes. At nearby salt lakes and beds, they mined salt, which they bartered (along with corn, beans, squash, piñon nuts, and cotton goods) in exchange for buffalo meat, hides, flints, and shells from Plains tribes to the east and Rio Grande pueblos to the west. This area, at the southern edge of the Manzanos, served as a major trade route, connecting tribes throughout the region.

Juan de Oñate visited in 1598, but Spaniards didn't move in until Franciscan priests settled alongside Indians early in the next century. The missionaries wasted no time converting the pueblo residents to Christianity and forcing them to build massive churches. Initially the Franciscans tried to prohibit the Indians from practicing their native religion, but their efforts failed, and the Indians eventually frequented both churches and their traditional kivas.

■ SALINAS PUEBLO MISSIONS NATIONAL MONUMENT
map page 65, B-3

Three pueblos, separately situated in a 25-mile radius around the ranching center of Mountainair have been preserved as Salinas Pueblo Missions National Monument. At Punta de Agua, a quiet hamlet on NM 55, a gravel road veers off to the west, leading to the mission ruins at **Quarai.** Sandstone walls still loom 40 feet above a grassy plain, much as they did in 1630, when the church of La Purísima Concepción de Cuarac was completed. A well-marked trail passes by the unexcavated mounds of pueblo dwellings, covered with patches of grass. Entering the nave of the church, you walk on some of the original flagstones. The dirt roof is gone, leaving an azure sky exposed. Outside, a kiva is submerged in the earth. Additional rooms that stretch to the mission's far walls, which surrounded the pueblo, most likely served as stables, hay and storage sheds, and animal pens. Close by the settlement, a grove of towering cottonwoods indicates the springs that were so vital to Quarai's survival. Today, these trees provide shade to picnickers who sit at tables and gaze over at the imposing church, perhaps speculating about what the original residents might have had for lunch—beef jerky and corn tortillas with beans, washed down with goat milk.

Seventeen miles southwest via NM 55 and U.S. 60, Indians at **Abo** erected their mission church in the late 1620s atop a rise in a wide valley surrounded by hillsides covered with piñon and juniper trees. Built of bright red sandstone, Abo's church was 30 feet high. Even though the roof is gone, its 2-foot-thick walls are still supported by stone buttresses—an unusually sophisticated building technique for 17th-century New Mexico. The church contained an organ, which was

About 1,500 people once lived at Gran Quivira, now part of Salinas Pueblo Missions National Monument.

accompanied by a choir during services. The narrow Abo River gently flows near the Indians' three-storied rock-walled homes, now covered with red soil and patches of pale-green desert grass. Only partial walls show above the earth.

South of Mountainair, NM 55 crosses vast fields of cholla cactus and brilliant orange-red Indian paintbrush. An occasional truck rattling along a lonely road disturbs the silence, and an occasional hawk floats in the sky. Then, looking up, you see the partial walls of the mission church at **Gran Quivira** materialize atop a distant mesa. Early Spanish visitors who arrived with Juan de Oñate in 1598 named the community Pueblo de los Jumanos (Village of the Striped Ones) for a stripe the Indians painted across their noses. Later explorers gave it its current name, perhaps wishfully thinking that it might hold the riches of the mythical Quivira that Coronado and Oñate sought.

Once, 1,500 people lived at Gran Quivira, growing beans and squash in well-watered fields. Though no water source is known to exist within 30 miles, historians believe the Indians may have captured rainwater in natural limestone cisterns or tapped a spring that has since dried up. The Indians here also hunted bison and fashioned pottery painted with black and white stripes. In 1659, forced by the Spanish, they erected the massive Mission of San Buenaventura, with 30-foot-high gray-blue limestone walls that were six feet thick. Nearby, they worshipped their traditional gods in underground kivas. By the 1670s, besieged by Apache attacks and drought, they left their homes to take refuge at pueblos along the Rio Grande, as did the other Indians of the Salinas Valley.

You can view generations of homes as you peer down into the pueblo's multi-level ruins. At the lowest level, the rock walls are ill-fitting compared with the well-crafted ones further up. Stone *metates* lie in the grass that has grown up between the walls. After walking through the ruins, you might want to sit on a stone bench, gaze out across the vast plains, and imagine children playing hide-and-seek among nearby stands of junipers, or think of the Indian women who once ground the day's cornmeal on these stone tools. From the top of this windswept mesa, the snow-capped peak of Sierra Blanca looms to the south; to the north you can see the Manzanos' deep-blue outline.

A visitors center for the three pueblos can be found on Main Street in Mountainair. *One block west of US 60 and NM 55; 505-847-2585.*

There was a time when **Mountainair** was known as the Pinto Bean Capital of the World. Like many of New Mexico's small towns, this ranching center has become popular among transplants from other states seeking an affordable and

The historic St. Augustine Church, Isleta Pueblo, ca. 1882–83.

safer lifestyle. The town's showpiece is the **Shaffer Hotel,** a whitewashed building adorned with orange and black squares and black swastikas (the Indian symbol for happiness). This 1929 masterpiece in the Pueblo deco style was the brainchild of Clem "Pop" Shaffer, a local folk artist who lived nearby at the equally whimsical Rancho Bonito, where he created his colorful works. Ownership of the hotel has changed often, and the current owner expects to reopen the Shaffer in 2004. Meanwhile, you can enjoy an enchilada or a burger and fries in the showpiece dining room, which has antique tin light fixtures and quirky geometric patterns. *US 60 (103 East Main Street); 505-847-2888.*

■ **ISLETA PUEBLO** *map page 65, A-2*

The imposing St. Augustine Church, built in the 17th century, remains the central focus of this large pueblo (population exceeding 3,000), established alongside the Rio Grande in the 14th century and located 13 miles south of Albuquerque. Inside the church's massive walls, several large paintings of saints important to the village stand out against the whitewashed background. Outside, simple one-story adobe homes typical of the state's pueblo communities sit in contrast. In even starker contrast is the Isleta Casino and Resort, a 300,000-square-foot complex that includes five restaurants, a 27-hole golf course, and a state-of-the-art concert venue.

Deer's Skull with Pedernal, *painted in 1936 by Georgia O'Keeffe, New Mexico's most famous artist.*

NORTH-CENTRAL
N E W M E X I C O

North-central New Mexico is framed by the pine forests, aspen groves, and craggy peaks of the Sangre de Cristo and San Juan Mountains and by the gentler slopes of the Jemez Mountains. In between are the russet-tawny-lavender cliffs near Abiquiu, the placid Chama River, and the more turbulent Rio Grande. Within this rugged, mountainous region, the light casts a daily spell. Sunsets turn deep green hillsides golden, then transform them into swaths of red; coyotes howl and owls hoot as the ink-blue of evening blankets the high country and lights switch on in the tiny villages.

Long ago, Indian agricultural communities flourished in the soft, crumbly tuff formed from ash and cinders left behind by volcanic eruptions. The ruins of some of these communities are preserved at Bandelier National Monument and the Puye Cliff Dwellings. Many of the state's surviving Indian pueblos are also spread throughout this region, near waterways that flow from the snow-packed Jemez Mountains. They look much like other rural New Mexican towns, their low-slung adobe buildings arranged around a central plaza. The most spectacular is the northernmost, Taos Pueblo—a stunning multilevel structure that has been occupied continuously since 1350.

Hispanic culture is pervasive here, with Spanish spoken as often as English—if not more so. Even the smallest hamlet displays a well-tended Catholic church, usually built of sturdy adobe; some isolated ranches have their own chapels.

The Rio Grande makes a dramatic entrance into New Mexico here from its headwaters in southern Colorado, cutting a 650-foot-deep gash through a sagebrush plain. The blue-green water kicks up through the Rio Grande gorge, churning itself into roiling rapids and deadly drops. One bridge passes over the deep volcanic chasm along U.S. 64; another rugged gravel road with no designation follows the Rio Hondo, slicing through the gorge's middle. The only other access to the river here is by steep trails.

Once through the gorge, the Rio Grande mellows. Towns such as Velarde and Alcalde tap its water to irrigate apple orchards before the river pools up behind Cochiti Dam. The Rio Grande also flows past Bandelier National Monument and Española, which bills itself as the Low Rider capital of the world—a place where

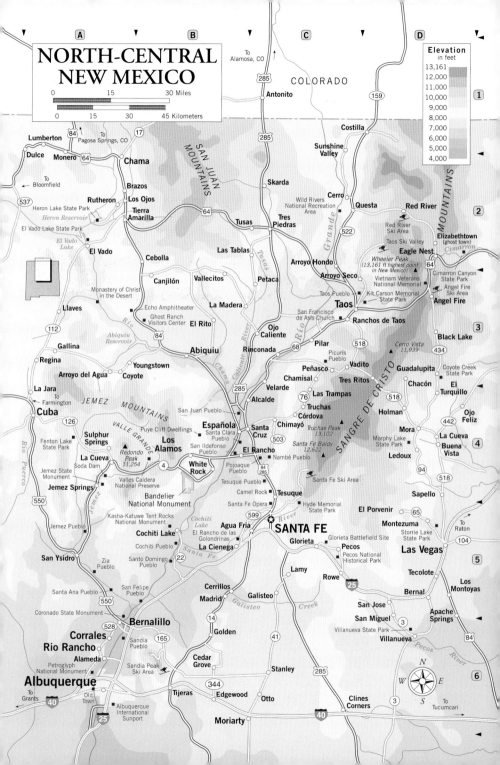

Deer's Skull with Pedernal, *painted in 1936 by Georgia O'Keeffe, New Mexico's most famous artist.*

the owners of these custom cars drive them slowly down the main drag, forcing others to admire their chain link steering wheels and low-slung body chassis.

Another of New Mexico's major waterways, the Chama River, enters the state with less fanfare at the western edge of this region. This gentle river, winding between alpine meadows and pine forests, forms reservoirs behind the Heron, El Vado, and Abiquiu Dams before joining the Rio Grande north of Española.

North-central's magical setting has attracted scores of artists, who have been coming since the 1920s to paint, sketch, and write about its sandstone bluffs, pine forests, and silent sagebrush plains, as well as the modest people rooted in its earth. Georgia O'Keeffe and D. H. Lawrence are the best known, but hundreds more have settled here. Galleries can be found in a good number of small towns; most of them exhibit paintings, pottery, weavings, and jewelry made by local artists.

■ INDIAN HISTORY

Around A.D. 1100, the Anasazi Indians began to leave their multitiered homes in Chaco Canyon in northwestern New Mexico and southern Colorado. Very likely, they had despaired of waiting for the unreliable seasonal storms needed to water their crops and decided to head toward water they could count on. Most ended up along the Rio Grande or one of its tributaries. In some cases, these farmers joined tribes already growing corn and beans in the fertile lowlands. Others formed new communities, building multifamily dwellings and, deploying methods developed at Chaco Canyon, diverting river water to irrigate crops. Some of these transplanted natives also broke with tradition and constructed their buildings according to a new organizing principle. Instead of carving out homes in canyon walls or lining a valley floor with multistoried structures, they built their new homes along streets and around open plazas.

During this transition, known as the Regressive Period, which lasted until 1450, ceremonial kivas varied from pueblo to pueblo; while some remained traditionally round, others were rectangular. Pottery styles changed from black-on-white vessels to black- or white-on-red, and designs also differed from pueblo to pueblo.

Pueblo Indians lived in flat-roofed buildings of multiple levels, with each upper level built behind the lower one so that access could be gained by climbing outside ladders. Inside there was a series of rectangular rooms with a central fireplace and a corner for grinding corn. Lower storage rooms were entered by a ladder through the ceiling, while additional ladders led to upper-story rooms. The Indians used whatever building materials were available; along the river where rocks were scarce, they prepared adobe by mixing water with the clay and sandy soil, then spreading this paste over a framework of sticks and brush.

By 1500, the Indians were concentrated in the Acoma-Zuni area and the Rio Grande Valley. Sixteenth-century Spanish explorers found nearly 80 pueblos scattered throughout northern New Mexico, some with as many as 300 residents. They were impressed with their ingenious structure, and the fact that the buildings were around plazas reminded them of the towns of their homeland, prompting them to call both the towns and those who lived in them by the Spanish word for town, "pueblo."

Indian religion reflected a deep reverence for nature: the sun and moon were gods; clouds, thunder, and wind were Pueblo spirits. Religious ceremonies dominated life. During summer, they focused on the growing of crops; in winter, on hunting. Produce consisted of beans, squash, melons, and several varieties of corn: yellow, blue, white, pink, red, and deep purple. Fresh vegetables were a treat in the summer and fall, but most were dried and stored for the cold winter. Likewise, buffalo meat was dried into jerky, the hides used as blankets and coats.

■ SPANISH HISTORY

Eleven years after Juan de Oñate carved out the settlement of San Gabriel, New Mexico's first capital, during his expedition of 1598, King Philip III of Spain designated New Mexico a royal colony, which placed it under the direct control of the Spanish Crown. This new designation meant that the Spanish government would pay the colony's expenses, along with those incurred by missionaries in their efforts to spread the Catholic faith. The following year Pedro de Peralta was dispatched from New Spain, with orders to establish a new capital. He chose a spot 30 miles south of San Gabriel in a grove of junipers and piñons, beside which ran a narrow stream that meandered down from the nearby Sangre de Cristo Mountains (named "Blood of Christ" for the color they reflect at sunset). At an altitude of 7,000 feet, the new capital, La Villa Real de la Santa Fé de San Francisco de Asís, enjoyed crisp, clean mountain air and looked westward to juniper-covered mesas and the soft curves of the Jemez Mountains.

(opposite) Pueblo Bonito, Chaco Canyon.

De Peralta proceeded to establish a town council, assign house and garden lots to citizens, and order construction of the Palace of the Governors, a walled compound that contained the governor's residence, government offices, and council chambers. From this fortress, 60 successive Spanish governors ruled New Mexico. All of this activity bespoke a sense of permanence, and Santa Fe to this day remains the capital of New Mexico, the oldest state capital in the United States. The Palace of the Governors, now a museum, is the nation's oldest government building.

During the next 65 years, aptly called the Great Missionary Period, 250 friars of the Franciscan Order traveled among the pueblos, building churches and tirelessly working to turn the Indians into devout Catholics. Missions sprang up from the town of Pecos to the western villages of the Hopi in eastern Arizona. Soon, the simple pueblo dwellings were dwarfed by colossal churches in their midst. Indians were ordered to erect these structures, assembling 30-foot-high walls with adobe bricks that weighed 60 pounds each and topping the buildings off with heavy vigas, *latillas* (smaller poles set between the vigas), dirt roofs, and a bell tower.

Church leaders didn't stop at converting the Indians. The Spaniards taught them painting, Latin, blacksmithing, carpentry, and weaving; they also showed them how to play the small pipe organs that had been transported in wagons from Mexico. As the friars and priests pressed their efforts to "civilize" the natives, they also set out to destroy Indian civilization—raiding ceremonial kivas, desecrating altars, and burning masks, prayer plumes, and fetishes in the plazas. Soon they had outlawed all Pueblo religious rites, singing, and dancing.

The crackdown on Pueblo religions came to a head in 1675, when Gov. Juan Francisco Trevino ordered the arrest of 47 medicine men, whom Spanish priests regarded as little more than devil worshipers. Three were hanged, another hanged himself, and the rest were whipped and jailed. In response, a group of Tewa warriors descended upon the capital, demanding the prisoners' release. Though Trevino obliged, the seed of revolt had been planted and Pueblo activists began plotting an uprising against the oppressive Spanish.

That day arrived one day in 1680, when Indian runners delivered a knotted yucca cord to each pueblo. A knot was to be untied each day, until none were left, signifying the day for battle. Led by Popé, a medicine man of San Juan Pueblo who had been humiliated by Trevino five years earlier, Pueblo Indians across New Mexico attacked settlers, burning their homes and killing entire families. The warriors directed their greatest wrath at the churches, giving vent to years of frustration by slaughtering priests at their altars and destroying holy symbols, smearing them with human excrement. Eleven days later, Gov. Antonio de Otermin surrendered Santa Fe and led a string of battered, frightened settlers southward. The Indians let them go.

The shattered Spanish settlers retreated 300 miles to El Paso, but within a year had regrouped and were making attempts to retake the territory. Armed Indians repelled them three times during the next decade. With the Spanish safely deposed, Popé encouraged the Indians to shed all ties to the Europeans and to return to their traditional ways. All Spanish influences—clothing, tools, livestock—were to be discarded, and everyone was to wash in the river with soapweed to remove the taint of baptism. Unfortunately for Popé and his followers, many Indians couldn't remember much about the days before the Spanish and their cattle, sheep, and horses. The pueblos did revive the independence they had

Don Diego de Vargas was the man chosen to recapture New Mexico from the Indians in 1692.

temporarily lost to the Spanish, but old feuds soon resurfaced, Popé lost his grip, and the nomadic Apaches, now on horseback, renewed their raiding on pueblos to a degree not seen since the onset of Spanish rule.

In 1692, when Diego de Vargas, accompanied by 60 soldiers and 100 Indian helpers, marched northward from El Paso, he passed one deserted pueblo after another before arriving in Santa Fe, which he found in a shambles. The Palace of the Governors had been converted into a pueblo. At first, the Indians countered his entrance into the city with a few bold refusals, but after a good long look down the barrels of the Spanish cannons, they surrendered, embracing de Vargas's promises of pardons and an unconditional return to the Catholic Church.

Despite this bloodless retaking, the next decade was rocked by more Indian uprisings—all unsuccessful. Thousands of Indians abandoned their Rio Grande

Famed potter Maria Martinez applies slip to a bowl at San Ildefonso Pueblo in 1941.

homes rather than return to Spanish rule, and many of these rebels moved in with the Hopis in eastern Arizona. Some eventually returned to the river, but others stayed on in Arizona. As New Mexico's Indians readjusted to the ways of their Spanish conquerors and resumed their subservient roles, church leaders wisely compromised: no longer did they raid sacred kivas, destroy religious symbols, or severely punish Indians who embraced Christianity while retaining their traditional religious practices.

Still, with their freedom gone forever, the Indians' spirits flagged. Diseases introduced by the Spanish took their toll on the natives, who had no resistance to measles, cholera, smallpox, and whooping cough. By the end of the 1700s, the pueblos had lost half their population, and of the nearly 80 pueblos that had flourished when the Spanish arrived three centuries before, only 19 remained.

The Spanish, however, thrived. Land grants were issued to entice colonists to the untamed province. They settled in villas laid out in fertile river valleys and on small ranches where they raised cattle and sheep, planted apple orchards, and cultivated squash, peas, and melons in fields irrigated by the Rio Grande, the Chama, and numerous streams that flowed from the mountains. As years passed, relations between the Indians and Spanish grew more cordial. Indian women shared their traditional methods for cooking bread, corn, beans, and chile. Both cultures traded herbs and healing plants, as well as their pottery-making and weaving techniques. The Spanish adopted the pueblos' flat-roofed architecture. And the two groups intermarried.

Today, mud-brick buildings blend into the chamisa-covered earth, cornstalks stand tall, and sheep munch on grass in small villages with names such as Abiquiu, Canjilon, Vallecitos, Santa Cruz, and Tierra Amarilla. These towns, which never prospered to any degree, still look much as they did 100 years ago. One of them, Hernandez, a mere cluster of adobe homes just north of Española, was made world famous by photographer Ansel Adams. After a disappointing day of photographing the northern New Mexico landscape in autumn 1941, Adams was passing through Hernandez when he noticed a full moon hovering high above the snowcapped peaks of the Sangre de Cristos. Standing atop his station wagon, he snapped a shot in which the moon cast an eerie light on the town's church and houses, illuminating crosses in its cemetery. "Moonrise Over Hernandez" proved to be the photographer's best-known work.

■ PUEBLO CULTURE TODAY

Despite a similar culture, history, and physical appearance, Pueblo Indians are not a single tribe with a common language. Today's 19 remaining pueblos share three language groups. Zuni is spoken only at Zuni Pueblo. Keres is the language at Acoma, Cochiti, Laguna, San Felipe, Santa Ana, Santo Domingo, and Zia Pueblos. The remaining 11 pueblos speak dialects of the Tanoan language family: Tiwa is spoken at Isleta, Picuris, Sandia, and Taos Pueblos; Tewa is spoken at Nambé, Pojoaque, San Ildefonso, San Juan, Santa Clara, and Tesuque Pueblos. Jemez Pueblo is the only one where Towa is spoken.

Pueblo Indians, stocky in build with piercing dark eyes, are reserved and very polite. They don't go for small talk, feeling that silence is part of the concentration that produces results. Accordingly, many of their rituals are cloaked in silence. Because towns have sprung up near most of the northern pueblos, many tribal members work at city jobs, returning to the pueblo on weekends and for ceremonies. This balancing of traditional demands with modern-day pressures often creates inner turmoil as people struggle to exist in two distinctly different worlds.

Further complicating this dilemma has been the introduction of Indian gaming in the state. Of New Mexico's 23 tribes, 13 operate casinos, some of which are part of first-class entertainment complexes that include golf courses and concert venues. The casinos have brought a new sense of financial security to some Indian communities, but they have also been accused of eroding traditional values.

The dice may roll, but Pueblo Indians continue to carry on their centuries-old creative traditions, weaving willow wickerwork baskets, beargrass and yucca bowls, and colorful cotton belts and headbands. They fashion beadwork jewelry and leather crafts, and painstakingly shape pottery without the aid of a potter's wheel. Clays usually are dug from sandstone mesas, then strengthened with volcanic ash. The potter shapes a pancake-like base, then patiently lays on rolls of coiled clay, one atop the other, until the desired shape and size are reached. Using a stone, the artist smoothes out the coils. Pots are polished and then fired outdoors in an open pit. If a red glaze is desired, the potter fires the pots with an oxidizing flame. To achieve the black-on-black pots made famous by Maria Martinez, cow dung is piled around and over the upside-down pottery, permitting the carbon to permeate the porous clay. To decorate the wares, potters use brushes of spiked yucca or soapweed leaves that have been chewed until only the stiff fibers remain.

Most pueblos also host a few silversmiths who continue the tradition of jewelry-making. Although metals were not commonly used for adornment until the 19th century, Pueblo craftsmen have for centuries been carving turquoise, shell, and other gemstones. Turquoise, once plentiful in the knobby volcanic rock of the Cerrillos Hills south of Santa Fe, is believed by the Indians to have beneficial powers: even a bead of the blue-green gemstone tied in an Indian's hair, they say, prevents disaster and ensures general well-being.

Another form of Indian artistic and religious expression can be found in kachinas, small doll-sized figures carved from a single piece of pine. Painted in bright colors and dressed in animal-like garb of deerskin, fur, feathers, and cloth, each kachina is unique and a constant reminder of the "real" kachinas—supernatural beings who live in the mountains, lakes, and clouds. These messengers dispense blessings, such as rain and good crops. All kachinas wear masks. Doll-like figurines of buffalo, deer, eagle, and snake dancers are not kachinas, although they often are sold alongside them.

Dances, held regularly, are the major measure by which Indians express their deep respect for nature. They dance to help the seasons follow one another in proper succession. They dance to promote fertility of plants and animals. They dance to encourage rain and ensure hunting success. Participation in these ceremonies is a duty and a privilege of all Pueblo people, who are trained to take part from early childhood. Every item of clothing and adornment involved in the dance has a special significance—from the hand-carried spruce or fir twigs, which symbolize physical longevity and everlasting life, to the feathers and tufts of down and cotton that are symbols of cloud and sky.

While some dances are open to the public, each pueblo has its own policy regarding guests. Some don't permit cameras or tape recorders, and those that do require approval from the tribal governor's office. Ceremonies are highly sacred to the pueblos and customs must be respected. Guests should stay clear of Indian performers or spectators, enter homes only when invited, and speak in hushed tones. Approach these ceremonies as if visiting a church of which you aren't a member.

A dancer at a Taos Pueblo powwow.

■ ABIQUIU   *map page 85, B-3*

Abiquiu (pronounced A-buh-kew) began as a farming and cattle center on the banks of the Chama River and later served as a stop on the Old Spanish Trail, the tortuous trade route from Santa Fe to Los Angeles. Shortly after Abiquiu's settlement in the 1740s, Spanish officials moved in a group of *genízaros* to help tame the barren land. These people were non-Pueblo Indians of mixed tribal blood but with Spanish surnames. Some had been captives of nomadic Apaches and Navajos who were sold to the Spanish as laborers and servants. At Abiquiu they fought alongside Spanish settlers, regularly fending off attacks of Ute Indians who came down from Colorado to terrorize the colonists. Arable land was scarce and could only be cultivated as far from waterways as irrigation ditches could be maintained. Timber was difficult to harvest because it had to be hauled long distances across open country. When not staging attacks, Ute Indians paid peaceful visits to Abiquiu, during which they traded deerskins for guns, horses, flour, and corn. ⌐

■ RELIGIOUS IMPULSES

The serenity of this spectacular red-rock country seemed to tap the spirituality of the Spanish who settled it. In Abiquiu, for instance, there were two *moradas,* or meeting houses, of the Penitentes, a confraternity of the Catholic Church that believed in experiencing the suffering of Christ by self-flagellation. The order was formed in the 19th century by Spanish men isolated in rural towns without resident priests. Seeking forgiveness for their sins, as well as for the sins of those who nailed Christ to a cross, the Penitentes performed community service, assisting the sick and poor, comforting the bereaved, and counseling those who were troubled. By voting as a block, they wielded much political power.

The high point of their year was Holy Week, its climax the reenactment of the crucifixion of Jesus. A procession of bare-backed men climbed a hillside, followed by a member chosen to represent Christ. As they marched, the men whipped themselves until they bled, and when they were no longer able to lash themselves, their companions took over the torture. "Christ" labored under a wooden cross that weighed as much as 100 pounds. Once atop the hill, the cross was erected and "Christ," bound tightly, hung there for about an hour.

Today, worship in the area takes many forms. Dar Al-Islam, a Muslim community best known for its stark, cream-colored adobe mosque, perches atop a piñon- and juniper-covered mesa in the Chama River Valley. The multidomed structure with arched walls was designed in 1980 by Egyptian architect Hassan Fathy. Next door, a series of barrel vaults covers a 10,000-square-foot Muslim school.

Farther south at Santa Cruz is a sizable Sikh community, where turbaned men are a common sight. Many of them are lawyers or own businesses in Española and Santa Fe. Each spring, the Sikhs sponsor a Peace Prayer Day, inviting their neighbors to share songs and stories. A few miles upriver, at the end of an unpaved road, sits the **Monastery of Christ in the Desert**. Here, Benedictine monks grow their own food, raise bees, weave, and make pottery and furniture. They worship in a stunning adobe chapel, with a floor-to-ceiling glass wall that seems to bring the nearby soft-hued red cliffs inside. The monastery is open to visitors interested in experiencing their

Saints and crucifixes at the Hacienda de los Martinez.

own silent retreat; they may wander in without appointment for a look around, but reservations, by fax only (419-831-9113), are necessary for overnight stays. *Off U.S. 84, 13 miles up Forest Service Road.*

■ **GHOST RANCH** *map page 85, B-3*

Ghost Ranch, established in 1766, is a collection of adobe buildings nestled among maroon shales and dusty orange and purple sandstone hillsides. It was named for the *brujas* (witches) said to inhabit its numerous canyons. In 1934, Arthur Newton Pack, a wealthy Easterner, turned the working cattle operation into a fancy dude ranch where wild horses, burros, and mountain sheep roamed nearby and rattlesnakes hid in the cool shadows of rocks. One of his early guests, who turned out to be his most famous, was Georgia O'Keeffe—one of the most important American painters of the 20th century. Once she set foot on Ghost Ranch, O'Keeffe rarely left it behind for long. Eventually, she bought a portion of it and lived there in a small U-shaped adobe house with whitewashed walls.

Painting class at Ghost Ranch.

Today, Ghost Ranch is operated by the Presbyterian Church as a conference center specializing in education and spiritual renewal. Retreats, workshops, and seminars take place year-round on topics ranging from paleontology, astronomy, and theology to pottery, wood carving, and conversational Spanish. Several lodging options and a dining hall cater to participants. *U.S. 84, between mileposts 224 and 225, 12 miles north of Abiquiu; 505-685-4333 or 877-804-4678.*

Two museums at Ghost Ranch highlight the area's natural history. The **Florence Hawley Ellis Museum of Anthropology** displays a re-created Spanish ranch house and interpretive exhibits of Indian pottery and crafts made by people living within a 60-mile radius during the past 12,000 years. The **Ruth Hall Museum of Paleontology** was built around a fossilized skeleton of Coelophysis, a 6-foot-long dinosaur that was capable of remarkable speed when it came time to catch dinner. The remains of many hundreds of these dinosaurs, who roamed the earth about 210 million years ago, were found in the Ghost Ranch area in the 1940s. Since then, Coelophysis has been named the state fossil, and the archaeological dig at the museum is ongoing.

■ **NORTH TO CHAMA** *map page 85, A-2/3*

North of Abiquiu, U.S. 84 climbs along the side of a red-rock mesa as it heads toward Abiquiu Lake. From this incline, one of the most magnificent views in the state unfolds southward. Distant mountain ranges line the horizon, and the sparkling blue Chama wends its way among the square plots of tiny farms; horses graze in moss-green meadows and red-tailed hawks circle overhead. Cliffs, colored variously in shades of purple, yellow, and pink, fall away to the east.

Three miles north of Ghost Ranch stands a beige sandstone cliff face rounded out by centuries of whipping wind and pounding rain. Called **Echo Amphitheater**, this is a lovely spot to enjoy a cold drink and sandwich at picnic tables maintained by the Carson National Forest Service. The 200-foot-high wall of sandstone is a 10-minute walk from the parking area. Be careful not to reveal any secrets along the way, because this isn't called Echo Amphitheater for nothing—your conversation will resound throughout the camping and picnic area.

Leaving Echo Amphitheater and still heading north, the road continues to climb toward a stand of ponderosa pines before it drops into the Chama Basin, where the tin roofs of **Tierra Amarilla** homes glint in the sun. Here in the broad valley, churro sheep graze alongside cattle. Tierra Amarilla, named for the yellow-colored soil of the area, began as a land-grant settlement in the mid-1800s.

Farther on, the tiny sheep-ranching community of **Los Ojos** was struggling to survive in 1981 when residents put their heads together and created Ganados del Valle, a collectively run economic development corporation. Today, the village is the home of **Tierra Wools** (91 Main Street; 505-588-7231), where weavers work on looms in the back of the store and shoppers can browse through clothing, tapestries, pillows, rugs, and piles of hand-spun yarn. Churro sheep produce the wool, and Los Ojos residents spin and weave it. Close by, the historic Parkview grocery store, reopened in 1990, operates as a general store that also sells locally made jams, tortillas, and handcrafts. Its coffee shop is the perfect place to sit and think about which of the Tierra Wools rugs to buy and ship home.

Across the valley, the waters of the Rio Brazos tumble through the steep walls of the Brazos Canyon. A narrow road follows the river up to the mouth of the dead-end box canyon, where two lodges nestle among tall ponderosa pines, shimmering aspens, and spruce trees. Look upward to see the 11,000-foot Brazos Cliffs looming overhead. This land is private, so it's best to ask permission to roam around.

■ **CHAMA** *map page 85, A-2*

This small town at the base of 10,000-foot Cumbres Pass retains its outpost feel, a reminder of its formative days in the mid-19th century, when lace curtains and window-box geraniums were signs of status. Residents don't have to store their home-grown vegetables in cool cellars anymore, but it still takes a hardy constitution to withstand the town's subzero winter temperatures and the piles of snow that reach to the rooftops. Homes are still simple, folks still friendly, and the railroad (built in 1878) still runs into town.

Nowadays, however, the **Cumbres and Toltec Scenic Railroad** no longer hauls cattle. Instead, it carries tourists aboard one of the nation's few remaining coal-fueled, narrow-gauge trains. Six days a week, from late May through mid-October, a jet-black locomotive and seven enclosed passenger cars pull away from the

(above) The Cumbres and Toltec Scenic Railroad carries tourists to Antonito, Colorado.
(opposite) A whisper can be heard from one side of Echo Amphitheater to the other due to its unusual acoustical configuration.

SEEING IS BELIEVING

Starting in September, in the valley, our eyes rise toward the mountains, waiting for the aspens to launch their melodramatic spectacle. Say what you will about their picture-postcard souls, the aspens make it official. If it is a bland, dry autumn, they take forever to turn. In other years, dampness and early frosts can trigger their excesses prematurely, and the show dies aborning. Occasionally, the foliage never truly ripens: it starts to flare, then suddenly nose-dives into mottled beiges, browns, and even blacks. And that robust cliché yellow we love to gawk at never happens. But oh, when all the elements fall together and great swathes of mountainside blossom with that scintillating radiance! Never mind if it has been versified and adulated to death, each year that the aspens truly turn gold renews our faith and our amazement. I nurture no belief in God, but when this beautiful death goes down I'm willing to grant to those who do trust in some hallowed deity at least a clever and arrogant magician out there, mischievously and with acute dexterity, amid a swirl of star-bedecked Arabian robes, working his or her overweening and yet totally captivating sleight of hand.

—John Nichols, *The Last Beautiful Days of Autumn,* 1982

Chama station, slice through groves of golden aspens, and struggle up the steep Cumbres Pass, belching charcoal-gray smoke. Passing lichen-covered craggy volcanic outcroppings, riders can watch eagles soar overhead and backpackers disappear along the banks of the meandering Los Pinos River. The train picks up speed as it emerges from the Toltec Gorge, sweeping past yellow-tipped chamisa and sweet-smelling sagebrush. The day-long journey ends in Antonito, Colorado, where passengers can either spend the night or return to Chama by van. *For reservations call 888-286-2737.*

After the trip, a great treat is a meal at **Viva Vera's Mexican Kitchen**, a spacious dining room where it's a challenge to complete the hefty portions of traditional New Mexican food that Vera Alcon has been serving for nearly 40 years. *2202 South NM 17; 505-756-2557.*

River-runners should consider rafting the Chama River from just below El Vado Dam to Abiquiu Reservoir. This 33-mile stretch of the blue-green Chama winds its way between 1,500-foot hills, past the dilapidated remains of an old homesteader's ranch, and beneath dusty orange rock faces and sagebrush meadows. Rounded orange globemallow, red and purple penstemons, bright purple thistles, and brilliant red-orange desert paintbrush blossom from the riverbank. The river's current virtually disappears at Monastery Lake, a flat stretch that occurs just before the Monastery of Christ in the Desert, but then the river picks up speed and heads into a series of rapids with names like Skull Bridge, Gauging Station, Screaming Left, and Sidekick. Before you know it, you're back on shore.

■ JEMEZ MOUNTAINS *map page 85, A/B-3/4*

One hundred and fifty million years ago the dinosaur Seismosaurus—which, at 120 to 140 feet long, may have been the longest creature ever to sprout from an egg and grow up—lumbered through the area that now holds the Jemez (pronounced HAY-mez) Mountains. Ten million years ago, camels, elephants, and horses roamed the tall grasses of northern New Mexico. Then, a million years ago, a mighty explosion—far greater than the blast that ripped the side off Mount St. Helens in 1980—changed the landscape forever. Ash and fiery lava streamed from a volcano that scientists estimate was between 14,000 and 27,000 feet high, blowing a hole in the ground 15 miles across and 3,500 feet deep. For thousands of years, eruptions poured forth, some of the ash flying as much as a thousand miles away. The build-up from all this violent activity left behind an entire mountain range whose tallest point, Redondo Peak, is a mere 11,254 feet.

Volcanic tuff from the massive explosion blanketed the landscape for miles, creating cone-shaped tent rocks and hoodoos (free-standing formations with a rock shaped like a pancake on top). Black volcanic glass, called obsidian, covered some of the tuff. The long-extinct volcano also left behind an extensive network of geothermal pockets. Many remain locked underground, while others have burst forth in hot springs scattered throughout the Jemez Mountains. Ironically, the volcano's caldera, known as Valle Grande, has turned into a lush green meadow upon which cattle graze contentedly. In 2000, the caldera became the **Valles Caldera National Preserve,** created to protect the ecosystem of magnificent forests, grassy meadows, and mountain streams of the Baca Ranch. Details for how hunters, hikers, fishermen—and wildlife and cattle—will share the 89,000 acres are still being worked out. *505-661-3333.*

■ **BANDELIER NATIONAL MONUMENT** *map page 85, B-4*
In the late 1100s, ancestors of the Pueblo Indians found tuff-covered cliffs in the protected Frijoles Canyon ideal for carving out homes. For centuries, these Indians lived in their cliffside homes and cultivated corn, beans, and squash alongside Frijoles Creek, which flowed nearby. Eventually, they moved away from the cliffs and built a communal house called Tyuonyi, a three-story, free-standing masonry pueblo with 400 rooms. A combination of famine, drought, soil-eroding flash floods, and disease eventually drove the Indians out, however, and by 1550 they had moved south along the Rio Grande.

Today, a 1.5-mile-long paved loop trail winds among the ruins of these early communities. Rough-hewn ladders reach to the carved-out cliff faces, where residue from ancient fires can be seen in faint black soot on ceilings. Ceremonial Cave sits 150 feet above the canyon floor and can be entered by climbing a series of spindly, but sturdy, ladders. Some anthropologists think the cool chamber, rather than the site of secret ceremonies, was a place where tethered turkeys were once held as they waited to become dinner. Bandelier was named for Adolph Bandelier, a Swiss-born, self-taught historian who documented the history of the Rio Grande Pueblo Indians by visiting them in the 1880s and balancing their oral histories against written records. He also wrote *The Delight Makers,* a fictionalized account of life in Frijoles Canyon when Tyuonyi was inhabited.

Besides the main loop, additional trails lead to the Rio Grande, north along Frijoles Creek, and through the monument's nearly 50 square miles of backcountry. The park closes at dusk, although visitors wishing to stay later can spend the night in one of two campgrounds. *Bandelier National Monument; 505-672-0343.*

More cliff homes, the **Puye Cliff Dwellings,** are preserved north of Bandelier on the Santa Clara Indian Reservation. A steep staircase of stone steps leads to the dwellings, which are one of the most extensive cliffside villages. Some were mere caves, others had porches or open rooms attached. Wooden ladders and steps carved into the volcanic tuff were used to go from one dwelling to another and to the pine-covered mesa above. Puye's residents, who lived there from 1250 until the latter part of the 16th century, constructed kivas on the cliff's edge, along its base, and on a ledge halfway to the top of the mesa. Their glazed red pottery was decorated with images of the serpents said to guard the springs on which their crops depended. The dwellings, which have been closed to visitors in recent years

To reach the cave entrances at Bandelier, visitors must climb rickety ladders up dizzying heights.

because of fires in the area, were the prehistoric homes of the Santa Clara Indians, who now live nearby on more than 40,000 acres of rich farmland, rangeland, and forests. *Ten miles west of Santa Clara Pueblo; 505-753-7326.*

■ **JEMEZ SPRINGS** *map page 85, A-4*

NM 4 crosses the gently sloping Jemez Range, passing by the Valle Grande, filled with pine-covered hillsides and meandering clear blue streams full of brown and rainbow trout. On the mountains' western edge, the smell of sulphur greets the nostrils, indicating that the supernatural-looking **Soda Dam** is right around the corner. Calcium carbonate and travertine deposits from a nearby hot spring have oozed into the river and hardened into a mushroom-shaped dam. Hot rocks under the surface cause the spring to simmer year-round, even when the rocks are covered with snow. In the winter, steam rises off the water's surface, adding to an already eerie atmosphere.

Two miles downstream is Jemez Springs, once the site of sheep wars, vigilante activities, and gambling enterprises, but more recently a winner of a national All America City award for civic excellence. The sleepy town, squeezed between steep red sandstone hills on the banks of the Jemez River, is known for its friendly atmosphere and its hot springs, some of which are harnessed at the Jemez Springs Bath House and at the **Bodhi Manda Zen Center**. This center, which backs up to

Stained glass at Los Ojos Bar in Jemez Springs.

the clear waters of the shallow Jemez River, welcomes overnight non-Buddhist visitors, but please call ahead (505-829-3854). If the state of your spirit is subject to the rumblings of your stomach, wander across the street to **Los Ojos Bar** (505-897-3587), the village's most popular gathering spot. Hearty burgers and heaping plates of enchiladas will fill your belly and in winter a huge stone fireplace will keep your toes warm.

Just north of town, the 8-foot-thick rock walls of the church of San José de los Jemez and the nearby prehistoric pueblo of Giusewa (a Tiwa word that means "Place at the Boiling Waters") are preserved at **Jemez State Monument**. The massive church was founded in the early 1620s by a Franciscan missionary, Fray Alonso de Lugo. A self-guided tour takes you inside the fortress-like church, built with small windows to help congregants defend it against anticipated invaders. A dirt path marked with small arrows leads past priests' quarters and the low walls of the adjacent Indian village. *505-829-3530.*

In the early 1630s, the missionary enterprise at Giusewa was abandoned, and **Jemez Pueblo** became the center of religious activities. Located 10 miles south of Jemez Springs, the pueblo's low adobe homes hug the brilliant brick-red earth. Coyote fences made with thin sticks form small corrals, and *hornos* (adobe ovens) the color of the rich earth appear beside nearly every home. Under shady ramadas that line NM 4 north of the pueblo, women sell bread they have baked inside these ovens. They also cook up frybread on the spot, and the pleasing smell of baking dough mingles with the sweet piñon scent of the fire. Young Jemez men are famous as cross-country runners and firefighters. Many spend their summers fighting forest fires throughout the United States. You can learn more about the pueblo at the Walatowa Visitor Center, just north of the pueblo on NM 4. *505-834-7235 or 877-733-5687.*

■ LOS ALAMOS *map page 85, B-4*

In 1918, educator Ashley Pond fulfilled a life-long dream by establishing the Los Alamos Ranch School, a school where young boys not only were taught standard book-learning but also rode horses, cut wood, and learned the common-sense values that only ranch living can teach. The school originally occupied an existing building on Pond's ranch, but after 1928, it moved into a two-story log cabin designed by famed Santa Fe architect John Gaw Meem. Called Fuller Lodge after a school benefactor, it was hidden among tall pines atop the finger-like mesas of the Pajarito Plateau.

UNWITTING EYEWITNESS TO HISTORY

While working on the top-secret Manhattan Project, Robert Oppenheimer, Niels Bohr, and other scientists often stopped at a tearoom near Otowi Bridge, which crossed the Rio Grande on present-day NM 502. The tearoom was run by Edith Warner, a Pennsylvania schoolteacher who had moved to New Mexico for health reasons. Nearly 40 and single, she agreed to live in a house by the bridge, which was also the railroad stop where supplies for the Los Alamos Ranch School were delivered. Her job was to secure the supplies until ranch employees retrieved them. To help make ends meet, she opened the tearoom and operated it for nearly 20 years, until her death. The story of her close relationships with her neighbors—both the San Ildefonso Indians and the scientists at Los Alamos—is told by Peggy Pond Church, Ashley Pond's daughter, in The House at Otowi Bridge. *For some of her information, Pond relied on Christmas letters Warner sent regularly to friends back East; among them was this post-war missive:*

"The climax came on that August day when the report of the atomic bomb flashed around the world. It seemed fitting that it was Kitty Oppenheimer who, coming for vegetables, brought the news. I had not known what was being done up there, though in the beginning I had suspected atomic research. Much was now explained. Now I can tell you that Conant and Compton came in through the kitchen door to eat ragout and chocolate cake; that Fermi, Allison, Teller, Parsons came many times; that Oppenheimer was the man I knew in pre-war years and who made it possible for the Hill people to come down; that Hungarians, Swiss, Germans, Italians, Austrians, French and English have been serious and gay around the candlelit table. It has been an incredible experience for a woman who chose to live in a supposedly isolated spot. In no other place could I have had the privilege of knowing Niels Bohr, who is not only a great scientist but a great man. In no other way could I have seen develop a group feeling of responsibility for presenting the facts to the people and urging the only wise course—international control of atomic energy and bombs."

—Peggy Pond Church,
The House at Otowi Bridge: The Story of Edith Warner and Los Alamos, 1960

During the summer of 1922, a young physics professor from Berkeley, J. Robert Oppenheimer, accompanied a pack trip from Frijoles Canyon into the Valle Grande. During subsequent trips into the Jemez wilderness, he often passed by the growing ranch school—and 20 years later, he thought of it when asked to help select an isolated site for a laboratory to develop the world's first atomic bomb.

So it happened that in 1942, the school was closed to make room for the Manhattan Project. Prefabricated apartment houses and wooden barracks were erected to house hundreds of scientists and technicians who arrived by train, many not even apprised of their destination. They were issued driver's licenses with only numbers—no names—and all mail was sent to a Santa Fe post office box. People who applied for jobs to empty trash were hired only if they were illiterate. Even the families that accompanied the scientists to the mountain outpost, which came to be called "The Hill," didn't know exactly why they were there. But they made the best of it: wives taught in classrooms, shopped in Santa Fe, and attended ceremonies at nearby pueblos.

On July 16, 1945, the secret was out. The first atomic bomb was detonated in the pre-dawn hours at Trinity Site, in the New Mexico desert about 240 miles south of Los Alamos. The atomic age had begun.

After the war, Oppenheimer and his chief assistants left, but Los Alamos National Laboratory stayed behind, continuing its nuclear weapons research and then branching off into other areas besides nuclear energy—such as cleaning up hazardous-waste sites and developing alternative energy sources. The town that grew up to support the lab is home now to one of the highest concentrations of Ph.D's in the country, and the original makeshift buildings have been replaced by permanent tan-colored concrete structures.

Although the laboratory still maintains high security, one of its components, the **Bradbury Science Museum,** in downtown Los Alamos, is open to the public. It documents the early days of Project Y, the code name given to the Manhattan Project. Replicas of the bombs dropped on Japan are on display, along with hands-on laser exhibits and examples of current research into the nature of atomic particles. *15th Street and Central Avenue; 505-667-4444.*

Further history of the community where nuclear energy was born is covered at the **Los Alamos Historical Museum** (1921 Juniper Street; 505-662-4493).

(following pages) The Rio Grande flows near Bandelier National Monument.

Housed in a guest cottage next door to Fuller Lodge, the museum has exhibits on physics and geothermal science, along with Anasazi artifacts and a bookstore well stocked with titles on Los Alamos and the Southwest. Fuller Lodge continues to be a community focal point; it houses the **Fuller Lodge Arts Center** (2132 Central Avenue; 505-662-9331), where rotating exhibits of New Mexico artwork are displayed and occasional concerts are performed. Fortunately, none of these buildings were damaged when a wildfire swept through the city in May 2000, destroying more than 200 homes and charring nearly 50,000 acres of nearby forest.

■ ENCHANTED CIRCLE   *map page 85, C/D-2/3*

An 86-mile loop strikes out from Taos and heads north between the craggy rim of the Rio Grande Gorge and the western edge of the Sangre de Cristo Mountains. It cuts through the tall ponderosa pines and Douglas firs of the rugged range and drops into the serene, spacious, ridge-rimmed Moreno Valley before returning to Taos along the meandering Rio Fernando de Taos. This so-called **Enchanted Circle** winds around the state's tallest peaks; at 13,161 feet, Wheeler Peak is the highest.

The first stop is **Arroyo Hondo,** the remains of a settlement created through an 1815 land grant; it straddles the rushing Rio Hondo, a runoff stream from the nearby mountains. The first Hispanic residents put in vegetable gardens along the fertile river plain and grazed cattle and sheep in tall grass meadows. It didn't take long for an enterprising Anglo to disrupt the tranquil lives of the settlers. In 1830, Simeon Turley established a prosperous cattle and sheep ranch here. He also planted acres of corn and wheat, dammed the Rio Hondo, built a gristmill, and hired Hispanic settlers and Taos Pueblo Indians to work for him. Turley was probably best known, however, for the "Taos Lightning" that he distilled. This moonshine often was the cause of drunken disruptions at fiestas in northern New Mexico.

During an uprising in 1847, when a group of Hispanics and Indians sympathetic to Mexican interests assassinated the new U.S. governor, Turley escaped after a two-day battle at his ranch, during which his mill was burned. He sought refuge at a neighboring ranch, only to be killed there by his pursuers.

In the 1960s, the canvas tepees of the New Buffalo commune sprang up near the village's earthen adobe homes. Part of a back-to-the-land movement, commune members dreamed of leaving modern urban life behind. Today, only a few members remain. A dirt road leads to the Rio Grande, passing by small gardens, barking dogs, and disinterested sheep. During the spring, trucks hauling inflatable rafts share the bumpy road with residents. At the John Dunn Bridge, which crosses the river where the Rio Hondo flows into it, boaters put in to run the Lower Taos Box, a 17-mile stretch of the Rio Grande that passes underneath the 600-foot-tall Rio Grande Gorge Bridge and through exhilarating boulder-choked rapids. Once beyond that bridge, no roads enter the steep volcanic canyon until the end of the trip. The remoteness and the challenging whitewater combine to make this the premier one-day river trip in the state.

North of Arroyo Hondo, atop a gravel ridge, **Questa** has changed from a farming and trade center to a community focused on the mining of molybdenum (an element used in the manufacture of lightbulbs, television tubes, and missile systems), which is removed from an ancient volcanic caldera on the steep banks of the Red River. The only trading Questa engages in these days is at its few gas stations, restaurants, and motels. The tiny village also markets honey, which can be purchased from the beekeepers themselves at their homes north of town.

NM 38 passes slopes scarred by the mining operation as it follows the Red River, a blue-green waterway that runs crimson after rainstorms, to a town named for it. **Red River** was platted in the late 1800s by the Mallette brothers, who sought to take advantage of a mining boom in the area. By 1905, the town supported 15 saloons, four hotels, two newspapers, a barbershop, a hospital, and a thriving red-light district. The miners' failure to strike it big spelled the end of Red River's first boom, but prosperity returned in the 1920s, when vacationers from the dusty plains of Oklahoma and Texas found its clear streams, radiant aspen groves, and stately pine forests—not to mention dust-free air—to their liking. Fishing, hiking, bicycling, and pack trips have ever since lured vacationers to the cool slopes in summertime, and construction of the Red River Ski Area in 1958 turned the town into a year-round resort. Shops, restaurants, and motels line the main street, making Red River a pleasant place to walk around and browse.

A few stone walls and cemetery grave markers are all that remain of **Elizabethtown**—the scene, from 1866 to 1875, of a gold rush during which thousands of prospectors feverishly scoured the flanks of 12,500-foot Baldy Mountain. Gold ore worth millions of dollars was removed from claims staked in the pine-studded hills before the ore played out. In 1903, a fire destroyed much of the dying town's business district. Baldy Mountain endures, of course: a rounded bare knob that stands like a beacon overlooking the tall grasses of the Moreno Valley.

Wheeler Peak is the highest in the Sangre de Cristo Mountains and in New Mexico.

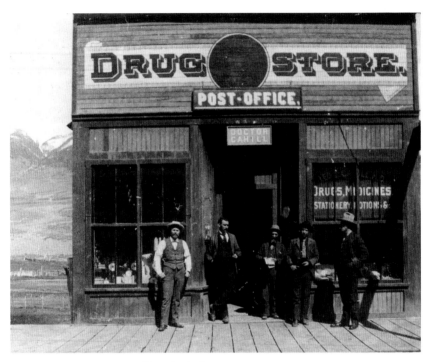

Cahill's Drugstore and Post Office, Elizabethtown, 1899.

In 1919, Charles Springer, a prominent cattleman, banker, and engineer, decided that the time had come to provide a stable water source for the vast fields of the Moreno Valley. He designed and built Eagle Nest Dam at the head of Cimarron Canyon; the resulting five-mile-long lake, named after the dam, today irrigates the fields nearby. The lake holds some of the state's biggest rainbow trout and kokanee salmon, which anglers go after even in winter through holes in the ice. A year after the dam went up, a village, Thermal, followed. The abundance of golden eagles in the mountains surrounding the lush Moreno Valley inspired residents to rename it **Eagle Nest**, and for years it was the largest town in the valley. Today, however, it's been relegated to the status of a stock-up and overnight stop because of newer developments nearby.

The **Vietnam Veterans National Memorial** sweeps upward from a hillside at the south end of Eagle Nest Lake. The solemn white structure—a shrine with 50-

foot-high front walls—was raised piece by piece by the family of Dr. Victor Westphall, whose son was killed in a 1968 enemy ambush in Vietnam. The first memorial to Vietnam vets built in the United States, it was completed in 1971 and is now recognized as a major national memorial site. It is open 24 hours a day; special programs take place on Memorial Day and Veteran's Day. *U.S. 64, five miles north of Angel Fire; 505-377-6900.*

After a shaky start in the mid-1970s as a ski area, **Angel Fire** has blossomed into a year-round resort with ample resources for golf, fishing, tennis, hiking, and horseback riding. From the area's 34 miles of trails, skiers can gaze out at the vast Moreno Valley unfolding below, with snowcapped Wheeler Peak visible in the distance. *See "Ski Areas," in Practical Information.*

■ **PECOS NATIONAL HISTORICAL PARK**   *map page 85, C-5*

By 1450, Indians in the Pecos River Valley were living in a tiered village on a rocky ridge overlooking both the river and the pine-studded mesas beyond. Dwellings rose five stories high and contained a total of 600 rooms and 22 kivas. These Towa-speaking Indians grew crops in the fertile valley and foraged for wild berries and nuts in the Sangre de Cristo foothills. By today's standards they were a small people; most women stood under five feet. Men draped themselves in animal skins, and women wore one-shouldered dresses and turkey feather robes.

When Franciscan friars arrived at the pueblo in the 1620s, they ordered the Indians to build the 170-foot-long, 90-foot-wide Mission de Nuestra Señora de los Angeles de Porciuncula. In addition to introducing Catholicism to the Indians, the friars taught them the Spanish way of life. They organized weaving rooms, tanneries, classrooms, and a carpentry shop; planted gardens of flowers and vegetables and fruit orchards; and brought in small bands of goats, sheep, cattle, and horses. In exchange, the Indians submitted to baptism and did the labor to maintain the community. That they didn't much appreciate the new lifestyle became evident when they enthusiastically participated in the 1680 Pueblo Revolt, burning the church and joining in the attack on Santa Fe.

When they were conquered again 12 years later, the Indians built a smaller church. By this time, repeated Comanche attacks, coupled with smallpox outbreaks, had severely reduced the population. Eventually, these Pecos residents moved to nearby villages or joined their brethren at Jemez Pueblo, the only other

The Eagle Nest Dam was built in 1920 to provide irrigation to the Moreno Valley.

remaining Towa-speaking community. By the mid-1800s, when travelers began to pass by on the Santa Fe Trail, the once-proud pueblo was a crumbling ruin.

The partial walls of the massive church still stand, testament to long hours of Indian labor. To the north are the ruins of the extensive pueblo. At a restored kiva, a ladder leads into a musty chamber that holds memories of many secret ceremonies. Push a button on one of the vertical support beams, and drumbeats and chanting voices fill the dank room, much as they might have hundreds of years ago. The Fogelson Visitor Center, named after the area's large landowner (actress Greer Garson's husband, Elijah "Buddy" Fogelson), provides both an excellent introduction and an in-depth look at the Indian and Spanish eras. Also under park management is the nearby site of the Civil War battle at Glorieta Pass (see "History"); rangers will take you on a guided tour if you plan ahead. *Pecos National Historical Park is four miles north of I-25 on NM 63; 505-757-6414.*

Two miles past the park, the tiny village of Pecos supplies campers and fishermen heading into the Pecos Wilderness. NM 63 follows the narrow, slow-moving Pecos River, penetrating the tall pines of the forest and ending at the hunting and fishing resort of Cowles. A few dude ranches and camps are spread out along the river, which is stocked with rainbow and brown trout.

Interior of kiva at Pecos National Historical Park.

GEORGIA O'KEEFFE

That first summer I spent in New Mexico I was a little surprised that there were so few flowers. There was no rain so the flowers didn't come. Bones were easy to find so I began collecting bones. When I was returning East I was bothered about my work—the country had been so wonderful that by comparison what I had done with it looked very poor to me—although I knew it had been one of my best painting years. I had to go home—what could I take with me of the country to keep me working on it? I had collected many bones and finally decided that the best thing I could do was to take with me a barrel of bones—so I took a barrel of bones.

—Georgia O'Keeffe, *Georgia O'Keeffe,* 1976

On a warm May day in 1929, Georgia O'Keeffe stepped off a train at the small station in Lamy, New Mexico, and beheld a landscape covered in bushy piñon and juniper trees, gray-green in the brilliant New Mexico sunshine. She was 41 years old and had ventured west without her husband, Alfred Stieglitz, to spend the summer painting whatever the dry, dusty desert presented as a subject. By then an established painter, O'Keeffe instantly was enamored with the radiant light and the sharp edges that the thin, dry air seemed to give the surrounding mountains, trees, and flowers. "No one told me it was like this!" she told her host, Mabel Dodge Luhan, a wealthy art patron who owned a sprawling compound in Taos.

After one of her paintings sold in New York for $6,000, O'Keeffe bought a black Model A Ford, which she used to explore the countryside. One day, motoring with Charles Collier, the son of the director of the Bureau of Indian Affairs, O'Keeffe reached the lavender, dusty orange cliffs of Abiquiu, about 60 miles west of Taos. Collier was searching for Ghost Ranch, a place he thought the painter would enjoy, but they never found an entrance. "This is my world, but how to get into it?" O'Keeffe remembered thinking at the time.

A few years later, she found the ranch, a cluster of low adobe buildings set in the shadows of a sandstone mesa speckled with piñons and junipers. Owner Arthur Newton Pack had just purchased the working cattle ranch and was turning it into a fancy dude ranch. O'Keeffe moved into a cottage and returned there every summer until 1940, when she purchased Rancho de los Burros, a U-shaped adobe house Pack had built for himself three miles from the main house. Whitewashed rooms surrounded a patio, and a huge bedroom window overlooked a flat-top mesa called the Pedernal, which lay 10 miles to the south. Behind the house to the north, rosy red, pale yellow, and coral cliffs rose to meet an azure sky. The colors of these corrugated cliffs shifted as the sun moved across the sky. The artist replaced adobe walls with huge panes of glass, and while the interior remained sparsely furnished, it overflowed with bones, rocks, shells, pine cones, driftwood, and feathers she collected on daily walks through the canyons and forests.

In 1945, O'Keeffe purchased a dilapidated house that overlooked the Chama River in the nearby village of Abiquiu. She had the place rebuilt to her specifications—once again, glass walls replaced older adobe ones, fireplaces were installed in every room, and village women plastered mud on the rounded fireplace walls.

The following year, Stieglitz died in New York, and shortly thereafter, O'Keeffe moved to New Mexico for good. She continued to paint the soft curves of Abiquiu's hills and flowers, casting many in ethereal poses. "Two walls of my room in the Abiquiu house are glass and from one window I see the road toward Española, Santa Fe, and the world. The road fascinates me with its ups and downs and finally its wide sweep as it speeds toward the wall of my hilltop to go past me," she said to describe two 1964 paintings of U.S. 84.

In 1972, a young impoverished potter came asking for work. After a few rebuffs, the aging artist hired him to do odd jobs at her Abiquiu home. Juan Hamilton subsequently became her constant companion, and as her eyesight failed, he managed her affairs. Their friendship lasted until O'Keeffe's death in 1986. She was 98. The house is open to visitors, but tour reservations must be made well in advance. *505-685-4539.*

Georgia O'Keeffe near Taos, 1929.

SANTA FE & TAOS

In Santa Fe, brown adobe houses, some nearly 200 years old, line narrow dirt streets, reminders of a past that doesn't feel too far away. Laid out in the protective foothills of the Sangre de Cristo Mountains, the town's crooked streets follow the contours of the uneven earth. Most buildings are one story high and painted in all shades of brown—from tawny to ginger to coffee. Even though many are of frame construction, nearly all reflect the flat-roofed, box-shaped, adobe building style that dominated the city's early architecture. Yards are often small, and shabby exteriors frequently belie elaborate interiors that accommodate pine vigas, corner kiva fireplaces, polished brick and tile floors, and fluid, curving walls and doorways.

Because of this indigenous architectural style, taken from Indian pueblos, the town blends in with the rolling landscape of piñon and juniper. At odd moments in the spare desert light it seems to have sprouted from the earth.

The town of Taos, 70 miles north of Santa Fe, was built on a high plateau between a deep chasm carved by the Rio Grande and the majestic peaks of the Sangre de Cristos. This smaller version of Santa Fe maintains the tradition of low-slung homes along winding dirt streets, which are rarely identified by signs. With its small population (5,300) and its isolated location, the village tends to be less fashionable and "hip" than Santa Fe. People choose lifestyles that meet basic needs, and their activities revolve around the Rio Grande and nearby mountains. Recycling takes on new meaning in homes built of old tires and empty aluminum cans. It's easy to be yourself in Taos, no matter how unusual you might be.

Both Santa Fe and Taos attract artists, writers, natural healers, psychics, and other creative minds from around the world who respond to the soft golden light of early morning and the crimson red of evening. The hustle-bustle of modern life is tempered, as people linger over cappuccinos or spend a day chopping and hauling piñon wood. Blue jeans and cowboy boots are de rigueur.

Both towns have an inordinate number of lodgings, galleries, museums, gift shops, bookstores, and restaurants. Taos attracts individualists with a keen appreciation of its outpost character. Santa Fe is more for the idiosyncratic cosmopolitan and gourmet.

Church of San Francisco de Asís, Ranchos de Taos.

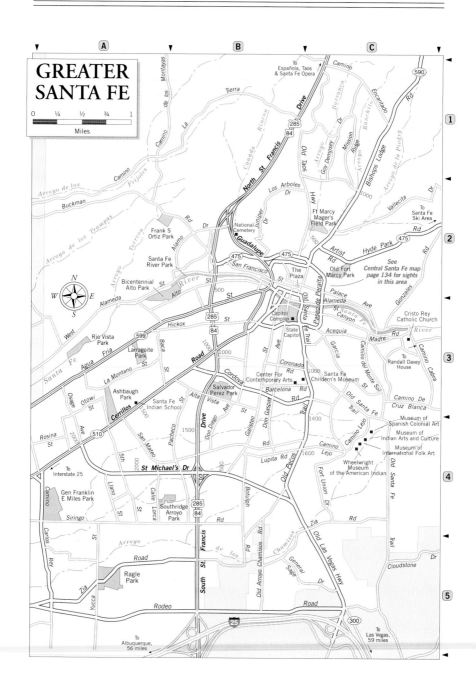

GREATER SANTA FE

0   ¼   ½   ¾   1
Miles

Both towns, however, are in danger of losing what makes them so appealing: their tricultural mixture of Indians, Hispanics, and Anglos. As urban outsiders descend upon the two communities, seeking clean air, simpler lives, and aesthetic sophistication, many longtime residents have been forced out by rising costs, taking traditions with them. Fortunately, that communal heritage—of roasting and freezing chiles, slapping out fresh tortillas, and sharing in the springtime ritual of clearing out irrigation ditches—continues to thrive in the smaller and less celebrated communities that dot the roads between Santa Fe and Taos.

■ HISTORY

Ancestors of today's Indian residents of Taos Pueblo lived nearly 1,000 years ago in small villages throughout northern New Mexico. By 1350, they had settled along the shallow waters of the Rio Pueblo, where they erected, tier by tier, the stepped walls of Taos Pueblo. Due to the isolation of this northernmost pueblo, Taos was a major target for the Comanche and Ute raiders who scoured the northern plains, but this same seclusion also kept away Spanish missionaries. Even though a mission church was built there in 1617 and the Pueblo Revolt of 1680 was plotted at Taos, few Spanish moved into the area until the 18th century.

Missionaries preferred to concentrate on pueblos closer to Santa Fe, established in 1610 as the capital of the new Spanish colony. During its formative years, Santa Fe was maintained primarily for the purpose of bringing the Catholic faith to New Mexico's Pueblo Indians. In 1680, however, the Indians rebelled against the Spanish and their religion. Colonists who escaped from their homes fled to the Palace of the Governors, an enclosed one-story compound that housed the town's chief political officers and their offices, a military chapel, shops, and work rooms. As the colonists huddled together inside the palace, the Indians outside set fire to a church and other buildings around the plaza, dancing and shouting victory chants. Then the Indians let them go, and the colonists marched in good order for 300 miles until they reached El Paso, where they remained for the next 12 years.

Diego de Vargas, a member of one of Spain's leading families, was assigned the task of restoring Spanish rule to New Mexico. In 1692, he led a squad of soldiers up El Camino Real to Santa Fe. There he surprised a group of Indians who had turned the governor's palace into a pueblo. After minor resistance, they surrendered peacefully, returning the battered capital to the Spanish. Every September since 1712, this reconquest has been celebrated as Las Fiestas de Santa Fe.

After securing the capital, de Vargas returned to El Paso, where he gathered colonists to resettle the territory. In October 1693, he ushered northward a ponderous entourage that included 70 families, 18 friars, 100 soldiers, 2,000 horses, 1,000 mules, and 900 head of cattle. Eighteen carts hauled heavy supplies, including three cannons. Accompanying this excursion was a small wooden statuette of the Virgin, known as La Conquistadora, which the retreating Spaniards had taken with them to El Paso in 1680.

Upon arrival, de Vargas discovered that the Indians had, in his absence, changed their minds and decided to resist the Spanish and keep Santa Fe. Well armed, de Vargas and his men took it back by force. Tradition has it that he attributed his success to the Virgin Mary, and today La Conquistadora stands on a gilded altar in the north chapel of St. Francis Cathedral. Every June, the statue is paraded through town to Rosario Chapel, the site of de Vargas's camp during the reconquest. A novena of masses is said before a procession returns her to the cathedral.

After a few more Indian uprisings were quickly quashed, the Spanish moved in in droves, settling the protective hills near the new capital and the high Taos Plateau, where they grew vegetables, wheat, and barley alongside streams that flowed from the nearby mountains. In 1617, Fray Pedro de Miranda built a mission near Taos Pueblo. An important landowner in the region was Fernando de Chávez, who left after his family was slain during the Pueblo Revolt and never returned. In 1710, when Cristóbal de la Serna petitioned for a land grant, he identified Chávez as the previous owner. Thus, the Spanish settlement became known as Fernando de Taos, later shortened to Taos. In 1716, a second community was established a few miles south and is known today as Ranchos de Taos.

Typically, homes were joined together by a solid rear wall that provided protection from raiding Comanches, who continually threatened settlers. During 1759, for example, 50 Spanish women and children were abducted by Indians. The following year, Spanish soldiers bent on revenge fought and killed 400 Comanches among the tall grasses of the high plains.

A regular event during these unsettled times was the annual Taos Trade Fair, at which Ute, Apache, and Comanche Indians—laden with buffalo hides, jerky, and buckskins—pitched tepees outside of town and traded with the Spanish for guns, knives, and ammunition, as well as vegetables and grains cultivated at the pueblos. Sign language was used to secure deals. Goods were bartered—no money changed hands. Spanish or Indian captives often accompanied the Indian traders, who sought to trade goods for their release. Sometimes the Spanish governor led a retinue from Santa Fe to oversee the noisy gathering.

Ill feelings were set aside during this boisterous occasion, and large amounts of local moonshine, called Taos Lightning, were consumed. By evening, everyone joined together at an all-night fandango. As soon as the fair ended and parties departed, however, tribes began plotting upcoming raids.

By 1821, Mexico had declared its independence from Spain. Nearly 1,400 miles north of Mexico City, Santa Fe became a far-flung outpost of the struggling new nation. A few decades later, however, the United States'

La Conquistadora, who accompanied Spanish colonists in their retaking of New Mexico from the Indians.

doctrine of Manifest Destiny brought Gen. Stephen Kearny and his troops to the Southwest to claim the territory for the United States. While most of New Mexico rolled over and let him fly the Stars and Stripes, a group of headstrong Taoseños loyal to Mexico mounted a resistance effort. On a January night in 1847, Hispanic settlers and Taos Indians converged on the Taos residence of Charles Bent, governor of the new U.S. territory of New Mexico, killed him, and paraded his scalp on a board through the streets. A week later, soldiers arrived from Santa Fe and defeated the insurgents, who had barricaded themselves inside the Taos Pueblo mission church.

Independence from Spain also opened doors to trade with the United States. Under Spanish rule, the northern province could trade only with Mexico, but Mexican leaders relaxed that edict and encouraged a business relationship with the United States. Once the Santa Fe Trail had been established as a major trade route between Santa Fe and Independence, Missouri, caravans rolled across the prairie, bringing goods as well as adventurous American settlers.

Santa Fe Trail

William Becknell knew a good deal when he saw one. Part of a carefree fivesome trapping and hunting horses in the Southwest in 1821, the veteran Indian fighter paid close attention to the dizzying profits his group reaped when they were invited to Santa Fe that September to celebrate Mexico's newly won independence.

Under Spanish rule, New Mexicans had been forbidden to trade with anyone outside Mexico. Traders of the day loaded *carretas* and pack mules with bearskins, piñon nuts, tallow candles, and wool and slowly made their way along the Chihuahua Trail, traveling 550 miles to Chihuahua City or another 900 miles on El Camino Real to Mexico City. There they exchanged their frontier goods for spices, chocolate, shoes, writing paper, and ink. Large caravans usually made the rough trip twice a year.

Because of this isolation, Santa Fe's residents rarely saw new wares. But once word reached the frontier capital of Mexico's independence, New Mexico's borders were flung open to new traders. When Becknell and his party turned up in town, they quickly sold the supply of brightly colored blankets, knives, kettles, and looking glasses that they had intended to trade with Indians. And their profits were three-fold!

Soon thereafter, Becknell hightailed it back home to Franklin, Missouri, where he restocked and headed west again. This time, instead of following the Arkansas River into southeastern Colorado and then heading south into New Mexico—up and over the Sangre de Cristo Mountains via the steep slopes of Raton Pass—Becknell veered south across the Arkansas River about 20 miles west of Fort Dodge, Kansas, crossing the Oklahoma Panhandle and the Cimarron River in a straight shot to Santa Fe.

For the next six decades, Becknell's Cimarron Cutoff was one of two principal trade routes to the Southwest. The main arm of the Santa Fe Trail continued into Colorado, where Bent's Fort became the largest trading post of the West. Although this main route, known as the Mountain Branch, took longer to traverse, wood and water were plentiful. The Cimarron Cutoff was shorter, cutting 10 days off the trip, but it entailed crossing 60 miles of bone-dry desert and hostile Indian country.

As the first major western trade route, the Santa Fe Trail preceded by two decades the Oregon and California Trails, which crossed farther north. By 1831, oxen were replacing mules as the preferred beasts of burden on the trail. Eight of the slow but steady animals could pull 2-plus tons of cooking pots, calico cloth, knives, and tools in a wagon with iron-rimmed wheels as tall as a man's head. Each spring, 100 of these wagons gathered in Missouri for the 900-mile trek across the plains of Kansas and the tall-grass prairies of northeastern New Mexico. The lumbering caravans averaged 15 to 20 miles a day; in New Mexico they passed by Rabbit Ears Mountain, Starvation

Peak, the abandoned Pecos Mission (Now Pecos National Historical Park), and Pigeon's Ranch. At the end of the trail in Santa Fe, tired oxen were sold or traded for fresh ones and the Conestoga wagons were loaded with gold, silver, wood, and furs.

This opening up of the West was not without its hazards. Pawnee, Apache, Comanche, and Ute Indians, unhappy with these intrusive caravans, often killed traders they encountered. But after the New Mexico territory won its independence from Mexico in 1848, forts were erected to protect traders from the aggressive Indians. The Civil War delayed the coming of the Santa Fe Railroad for a time, but in 1880 the iron horse began inching its way across the Mountain Branch of the Santa Fe Trail, tunneling through mountains in Raton Pass and chugging across northern grasslands before it reached Lamy, outside of Santa Fe.

Today, tall grass obscures the deep indentations carved into the soft earth by wagon wheels creaking across the now-silent prairie. These ruts, which stretch to the eastern horizon, are all that remains of the Santa Fe Trail. Congress has since designated it a National Historic Trail, setting aside funds to preserve and mark the vestiges of this once-vital lifeline.

The 1848 Treaty of Guadalupe-Hidalgo ceded New Mexico to the United States, which immediately began wielding its influence. Lawyers, newspapermen, and shopkeepers flocked to the newly opened frontier. In Santa Fe, Archbishop Jean Baptiste Lamy arrived in 1851 and promptly began molding New Mexico's laid-back clergy into disciplined church leaders. He also designed a cathedral in the Romanesque style of his native Auvergne, France. Begun in 1869, it took 17 years to complete St. Francis Cathedral, which today dominates the end of San Francisco Street in downtown Santa Fe. Built of volcanic stone quarried in hills south of town, the cathedral stands as a monument to Lamy, who went on to build 45 more churches and bring a handful of parochial schools to the wild New Mexico Territory. The bishop lived for a time at a ranch a few miles north of town, among the foothills of the Sangre de Cristos, and today you can play tennis and ride horses at **Bishop's Lodge Resort and Spa**, where the bishop's gardens still flourish. *Bishop's Lodge Road; 505-983-6377 or 800-732-2240.*

Outside of Santa Fe, however, New Mexico continued to be ruled by the smoking gun. In 1878, President Rutherford B. Hayes appointed Lew Wallace as governor to enforce law and order. In between trying to negotiate the capture of Billy the Kid and administer the state, Wallace penned the novel *Ben-Hur* in 1880, while he was living at the Palace of the Governors.

In 1879, the Santa Fe Railroad reached Lamy, 18 miles south of Santa Fe (the closest passenger trains ever came to Santa Fe itself). With this comfortable mode of travel, ever more immigrants from the United States arrived, bringing with them their own ideas and traditions. Redbrick Victorian houses with double-hung windows were soon being built alongside brown adobes with rough-hewn panes.

Seventy years later, in 1949, Ernie Blake arrived in Santa Fe to help build the Santa Fe Ski Basin on the western slopes of 12,409-foot Lake Peak. The Swiss-born mountaineer managed the small ski area for five years, until he discovered the perfect location for his dream resort at the abandoned copper mining camp of Twining, north of Taos. Against the advice of friends who warned him the slope was too steep and would scare off skiers, Blake installed the first lift in 1956 and went on to mold Taos Ski Valley into one of the world's most popular resorts. Today, the mountain offers skiers some of the most challenging terrain in the West.

■ ARTISTS ARRIVE

In 1848, two Philadelphians, Edward and Richard Kern, arrived at Taos. Their stay was brief—just long enough to earn the brothers the distinction of being the first artists to visit the town. Fifty years later, a broken wagon wheel detoured painters Bert Phillips and Ernest Blumenschein, who were on their way to Mexico. They found themselves enthralled with the handsome, chiseled faces of the Taos Indians, the deep dark eyes of Hispanic farmers, and the pine-covered mountain ridges. They stayed to establish what came to be known as the Taos School—a group of painters who became internationally renowned for their spiritual canvases of Indians and mountains, awash with the ethereal New Mexico light.

Taos became firmly established as an art colony in 1915, when the Taos Society of Artists was formed. In addition to Phillips and Blumenschein, members included Kenneth Adams, Oscar Berninghaus, E. Irving Couse, Victor Higgins, J.H. Sharp, and Walter Ufer. The following year, a bored wealthy Easterner by the name of Mabel Dodge Sterne moved to Taos, and in 1923 she married Tony Luhan, a Taos Indian. To her wide circle of friends back east she wrote of sunsets that transformed the high plateau and pine-clad mountains into a luminescent tableau, and of Indian people living a simple life of survival in multilevel adobe structures with no electricity or plumbing.

Blumenschein House in Taos is a fine example of "Santa Fe Style."

Artists who came at her invitation included Ansel Adams, Andrew Dasburg, Marsden Hartley, John Marin, and Georgia O'Keeffe. Perhaps her most famous visitor, D.H. Lawrence, arrived in 1922. He and his wife, Frieda, spent the fall and winter of that year, and the summer of 1924, at Kiowa Ranch, a property north of Taos that the generous Mabel Dodge Luhan gave them as a gift.

Though his time in New Mexico was short, Lawrence wrote that the state changed him forever. Overwhelmed by the setting of the ranch—the "vast amphitheatre of lofty, indomitable desert, sweeping round to the ponderous Sangre de Cristo mountains on the east, and coming up flush at the pine-dotted foot-hills of the Rockies!"—he waxed eloquent about the "splendor of it all," and he too tried his hand at painting. He left behind half a dozen stylized works displaying an amateurish quality that fell far short of the sophisticated prose of his novels and essays. Mostly renderings of plump, bare-breasted women with piercing eyes, they now hang in a gallery at La Fonda de Taos, a hotel on the Taos town plaza. For $3, you can also view photographs—many signed—of Frieda Lawrence and some other famous Taos residents, including painter Andrew Dasburg and film actor and director Dennis Hopper.

In 1930, Lawrence died in France of tuberculosis. A few years later, Frieda returned to Taos with his ashes and her new lover, Angelo Ravagli. Today, the ashes are housed in a small chapel at the ranch that Frieda bequeathed to the University of New Mexico. Her own grave is nearby.

D.H. LAWRENCE IN TAOS

D.H. Lawrence and his wife Frieda spent the fall/winter of 1922–23 and the summer of 1924 at a ranch outside Taos.

We leave the ranch quite wild—only there's abundant feed for the five horses. And if we wanted to take the trouble, we could bring the water here as McClure did, and have a little farm.—There's quite a lot of land, really—I'd say 180 acres, but it takes a terrible long time to go around the fence, through the wild forest.—We got lots of wild strawberries—and we still get gallons of wild raspberries, up our own little canyon, where no soul ever goes. If we ride two miles, we can get no farther. Beyond, all savage, unbroken mountain.

We get our things from Taos—17 miles—either by wagon or when someone is coming in a car. Our road is no road—a breaking through the forest—but people come to see us. Every evening, just after tea, we saddle up and ride down to Del Monte Ranch for the milk, butter, eggs, and letters. The old trail passes their gate, and the mailman, on horseback, leaves all the mail in a box nailed on a tree. . . . During the day there's always plenty to do—chopping wood, carrying water—and our own work: sometimes we all paint pictures. Next week the Indian Geronimo is coming up to help me mend the corral, and build a porch over my door, and fix the spring for winter. . . . It gets very cold, and snow often knee deep. Sometimes, for a day or two, no getting away from the ranch.

—D.H. Lawrence in a letter to his niece, 1924

Most artists and writers who came to the state arrived by train, and many of them preferred the juniper foothills of Santa Fe to the plateau outpost of Taos. These included Mary Austin, Willa Cather, and Oliver La Farge, who won a Pulitzer Prize in 1929 for a Navajo love story called *Laughing Boy.*

One group of Santa Fe artists—who met while painting the high desert countryside and the people of Santa Fe—formed Los Cinco Pintores (The Five Painters), but were dubbed by others "the five nuts in five mud huts." The goal of members Jozef Bakos, Fremont Ellis, Walter Mruk, Willard Nash, and Will Shuster was to "bring art to the people." The group's first exhibition was held at the Museum of Fine Arts in 1921. All built homes on Camino del Monte Sol and worked in studios along and near Canyon Road, which today is the most concentrated art district in the city.

Will Shuster briefly broke away from painting in 1926 to help create Zozobra, a menacing 40-foot-tall marionette that has come to symbolize Las Fiestas de Santa Fe, the celebration commemorating the 1692 reoccupation of Santa Fe. The weekend event begins begins at dusk on the Thursday following Labor Day at Fort Marcy Park. Zozobra, also known as Old Man Gloom, eyes gleaming with anger, waves his arms and groans in anguish, trying to dissuade the fire spirit dancer from igniting his papier-mâché body, which is clad in flowing muslin and stuffed with shredded paper (including obsolete police reports and divorce papers) with a flaming torch. The effigy always loses and goes up in a burst of flame to the cheers of 40,000 spectators, gleeful to see gloom disappear for another year.

Many others followed these early artists to northern New Mexico, including woodcutters Gustave Baumann and Nicolai Fechin, and painters Robert Henri and Leon Gaspard. The growth of the Santa Fe and Taos art colonies also fostered a new respect for Indian artists, such as Allan Houser, Dan Namingha, Michael Naranjo, and Pablita Velarde, whose works hang in museums and galleries.

■ SANTA FE SIGHTS AND ATTRACTIONS

The early Santa Feans adopted the earthen building styles of the neighboring Pueblo Indians in order to deal with an intense summer sun, spring winds that whipped up the sandy soil, and a white winter carpet that turned streets into mud bogs each spring. But they steadfastly retained the colorful dress of their Spanish forefathers in the Old World or to the south in Mexico.

From these influences, these hardy and ingenious people developed a unique and indigenous fashion statement known as "Santa Fe Style" that today can be found in all corners of the United States. Dirt-and-straw adobe bricks may survive only in dry climates, but vigas and *latilla* ceilings and red-brown clay tiled floors can go anywhere.

But it's in New Mexico where these elements most naturally belong. Cozy corner kiva fireplaces warm up cold nights, flat roofs become gardens during summer months, and doorways curve into adobe benches underneath cobalt blue, wood-trimmed windows. Navajo and Chimayo textiles adorn walls and floors. Chairs, tables, and cupboards are intricately carved in the old Spanish Colonial style. Tin light fixtures and frames hang on white plaster walls.

In the early 1900s, a group of Santa Fe painters, writers, architects, businessmen, and politicians began a movement to preserve this Spanish-Pueblo style of

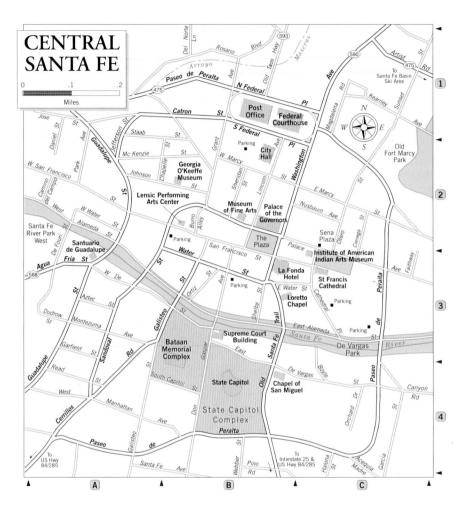

architecture. The movement resulted in important new buildings that celebrated their vision: the Museum of Fine Arts, La Fonda, the New Mexico School for the Deaf—all sporting vigas, deliberately uneven walls, and kiva fireplaces.

But as Santa Fe Style has gained in popularity, so have its travesties multiplied. One newcomer, an apartment manager, wanted to erect a 15-foot-high, turquoise-colored coyote outside the apartment complex because she thought it was the town's symbol. Indeed, coyotes howling at the moon—small wooden sculptures of them, that is—are everywhere in the "City Different," one of Santa Fe's labels.

They come in a multitude of colors, from fire-engine red to sea foam green, and often wear a bandana around their necks. Brightly painted wooden snakes are another cliché, writhing as if to escape their cuteness. Other flamboyant items include cow and ram skulls with horns, finely worked silver concha belts, and 20-pound squash blossom necklaces strung with enough turquoise to fill a small safe. Put them together and you've got what many people call "Santa Fe Tacky."

Tacky or stylish, Santa Fe is a city unlike "the deadly monotony of 10,000 American towns," as Santa Fe painter Carlos Vierra described the rest of the United States in 1917.

■ **GALLERIES AND SHOPS**

More than 250 galleries line the plazas and winding streets of Santa Fe. They are stocked with items ranging from the sublime to the ridiculous—Western landscape paintings, cowboy portraits, acrylic abstracts, old and new pottery, the ubiquitous bandana-bedecked howling coyotes, bronze buffaloes, and the works of a few European masters. Roy Rogers floor lamps stand next to glass cases stuffed with exquisite Hopi silver bracelets and earrings. Ancient pottery made by the Mimbres Indians in southwestern New Mexico and yucca water baskets are for sale next to saddles and silver spurs. In many galleries and shops, a friendly house cat or hound extends the initial greetings.

Canyon Road, an old Indian trail that leads into the piñon foothills, provides a total immersion into the town's eclectic art world; nearly a hundred galleries, shops, and restaurants line its narrow length. Coming from the Plaza, you might stop first at the **Gerald Peters Gallery,** just past the entrance to Canyon Road. This elegant space, filled with a broad range of works by distinguished artists, both local and national, feels more like a museum than a gallery. It serves as a good primer on the paintings of the early Taos and Santa Fe artists and displays works by Western masters, such as sculptures by Frederic Remington. Contemporary artists are represented as well. *1011 Paseo de Peralta; 505-954-5700.*

Backtracking a little and turning into Canyon Road, on a chilly winter day you'll encounter the sweet smell of piñon smoke wafting from kiva fireplaces, which provide welcome warmth. The uncluttered, wood-floored interior of the **Turner Carroll Gallery** (725 Canyon Road; 505-986-9800) and its international modern art collection contrast with the homey feeling at **Kania-Ferrin Gallery** (662 Canyon Road; 505-982-8767), where you walk through the kitchen to view a Fiji war club. The exhibitions and the artists change regularly at **Bellas Artes**

(653 Canyon Road; 505-983-2745), where the focus is on innovation—whether the medium is photography, painting, or mixed media.

Two horse chestnut trees and a turquoise picket fence mark **El Zaguán** (545 Canyon Road; 505-983-2567), a 19th-century hacienda that has been turned into private apartments. The west garden of this rambling adobe was designed by Adolph Bandelier in the late 1800s, and its peony bushes were imported more than a century ago from China. The garden's wrought-iron benches are a pleasant place to rest and listen to the songs of birds and the hum of nearby traffic.

On Christmas Eve, *farolitos*—votive candles in paper sacks weighted with dirt—line walls, rooftops, and the narrow streets in the Canyon Road vicinity. Those strolling among the flickering lights may stop to warm their hands at small bonfires of stacked piñon wood. Neighbors play guitars and share hot apple cider and *bizcochitos*—small anise-flavored sugar cookies. When spring comes, the white and pink blooms of cosmos mix with other wildflowers, leaving barely a sidewalk for folks on foot. Coyote fences (wooden posts strung together with wire) and stone walls ensure privacy for the few residents who live along this scenic thoroughfare.

Where Canyon Road joins Camino Cabra, **Cristo Rey Catholic Church** stands as a memorial to Francisco Vásquez de Coronado. Dedicated in 1940, the 400th anniversary of the Spanish explorer's travels in the Southwest, the massive adobe structure was designed by John Gaw Meem, Santa Fe's most famous architect and a central figure in the revival of Spanish Pueblo style. A total of 180,000 adobe bricks were used in constructing the building, all molded from the soil on which it stands. The church was built primarily to house a magnificent stone *reredos* (altar screen), the most famous piece of ecclesiastical art created in New Mexico during Spanish colonial times. The screen—clearly the focal point of the otherwise austere sanctuary— was commissioned in 1760 and served as the prototype for the numerous wooden altar screens found in churches throughout the state.

Farther into the foothills, on Upper Canyon Road, is **Randall Davey House.** The New Jersey–born artist purchased the home when he moved to Santa Fe in 1920; it has been turned into the Audubon Society's state headquarters, and nature trails wind through its grounds at the mouth of Santa Fe Canyon. *1800 Upper Canyon Road; 505-983-4609.*

Offsetting the regionalism of the Santa Fe art scene is **Site Santa Fe**, a contemporary exhibition space southwest of the Plaza. The nonprofit arts organization is

In Santa Fe, as in Albuquerque, buying jewelry from the Indians who make it is high on any traveler's to-do list.

best known for its international biennials, but it continues to develop a strong year-round exhibition program that showcases established conceptual artists along with cutting-edge newcomers. *1606 Paseo de Peralta; 505-989-1199.*

■ MUSEUMS

More than 450 years of New Mexico history is represented in the **Palace of the Governors**, nearly 400 years old and the oldest public building in the United States. The block-long adobe palace was built around a courtyard, and its rooms attach to each other, beckoning exploration from one to the next. Exhibits follow a chronological order and include ancient Indian pottery, a rebuilt two-wheeled *carreta,* maps of 18th-century Spanish America, and a 19th-century chuck wagon. *105 West Palace; 505-476-5100.*

Rain or shine, warm or cold, on every day of the year Indian artists sit patiently on the brick sidewalk outside the restored government building, beside blankets spread with their crafts, artwork, and handmade jewelry. Prices are reasonable and the artists enjoy talking about their work.

Across the street from the palace is a building as wonderful as the art contained within. The **Museum of Fine Arts** houses a permanent collection of more than 8,000 works, including seven paintings by Georgia O'Keeffe and other pieces on regional subjects by Gustave Baumann, Marsden Hartley, John Marin, Will Shuster, and painters of the Taos School. Completed in 1917, this massive structure was the first example of the Pueblo Revival style to be built in Santa Fe, and it acted as a stimulus to the development of the city's emerging art colony. Changing shows display works from the permanent collection, along with contemporary local and regional painting, sculpture, and photography. *107 West Palace Avenue; 505-476-5072.*

Southeast of downtown amid a cluster of juniper and yellow-tipped chamisa is **Museum Hill,** on which four of the city's most impressive museums are to be found. The **Museum of International Folk Art** is a whimsical, fascinating world of toys, textiles, and crafts collected from 100 countries. A walk through the wonderful Girard Wing introduces visitors to the one-of-a-kind collection gathered by architect Alexander Girard and his wife, Susan, during a lifetime of travels. Their 106,000 pieces of folk art create a mesmerizing fantasy world of African puppets, antique dolls from around the world, Russian icons, and table settings complete with plastic vegetables and rubber hamburgers. Tiny figurines depicting people of all ages populate a miniature Mexican village that includes green shrubbery. Doll

The Museum of Fine Arts, opened in 1917, was the first Pueblo Revival building in Santa Fe.

houses line the streets of a typical American town, and an array of intricately carved boats, mostly Oriental, line up in a busy harbor ready to unload their wares.

Elsewhere in the museum, the Hispanic Heritage Wing houses the largest collection of Spanish colonial folk art in the United States. Changing exhibits display tinwork, Spanish colonial furniture, folk costumes, and textiles. Religious figurines—*bultos* and *santos*—reveal an evolution of style through nearly three centuries. The Neutrogena Wing contains exquisite textiles and garments as well as objects. *706 Camino Lejo; 505-476-1200.*

Across a plaza, the **Museum of Indian Arts and Culture** details the history and contemporary lives of Pueblo, Apache, and Navajo Indians. Their story is told through diagrams and displays of Clovis points, ancient cookware, and clothing. Exhibits draw from collections of the Laboratory of Anthropology, located next door and founded in the 1920s by John D. Rockefeller, and include the first black-on-black pot fired by famed potter Maria Martinez, a bridle that once belonged to Apache leader Cochise, a 151-foot-long hunting net made of human hair dating to 1100, and more than 75,000 baskets, pots, and examples of jewelry, carving, and weaving—among them a large number of fine 19th-century Navajo blankets. In addition, modern Indian artists demonstrate their craftsmanship, weaving on looms and molding pottery. *710 Camino Lejo; 505-827-6344.*

The **Wheelwright Museum of the American Indian** focuses primarily on traditional and contemporary Southwestern Indian art. The building's design resembles a giant Navajo hogan—the one-story, eight-sided structure used for ceremonies and residence. As in all Navajo dwellings, the entrance faces east, to achieve a sense of harmony with the sun streaming in every morning. The museum is dedicated to preserving and furthering Native American traditions and contains textiles, baskets, pottery, jewelry, folk arts, fine arts, and clothing, mostly of Navajo origin. In addition, the Wheelwright's collection of 600 Navajo sandpainting reproductions is the largest in the world. Pueblo, Plains, and Apache Indians also are represented in the exhibits, which include the Case Trading Post, a replica of an early 20th-century reservation store. *704 Camino Lejo; 505-982-4636.*

The newest addition to Museum Hill is the **Museum of Spanish Colonial Art**, which opened in 2002 in a 1930s house that is another example of the work of famous Santa Fe architect John Gaw Meem. As you walk through the cozy rooms, you can admire the workmanship of silver hair combs, hand-hewn furniture, and stylized santos created during the 18th and 19th centuries, when New Mexico was struggling to establish its identity. *750 Camino Lejo; 505-982-2226.*

The **Georgia O'Keeffe Museum**, downtown, is dedicated to the work of one of the 20th century's most influential women painters. Located two blocks off the Plaza, the museum houses the largest concentration anywhere of the pioneering modernist artist's paintings, drawings, and sculpture. The collection is on display throughout the year, alongside changing exhibitions that celebrate various aspects of O'Keeffe's life and the work of her colleagues (including, for example, photographs by her husband, Alfred Stieglitz, or by her friend Mary Chabot, another photographer, who spent time with O'Keeffe in New Mexico). *217 Johnson Street; 505-995-0785.*

Fifteen miles south of town, Spanish colonial life comes alive again at **El Rancho de las Golondrinas**. This living history museum is located at what was, during the 18th century, the last stopping place on the journey from Mexico to Santa Fe on El Camino Real. On select summer weekends, the restored ranch brims with activity as the ranch's churro sheep are sheared, cloth is woven on looms, and molasses is made from sorghum cane. *334 Los Pinos Road; 505-471-2261.*

In the Sculpture Garden at the Museum of Indian Arts and Culture.

■ SANTA FE WALK

The winding streets of Santa Fe, which often seem too narrow for cars, are perfect for a leisurely stroll. Following is a suggested walk that starts at St. Francis Cathedral. It is only a taste of old Santa Fe, however; nearly every street surrounding the Plaza contains its own treasures and is worth exploring.

Built of sandstone and a lightweight volcanic rock, the towering Romanesque **St. Francis Cathedral** looms at the end of East San Francisco Street, in stark contrast to nearby low earthen-colored adobe buildings. Originally, plans included a 160-foot steeple on each of the two towers, but today the only visual evidence of such intentions are supports that jut from the left tower.

As you enter the grounds, you'll see the statue of Archbishop Jean Baptiste Lamy, the driving force behind this mammoth undertaking. Inside, 55-foot-tall taupe walls are decorated with intricate geometric designs painted on the many sweeping arches that reach up to support the vaulted ceiling. The brightly colored stained-glass windows are finely crafted and exquisitely detailed. The serene La Conquistadora, the statue first brought by Spanish colonists to Santa Fe in the early 1600s, stands proudly on her own altar in her own chapel. She wears a delicate lace veil and a billowing gown that is changed with the season or holiday: at Christmas it is kelly green.

Across from the cathedral and commanding an entire block is **La Fonda,** a hotel steeped in history. The site has been occupied by a hotel since the city was founded in 1607; the current four-story structure, in the Pueblo Revival style, was built in the 1920s. Then, as now, La Fonda represents the essence of the city's style. Details include a polished tile floor, whimsically painted furniture, murals created in the 1920s by Gerald Cassidy, and panels of colorful windows that surround the hotel's La Plazuela restaurant. A popular hangout for locals, you might find a goateed artist buying the daily newspaper or a Hollywood star on vacation in the lobby. Take a seat in one of the lobby's comfortable leather chairs and watch the bustle of Santa Fe life, then take in the sunset from the Bell Tower Bar. *100 East San Francisco Street; 505-982-5511 or 800-523-5002.*

To the south of La Fonda is another of Archbishop Lamy's projects, the **Loretto Chapel.** The small Gothic chapel was designed to meet the spiritual needs of Loretto Academy, founded in 1853 by the first six nuns to arrive in

Baking bread the old-fashioned way at El Rancho de las Golondrinas.

New Mexico. Fashioned after Sainte Chapelle in Paris, it offers a lot for its size: European-made stained-glass windows, Italian statues depicting the stations of the cross, and a faux-marble wooden altar. Most impressive is a 33-step wooden staircase that twists in a double helix—and was built without a nail, screw, or support of any kind. Known today as the "miraculous staircase," this wondrous feat of carpentry contains no imprint of its master builder, a mysterious man equipped with a hammer, saw, and T-square. He appeared out of nowhere, in answer to the nuns' prayers, when the chapel was near completion but with no space remaining to construct a conventional staircase to the choir loft. His only request was for two tubs of water. He accepted no payment and disappeared after completing the project. Some believe he was St. Joseph, the carpenter saint; others say he was Yohon Hadwiger, a carpenter visiting from Vienna, Austria. *277 Old Santa Fe Trail; 505-982-0092.*

Farther south, Old Santa Fe Trail crosses the Santa Fe River, which rushes with water in the spring, but becomes a dry ditch by fall due to dams and reservoirs high up in the mountains.

Across the river is **Barrio de Analco**, Santa Fe's oldest neighborhood, originally settled in the 1600s by Tlaxcalan Indians from Mexico who accompanied early Franciscan missionaries and Spanish officials to the new territory as servants. Narrow brick sidewalks buckle and porch roofs slant, showing their age. The **Chapel of San Miguel** stands in the center of this historic district, protected from the busy street by a finely crafted stone wall. Inside the simple adobe church, a very expressive gilded statue of St. Michael, the chapel's patron saint, stands centered on an ornate wooden altar.

Cottonwoods provide shade, and a cloyingly sweet fragrance emanates from purple wisteria blossoms as the ancient and narrow De Vargas Street leads west to the **Santuario de Guadalupe,** a chapel at the corner of Agua Fria and Guadalupe Streets. Built sometime between 1776 and 1795, this adobe shrine to Our Lady of Guadalupe, patron saint of Mexico, displays one of the finest *reredos* in the Southwest. Painted in 1783 in Mexico, this oil-on-canvas altar screen was made expressly for the Santa Fe sanctuary and was hauled up the Chihuahua Trail in an oxcart. Carved vigas and corbels adorn the high ceiling, and the windows are stained glass. Today, the small chapel, no longer used as a church, is often the site of theatrical and musical performances. *505-988-2027.*

The Loretto Chapel and its famous staircase.

SANTA FE OPERA

The pleasures of summertime opera festivals can be enjoyed in locations across the United States, outdoors in parks and in partially enclosed theaters. But the Santa Fe Opera, whose season is in July and August, may have them all beat. The impressive theater, a 1998 state-of-the-art renovation of the Opera's original performance space, sits on 155 acres and seats 2,128. The surrounding panoramic view of the Jemez and Sangre de Cristos Mountains virtually begs to be incorporated into the onstage scenery. The building's dramatically curved roof is its architectural highlight; its undulations were designed to follow "the shape of the sound"—the acoustic reflections that connect the stage to the audience.

When in the 1950s impresario John Crosby decided to found a new opera company, feeling that young American singers lacked opportunities to develop their art in this country, he selected Santa Fe as the ideal site. As he explained in a recent interview: "It was a community that had a flourishing art colony: painters, poets, writers, sculptors. Strangely, music was missing. It seemed to me that the community would receive this missing link warmly." Crosby bought and converted an old ranch north of the city, and in July 1957 the Santa Fe Opera introduced itself to the public with Puccini's *Madama Butterfly,* performed in the company's original 480-seat open-air theater. It wasn't long before world-class singers such as Marilyn Horne and Kiri Te Kanawa were lured to New Mexico, as were movie star Jose Ferrer (singing his first operatic role) and ballerina—and Santa Fe resident—Vera Zorina.

The company was taken seriously from the start by critics and the international musical community. A two-week Stravinsky Festival was mounted in 1962, honoring the composer's 80th birthday, and the next year, Santa Fe had the distinction of producing the first U.S. performances of Alban Berg's *Lulu,* and in subsequent seasons gave the American stage premieres of Richard Strauss's *Daphne* and Nino Rota's *The Italian Straw Hat.* Known for its diverse repertoire, and never unfriendly to contemporary works, Santa Fe commissioned and produced three new American operas in the mid-1990s, one of which, Tobias Picker's *Emmeline,* was telecast by PBS.

Santa Fe Opera's artistic standards are high but its community spirit is heartily down-home. The parking lots open three hours before each performance to accommodate al fresco tailgate parties, and picnic suppers are available from the catering kiosk. (The Opera Cantina is open for more elaborate meals.) Shuttle buses convey ticket-holders from several downtown hotels. *On U.S. 84/285, 7 miles north of downtown; 505-986-5900 or 800-280-4654.*

—John Morrone

Montezuma Avenue leads to a complex of state government buildings. The most impressive and unique is the circular **State Capitol,** a 1960s structure whose design combines that of the ceremonial Indian kiva and the Zia sun sign, which appears on the state flag as well as on New Mexico license plates. A stroll through the rotunda takes you to Old Santa Fe Trail, which leads back to the Plaza.

■ EATING IN SANTA FE

Finding a great place to eat in Santa Fe is never a problem, but during the summer, getting a seat in a restaurant can be a different story. More than 200 restaurants (not including chains and franchises) can be found along major thoroughfares or tucked into back-alley adobes. Menus offer everything from dim sum to pasta, from bean burritos to rabbit confit enchiladas with orange-jicama salsa—a cuisine that represents the city's varied cultures, especially the newly transplanted ones.

The tony **Coyote Cafe** (132 West Water Street; 505-983-1615), while beyond the pocketbooks of most Santa Feans, is probably the city's most famous eatery. When chef Mark Miller opened it in 1987, his unique combination of ingredients and techniques from Mexico, New Mexico, France, and Northern California won near-instant success and helped foster a Southwestern cooking craze that spread across the country. Local restaurants responded as well. Tapas are now served in the cozy confines of **El Farol** (808 Canyon Road; 505-983-9912); the **Zia Diner** (326 South Guadalupe Street; 505-988-7008) replaces mundane pinto beans with sleeker black ones; and blue corn tortillas have nearly run the traditional yellow variety out of town.

Still, traditional New Mexican cooking holds its own: dishes such as breakfast burritos, chile rellenos, tamales, and enchiladas represent the food of choice. Try the blue-corn enchiladas smothered in red chile at **The Shed** (113 East Palace Avenue; 505-982-9030) or the same dish with green chile at its sister restaurant, **La Choza**—Spanish for "shed"—(905 Alarid Street; 505-982-0909). Both are owned by the same folks, and at either spot the mocha cake is worth saving room for. At **Maria's New Mexican Kitchen** (555 West Cordova Road; 505-983-7929), choose from 100 different types of margaritas to go with a steaming plate of fajitas or enchiladas.

When the urge to take a rest from afternoon shopping takes over, treat yourself to the British tradition of afternoon tea, which is served daily in the lobby of the **Hotel St. Francis** (210 Don Gaspar Avenue; 505-983-5700).

For a romantic evening, try **Geronimo** (724 Canyon Road; 505-982-1500), where you might enjoy elk tenderloin with apple wood–smoked bacon or white prawns with jasmine rice cakes. Things are livelier at **La Casa Sena** (125 East Palace Avenue; 505-988-9232), where the waitstaff serenades diners with Broadway show tunes while serving up grilled lamb chops marinated in papaya with yucca root–plaintain puree. When eating out in Santa Fe, expect to pay a few dollars more than anywhere else in the state, but after all, location is everything.

■ THE HIGH ROAD *map page 85, C-3/4/5*

Most of the small Hispanic farming villages that line what has become known as the "high road," linking Santa Fe and Taos, were settled in the 18th century. Remarkably, these picturesque hamlets—with their weathered log barns, adobe-walled homes, and tin roofs that reflect the shimmering sunlight—appear much as they did 200 years ago. Most people speak Spanish as easily as English. Every spring, members of community *acequía* associations, armed with shovels, rakes, and pitchforks, clear debris from irrigation ditches to ensure an uninterrupted flow of mountain runoff throughout the summer. Fall brings a harvest of beans and apples and day-long wood-cutting expeditions to the nearby mountains.

Heading north out of Santa Fe, this scenic route starts out by passing **Tesuque, Pojoaque,** and **Nambé** pueblos. Situated between the pueblos, the town of **Española** boasts the state's most concentrated population of low riders, automobile aficionados devoted to customizing their vehicles with chain-link steering wheels, hydraulic suspension systems, and one-of-a-kind paint jobs. As you make your way through town, you'll likely be slowed by one or more of these custom cars showing off its individuality.

■ CHIMAYO TO PEÑASCO *map page 85, C-3/4*

Winding among rolling hills, the high road drops into the village of Chimayo, which is tucked into a cottonwood-shaded valley. Here, Hispanic weavers craft brightly colored clothing and blankets, characterized by bold stripes. Originally, Spanish colonial artisans wove these beautiful textiles for their own use. For a time, interest in the craft flagged, but in the early 1800s Santa Fe residents sent to Spain for expert weavers to revive the art and teach their children. Two of these artisans, Juan and Ignacio Balzan, rejected the capital city for the sheltered hamlet of Chimayo and taught weaving to residents there. **Ortega's Weaving Shop** (505-

The Santuario de Chimayo is visited by thousands of religious pilgrims every Holy Week.

351-4215; 877-351-4215) is now headed by David Ortega, a member of the sixth generation to live and work in this spot. His two sons are also weavers.

This peaceful town is also known for the **Santuario de Chimayo**, which attracts thousands of pilgrims every year during Holy Week. Some worshipers walk along the shoulders of freeways and two-lane highways from as far away as Albuquerque, 80 miles south. They come to express their faith at the small adobe chapel whose bell towers rise above the ancient cottonwoods. The chapel was built between 1813 and 1816 by Bernardo Abeyta, who, as the story goes, was deathly ill when a vision led him to a spot where he was immediately cured. To give thanks, he erected the chapel at the site.

According to legend, fire and smoke once erupted here, leaving a pool of mud that Pueblo Indians used for medicinal purposes, eating it or smearing it on their bodies. From a tiny hole in the ground inside a small candlelit room built onto the chapel, today's faithful collect samples of the same *tierra bendita* (sacred earth), in the belief that it has healing powers. Discarded crutches hang from the adobe walls of a small adjoining room, along with other testaments that many others believe in the site's healing abilities.

Before leaving town, a perfect rest stop is **Rancho de Chimayo** (505-351-4444), the restored 1880 home of the Jaramillo family, now a restaurant. A strain of chile grown only in the fields of this area is used in Chimayo's style of New Mexico cuisine. Diners can bask in the warmth of a kiva fireplace in a wooden-floored dining room, or sip a margarita in cool shade on the outside patio. Another Jaramillo family home has been turned into a quaint bed and breakfast, the **Rancho de Chimayo Hacienda Bed and Breakfast** (505-351-2222). The Jaramillos were early Chimayo settlers, and both operations are run by their descendants.

Córdova, a tiny enclave tucked into a narrow valley, has long been home to traditional woodcarvers. Look for signs that mark their workshops.

With the stunning 13,000-foot Truchas Peaks as a backdrop and the Rio Grande Valley in the distance, the tin roofs of **Truchas** (Spanish for "trouts") rise from fertile vegetable and bean fields. Wild herbs, scrub oak, and cattails prosper in backyards. It's easy to see why, in the mid-1980s, Robert Redford filmed *The Milagro Beanfield War* in this bucolic setting. Many trails branch out of town into the piñon and ponderosa pine hills of the Carson National Forest. Fittingly, rainbow trout can be found in the nearby Truchas River.

One of the finest 18th-century Spanish Pueblo–style churches survives at **Las Trampas**, on high ground next to the road. In contrast to the more refined restoration at the Chimayo sanctuary, San José de Gracia at Las Trampas retains a rustic simplicity. The Las Trampas church initially was known as the Church of the Twelve Apostles, and it has been said that only 12 men at a time were permitted to erect its 4-foot-thick adobe walls. The church, which stands 34 feet high, was built with an outdoor choir loft so the chorus could move outside to sing during religious processions. Inside, plain wooden benches rest on uneven wood-planked floors. Painted vigas and corbels, along with elaborate paintings, add decoration to the stark interior. If visitors should find the church locked, they can ask a neighbor to open the heavy wooden doors.

Picuris Pueblo, small but growing, is situated in a hidden valley in the Sangre de Cristo Mountains. A tribal museum tells the story of the isolated pueblo, which today has 150 residents. Guides take visitors past the remains of its prehistoric village, which stands near modern-day residences.

Abandoned movie theaters and car dealerships attest to the long-lost prosperity once enjoyed by the village of **Peñasco**. Established in 1796 as three settlements along the Rio Santa Barbara, Peñasco still stretches along the waterway. But as its younger residents move away in search of better jobs, the small farms and ranches that gave the village its identity are disappearing. Many historic adobe homes, dance halls, and restaurants remain, but some are no longer occupied.

A dirt road follows the shallow, tree-shaded Rio Santa Barbara into the **Pecos Wilderness.** There, campgrounds are surrounded by fields of wildflowers, and trails lead to mountain lakes and the high peaks that protect the valley settlements.

■ **NM 518 TO TAOS** *map page 85, C/D-3*

The paved road to Taos, NM 518, climbs steeply just past Peñasco, leaving behind the fertile valleys and entering into the tall pine forests and mountain meadows of the Taos Plateau. **Fort Burgwin Research Center** straddles the road. Restored and run by Southern Methodist University, the fort was built in 1852 to protect Taos from Comanche and Ute raiders. Research is focused on ruins of Anasazi dwellings on the site that date to 1100. During summer months, concerts and lectures take place here. *505-758-8322.*

The road ends at **Ranchos de Taos,** a few miles south of the town of Taos. This small village was established by Spanish homesteaders in 1716, and Comanche raids made life unpredictable for its settlers until the end of the 19th century. Many fine adobe buildings have been restored in this hamlet, which can claim one of the most photographed and most painted 18th-century missions, the Church of San Francisco de Asís, built in 1730. Burros hauled huge adobe bricks up earthen ramps to construct this fortress-like church, whose walls are 13 feet thick at the base and supported on the outside by heavy adobe buttresses. Like most others of its day, the Ranchos church supports two bell towers. Unlike many, however, the left tower is slightly taller than the right. One artist attracted to the church's irregular lines was Georgia O'Keeffe. "Most artists who spend any time in Taos have to paint it, I suppose, just as they have to paint a self-portrait. I had to paint it—the back of it several times, the front once."

Inside, enormous vigas and corbels support a high ceiling. Most notable among the collection of European and New Mexican artwork is a painting that is said to glow in the dark.

(following pages) The adobe church of Las Trampas.

■ Taos Sights and Attractions   *map page 155*

Like many New Mexico towns, Taos grew up around a central plaza, and wandering through nearby streets you'll see a number of restored historic buildings that now double as museums. At the **Old Taos County Courthouse,** which faces the Plaza, 10 allegorical murals depicting classical scenes with moralistic themes (such as Reconciliation and Transgression) grace the walls of the second-story courtroom. The impressive 1934 frescoes were the work of Emil Bisttram, Bert Phillips, Victor Hughes, and Ward Lockwood and were commissioned by the Works Projects Administration. An 11th mural by Frederico Vigil was added in 1995.

Occasionally a crow calls from the treetops above the **Gov. Bent House and Museum,** where Charles Bent, New Mexico's first American governor, lived and where he was killed during the Taos Rebellion in 1847. Pink plaster is peeled away where his wife and two other women dug into the thick adobe wall in their attempt to escape Bent's killers. (The women were spared.) A black cloth Penitente mask and leather whip are protected in a glass case as a reminder of the days when that self-torturing Catholic confraternity flourished in northern New Mexico. A broad-backed Bent family wooden chair with leather seat sits in a room next to a marble-topped dresser. *117-A Bent Street; 505-758-2376.*

Kit Carson, who at age 16 signed on with a wagon train heading across the Santa Fe Trail, made Taos his home. Even though the famous trapper and Indian fighter spent most of his time on the road, in 1843 he bought and presented his new bride, Josefa Jaramillo, with a 12-room adobe home built 18 years earlier near the central plaza. Seven of the Carsons' eight children were born inside the 30-inch-thick adobe walls of the U-shaped building, occupied by the family for 25 years. Today, the **Kit Carson Home and Museum** is one of three historic museums operated by the Kit Carson Foundation. In the meandering dirt- and wood-floored rooms visitors can see where the couple's children played and helped their mother prepare meals, and where Carson met with traders, dignitaries, and military men who passed through New Mexico. On display are shotguns that probably accompanied the Kentucky-born scout on his many missions into the wilderness, as well as one of Josefa's narrow-waisted tan and brown silk dresses and a fringed beige shawl, protected inside a glass case. The living room, with Carson's black wooden desk in a corner and wooden organ along a wall, seems to be awaiting the return of its inhabitants. *113 Kit Carson Road; 505-758-0505.*

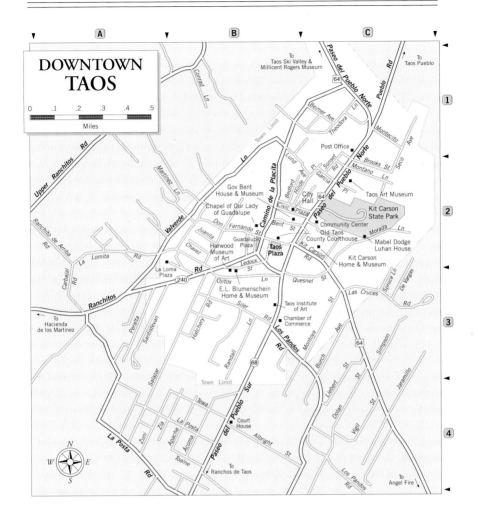

DOWNTOWN
TAOS

0   .1   .2   .3   .4   .5
Miles

From 1919 until his death in 1960, artist Ernest Blumenschein, along with his wife, Mary, lived and worked in a 12-room, 18th-century adobe house in downtown Taos. Today, the **E.L. Blumenschein Home and Museum** appears much as it did when the painter lived there. Wooden armoires shipped from France stand against adobe walls, and a cedar table and matching sideboard made by a Taos craftsman fill the dining room. Paintings by Blumenschein, his wife, their daughter Helen, and other Taos artists line the walls. *222 Ledoux Street; 505-758-0505.*

Kit Carson and his wife Josefa fed their eight children out of this kitchen.

Just northeast of the Plaza, on the edge of the Taos Indian Reservation, is where Nicolai Fechin settled when he arrived in Taos in 1927. Already a celebrated artist in Russia, he was spurred by the hardships following the Bolshevik Revolution to find a better life for his family in the United States. He bought a house and began improving upon it, carving intricate patterns into doors and window frames and embellishing his own handcrafted furniture. After seven years, he moved to Santa Monica, California, but he left behind a showpiece, which now houses the **Taos Art Museum,** where you'll be able to admire not only Fechin's woodworking talents, but also his paintings and drawings, along with a permanent collection of works by members of the Taos Society of Artists and by a group of abstract artists who painted in the 1940s and 1950s and are now known as the Taos Moderns. *227 Paseo del Pueblo Norte; 505-758-2690.*

A luminary in the art world who continues to make her home in Taos is Agnes Martin, whose minimalist paintings are found in museums around the world. Seven of her ethereal works hang in their own gallery inside the **Harwood Museum of Art.** (She enjoys showing up to observe visitors' reactions to them.) The museum, operated by the University of New Mexico, also features paintings by early Taos artists and other modernists, along with traditional Hispanic artwork. *238 Ledoux Street; 505-758-9826.*

More than 50 art galleries are scattered throughout the town's dusty streets. Most of them hug the narrow lanes and historic sites surrounding the central plaza, so it's easy to sample them on foot. Representative of the variety of art to be found are the **New Directions Gallery** (505-758-2771; 800-658-6903), on the plaza, where works of emerging Taos-area artists are on display, and R.C. Gorman's **Navajo Gallery** (210 Ledoux Street; 505-758-3250), where the walls are lined with pastel portraits of Indian women by this Navajo artist, who has lived on the outskirts of Taos since 1968.

Two miles outside of town is the **Hacienda de los Martinez**, set inside imposing adobe walls that were built for protection from Indian attacks. Construction of the home, begun in 1804, was often interrupted by Comanche and Apache raids. Even after completion, tending sheep outside its protective walls was hazardous. Antonio Severino Martinez, one of the area's chief traders, used two-wheeled *carretas* and pack mules to haul tallow candles, piñon nuts, jerky, beaver pelts, wool, and woven belts to Mexico via the Chihuahua Trail. On the return trip, he brought back cloth, nails, tools, sugar, and chocolate. Martinez, who also served as mayor of Taos, turned his home into a showpiece, with 21 rooms surrounding two courtyards. Each room reveals a different *latilla* construction, with split pine, juniper, or aspen pole, all obtained from nearby mountains. A shepherd's fireplace, set deep enough into the adobe wall so that large pots could fit inside, takes up one corner of the kitchen. Today, local weavers and quilters spin wool, work on wooden looms, and sew in rooms off the rear courtyard, much as they might have done 150 years ago. *Ranchitos Road; 505-758-0505.*

Millicent Rogers, a Standard Oil heiress, came to New Mexico in 1948 for a short visit and, caught by its spell, built a home north of Taos. From then until her death in 1953, Rogers amassed an extensive collection of ancient Indian pottery, 19th-century Navajo blankets, kachinas, jewelry, and Spanish Colonial *bultos,* pressed tin light fixtures, and frames. In 1956, her son, Paul Peralta Ramos, established the **Millicent Rogers Museum,** which includes a fabulous assortment of Indian turquoise and silver bracelets, squash blossom necklaces, concha belts, and other adornments accumulated by this woman of style, as well as one of the largest collections anywhere of black-on-black pottery by Maria Martinez. A large deer-motif pot dates to 1919, the year Maria and her husband, Julian, devised the technique, and one room is dedicated to Maria and her family, some of whom are also potters. Photographs depict the precise, time-consuming process of coiling the clay and achieving the shiny black glaze. *1504 Millicent Rogers Museum Road, 4 miles north of the plaza on NM 64; 505-758-2462.*

North of town is perhaps the most photogenic of New Mexico's 19 pueblos. For more than 600 years, Tiwa-speaking Indians have lived in two five-story apartment complexes on opposite banks of the Rio Pueblo de Taos. **Taos Pueblo** has changed little during that time; even today, it has no running water or electricity. About 150 people live here, with 1,900 others residing on reservation lands nearby, returning to their pueblo homes for ceremonies. One of the most anticipated events is the San Geronimo Feast Day on September 30. Foot races start the day, followed by buffalo, Comanche, and corn dances. In mid-afternoon, the Koshares arrive. These are Pueblo men painted in black-and-white stripes, wearing only loin cloths. First, they play tricks on spectators; the dancers are even known to throw children in the creek. Eventually, they make their way to a 50-foot-tall pole draped with ropes. Bundles of gifts, along with a dead sheep, are suspended from the top. After many more antics climbing the ropes, one dancer reaches the gifts and sheep and presents them to Pueblo elders seated close by. The pueblo is open daily except during religious ceremonies. *505-758-1028.*

At the end of the day, a great place to end up is the **Taos Inn,** a collection of buildings that stretches along Paseo del Pueblo Norte, near the Plaza. The hotel opened in 1936 and has served as the town's social hub ever since; locals and visitors mingle over margaritas in the cozy Adobe Bar or enjoy a meal in Doc Martin's restaurant, named for the county's first and, at the time, only doctor, who bought the building for his home in the 1890s. Most of the rooms have a corner kiva fireplace. *125 Paseo del Pueblo Norte; 505-758-2233 or 888-518-8267.*

■ **EATING IN TAOS**

On the whole, Taos restaurants are less interesting than those in Santa Fe—but that doesn't mean there aren't some gems. You'll find innovative pastas and seafood at the **Apple Tree** (123 Bent Street; 505-758-1900), where an apple tree planted in 1903 still commands pride of place on the patio; blue corn–dusted trout or goat-cheese charlotte at **Doc Martin's** (125 Paseo del Pueblo Norte, in the Taos Inn; 505-758-1977); and grilled ginger shrimp at **Lambert's of Taos Restaurant** (309 Paseo del Pueblo Sur; 505-758-1009), housed in a building where teen dances were held in the 1950s. Otherwise, the choices are mostly traditional New Mexican. In keeping with its Pueblo-Spanish decor, even the fast-food outlets boast stuccoed mud-colored exteriors (with no golden arches on view). For quick, non-traditional fare, try a Greek pizza at the **Taos Pizza Out Back** (712 Paseo del Pueblo Norte; 505-758-3112); bangers and mash at **Eske's Brew Pub and Eatery** (106 Des Georges Lane; 505-758-1517); or a club sandwich at the **Bent Street Deli and Café** (120 Bent Street; 505-758-5787).

Breakfast cooks seem to think everyone is on their way to the ski slopes. At **Michael's Kitchen,** (304 Paseo del Pueblo Norte; 505-758-4178), a popular local hangout, no matter what you order, you'll get more than you can eat. You can catch up on the local gossip over chile and eggs at **El Pueblo Cafe,** north of town in the village of El Prado (625 Paseo del Pueblo Norte; 505-751-9817) or wait to pick up a breakfast burrito at **Tim's Stray Dog Cantina** at Taos Ski Valley (105 Sutton Place; 505-776-2894).

NORTHWESTERN
N E W   M E X I C O

Sandstone bluffs and mesas rimmed in muted shades of red and gray rise above the box canyons and grama grass meadows of northwestern New Mexico. Parched riverbeds, which swell with muddy water after a summer cloudburst only to dry up again, meander throughout rangeland dotted with chamisa and saltbush. The rugged El Malpais lava flow, with its chilly ice caves and hardened tubes of lava, intrudes upon this gentle landscape. In the Bisti/De-na-zin Wilderness, the fossils of horned dinosaurs lie strewn among eerie mushroom-shaped spires, and Shiprock, a basalt core that once filled the center of a volcano, now stands like a beacon in the desert. Nearby flows the blue-green water of the San Juan River as it wends its way toward Utah.

· Among these buttes, abrupt rock cliffs, and sprawling mesas is a treasure trove of Native American dwellings, old and new. Ragged remains of ancient Indian villages lie scattered throughout broken mesas and cliffsides. Some have been excavated and preserved, others are covered with mounds of windswept soil. Indian influence, past and present, is greater here than anywhere else in the state, and much of the land belongs to New Mexico's three major Indian groups: the Navajos, Apaches, and Pueblo Indians.

The Anasazi, ancestors of the Pueblo Indians, lived alongside riverbeds that once flowed year-round, where they cultivated beans and corn and erected rock buildings held together with mortar. Excavations at 11 of these sites have revealed the most extensive ancient Indian ruins in the United States. On the other hand, little evidence remains of the ancestors of the Apaches and Navajos, nomadic hunters and gatherers who moved about in search of food.

Northwestern New Mexico is still largely rural, with many Indians living in small communities or on isolated ranchos spread across their reservations. Of the few sizable towns, Gallup, at the southern end of the Navajo Reservation, is the major trading center for Indian wares, and Farmington, at the reservation's northern border, serves as a business hub.

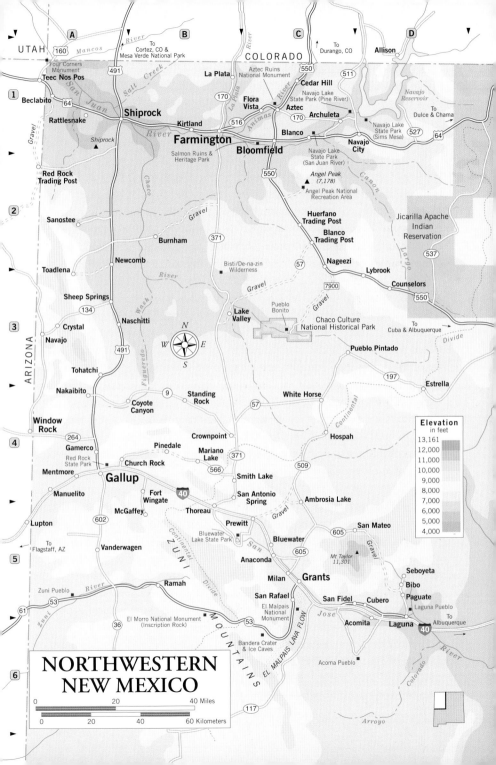

■ **CHACO CANYON** *map page 161, C-3*

Today, most of the state's 19 pueblos hug the Rio Grande, clustered in the north-central part of New Mexico. But it wasn't always that way. Between A.D. 900 and 1200, the ancestors of these Indians made their homes farther west, alongside the flowing Chaco River and atop high desert mesas. More than 2,000 sites have been documented throughout the northwestern region, and it is likely there are more to be found. Until recently, we have known these early people as the Anasazi, a Navajo term meaning "enemy ancestors." Because of the term's pejorative connotation (although not for the archaeologists who continue to use it), their descendants prefer that we call them Ancestral Puebloans. We know that during the Chaco years, they made a giant evolutionary leap forward in their approach to life.

As many as 5,000 Indians grew corn, beans, and squash in irrigated fields beneath sandstone walls in Chaco Canyon during what has come to be known as the Anasazi Golden Age. They built multistory stone and mortar homes, with rooms several times larger than those in the previous stages of their culture. River water was diverted through complex irrigation systems into ditch-fed fields, and an elaborate network of roads connected more than 75 pueblos scattered across the region. These 30-foot-wide roads were laid out in straight lines unimpeded by rough terrain, and where they passed over bare rock the roads were bordered by masonry walls or a line of boulders. This 400-mile transportation and trade network probably was used by communities spread throughout northwestern New Mexico to exchange crops, pottery, and clothing made from deer, elk, and antelope hunted in nearby mountains. Seashells, copper bells, and the remains of parrots and macaws found in the crumbling ruins prove that the Indians also had contact with tribes as far south as Mexico.

We know that by A.D. 1000, Chaco had established itself firmly as an important center, but its exact importance remains fuzzy. Was it the political, economic, or religious center of the area—or was it all three? Researchers continue to unravel the Chaco story, trying to determine whether the site was used solely for ceremonial purposes or was a working community. There are nearly as many theories as there are people working on the mystery.

In any event, these productive people also enjoyed the leisure to develop their artistic abilities. They etched petroglyphs of snakes and spirals into the soft sandstone, wove baskets and sandals from desert grasses, and fashioned clay bowls, pitchers, water jars, and mugs with detailed black-on-white geometric designs.

The Anasazi had mysteriously disappeared from the canyon by the 14th century. Theories abound as to why they abandoned their pueblos at the height of their culture. Archaeologists attribute the exodus to drought, to disease, to roving bands of Indians who continually threatened these people, or to outbreaks of fighting among the Anasazi themselves. One thing is certain: a drought lasting 25 years struck the region in 1276. The residents may have traveled south to build new homes near more reliable sources of water, such as the Rio Grande.

When the Navajos entered the area in the 1770s, they found the broad basin unoccupied. The once-flowing river was dry and ran only after summer rainstorms. The fields of corn and beans had been overtaken by desert grasses and sagebrush, and the voices of a once-vibrant culture were silent.

Today, the wind whistles through the canyon and carries new voices: those of visitors at **Chaco Culture National Historical Park,** where extensive rock ruins blend with the towering sandstone cliff faces that provided the ancient masons with their building materials. At Pueblo Bonito, the Anasazi shaped thousands of rocks of all sizes with crude stone hammers and axes, constructing more than 600 rooms and 40 kivas. The varying construction techniques reflect the order in which these carefully crafted walls were built. The oldest walls were one stone thick, with generous applications of mud mortar; later walls had thick inner cores of rubble topped by a veneer of stonework so precisely fitted that little mortar was needed.

Across the dry wash from Pueblo Bonito is the giant kiva of Casa Rinconada, which was built apart from other communities, possibly indicating that it was used as some sort of community center. An occasional gust of wind disturbs the silence, and the musty smell of sandstone mingles with imagined memories of the many ceremonies that must have taken place here, at one of the largest "great kivas" in the Southwest.

Tours of the park are offered daily, and pamphlets for the self-motivated are available at each of eight restored ruins connected by well-marked hiking trails.

Two gravel roads lead to the park. The road from I-40 to the south is not recommended, although it is usually passable by four-wheel-drive vehicles. The preferred route is to come in from NM 550 to the northwest, but check with the visitors center regarding accessibility, as storms can create impassable conditions. The only accommodation at the park is a campground; no food is available, only a soda-pop machine. *505-786-7014.*

■ **CHACO OUTLIERS** *map page 161, C-1*

While most of the prehistoric villages served by the Chaco road network have remained unexcavated, two outlying sites are preserved and have been partially reconstructed.

The communal dwellings at **Aztec Ruins National Monument** were built on a rise overlooking the blue-green Animas River in what is now the town of Aztec. (The name comes from 19th-century settlers who mistakenly assumed the pueblo was built by the Aztec Indians of Mexico.) A walk through the largest pueblo, a U-shaped village that covered two acres and contained 500 rooms in three stories, allows you to look across the decaying walls into a maze of adjoining square and rectangular rooms and to crawl through tiny doorways. Anchoring the pueblo is the Great Kiva, constructed in the 12th century and reconstructed in 1934. This grand underground space, the sole reconstructed great kiva in the Southwest, was broken only by massive columns that supported a roof estimated at 90 tons. As you descend into the flat-topped, underground sanctuary, push a button to hear recorded Native American music, then take a seat on the rock bench and try to recapture the solemnity that must have pervaded Anasazi religious ceremonies.

Much of this site remains unexcavated under sandy mounds scattered in the shade of cottonwood trees. No one knows whether the mounds cover dwellings or trash heaps. *505-334-6174.*

Salmon Ruins and Heritage Park sits on top of a bluff overlooking the farmland of the San Juan River valley, 2 miles west of Bloomfield. A well-traveled Chaco road leads directly north from Chaco Canyon for 50 miles through dusty arroyos and across desert mesas to the C-shaped, 250-room pueblo. Most building materials here were imported: sandstone was quarried at sites 30 miles distant, and timbers used for the vigas were hauled from southern Colorado. Nearby petroglyphs depict ears of corn on a stalk, and some archaeologists speculate that the small community was developed as an agricultural center to serve the main Chaco Canyon villages. Salmon Ruins was named for George Salmon, an 1880s homesteader who protected the site from vandals and thieves in search of ancient pottery. His home still stands nearby. *505-632-2013.*

The pueblos of Aztec and Salmon were abandoned by the middle of the 12th century, only to be reoccupied in the early 13th century by Indians from the nearby Mesa Verde area of southwestern Colorado. Later that century they, too, abandoned it, never to return.

Consisting of more than 600 rooms, Pueblo Bonito is considered one of the most sophisticated examples of Anasazi architecture.

■ **AZTEC** *map page 161, C-1*

Aztec is a town of tree-shaded streets filled with Victorian-style brick buildings. Main Street shops and businesses have retained an early-20th-century Midwestern appearance, and the only modern touches are a few pastel-painted storefronts.

Aztec lays two claims to fame: first, it's home to "6,000 friendly people and six old soreheads," a tradition begun in 1969, when a good-natured Chamber of Commerce erected a welcoming sign that listed its population that way. Townsfolk loved it and clamored for sorehead designation, so the matter was put to a secret vote. The identity of the winners was never revealed, although they posed for the local newspaper—with bags over their heads and their backs to the camera. The tradition lapsed for a while, but every year since 1987, new soreheads have again been elected, these days as a fund-raising stunt. Once nominated, the sorehead candidates, bags on their heads, parade around town collecting "votes" in the form of money. Those with the most "votes" win, their identity is revealed, and the money is donated to charity.

Aztec's second claim to fame is as an All America City, an award it received in 1963 after its citizens built NM 173, a two-lane road that connects the town with the San Juan River just below Navajo Dam. No government funds were used in construction: businesses donated supplies, men and women volunteered labor, and children held fundraisers to help cover expenses.

The road now takes them to the marina that serves boaters at **Navajo Lake State Park**, 34 miles east of town. Downstream from Navajo Dam, in the San Juan River's clear, cold, blue-green waters, is the finest trophy stream fishing in New Mexico. A nearly four-mile stretch called the Quality Waters harbors big, fat trout that will give you a fight to the finish. Strict restrictions apply. Fishermen must use hooks without barbs and may not take home more than one 20-inch lunker. The locals say that once you've fished these waters, no other New Mexico stream will ever satisfy you. *505-632-2278.*

■ JICARILLA APACHES   *map page 161, D-1/3*

Jicarilla (pronounced hik-a-REE-ya) is a Spanish name meaning "little basket." It was given to this band of Apaches by colonial settlers, who were impressed by the beautiful baskets the Indians fashioned—especially small drinking cups (*jícara* means "small cup") and two-handled vessels coiled and stitched with sumac twigs.

Until a century ago, the Jicarillas roamed freely throughout the forests and canyons of northwestern New Mexico. When the federal government placed them on 722,000 acres of land along the Continental Divide, it seemed clear to everyone that the Indians had received a bad deal. They were used to a nomadic existence— hunting deer, gathering nuts and berries, and (later) pillaging wagon trains for their survival. They had a difficult time settling down to an assigned spot, and with little experience in farming, their attempts at cultivating the sandy soil they'd been given were not always successful. Their new home had variety, however, with pine- covered mountains, tall grass meadows, canyons, mesas, and sagebrush prairies. And as it turned out, the land also was rich in fossil fuels, namely oil and natural gas. The sale of leases has made the Jicarilla the richest tribe in the state.

The Jicarilla have also capitalized on their diverse landscape. At **Stone Lake Lodge,** they cater to fishermen and to hunters who flock to the reservation for its prize deer, elk, turkey, cougar, and waterfowl.

North of the lodge is the town of **Dulce,** the reservation's capital, where most of the tribe's approximately 2,750 members make their homes. You won't find many of the Jicarilla's namesake baskets for sale in the gift shop at the **Tribal Arts and Crafts Museum** (U.S. 64, Dulce; 505-759-4274), but oil paintings, leather craft, and intricate beadwork are plentiful. *Tribal headquarters: U.S. 64, Dulce; 505-759-3242.*

■ **FARMINGTON AREA** *map page 161, A/B-1*

To the Navajos, the area of present-day Farmington was known as To-tah, which means "among the waters." The town is in the midst of three of the region's major waterways: the gently flowing Animas River skirts Farmington's eastern edge, then empties into the wide San Juan River south of town, while the smaller La Plata enters the San Juan west of town after irrigating fields of hay and corn.

When local residents think of the Farmington area, they think of an outdoorsman's paradise: fishing, hiking, and great skiing (nearby in Colorado). Business

Morning light in the Great Kiva at Aztec Ruins National Monument.

folks eye the Farmington area's large deposits of oil, natural gas, and coal, which lie beneath some of the most unusual land formations found in the state. Farmington's main thoroughfares are crowded with small businesses, restaurants, shops, and some fine places to replenish coolers and tackle boxes.

■ SHIPROCK *map page 161 A-1*

Along the wide, placid San Juan River, fertile fields suggest the origins of Farmington's name. Today, small farms and orchards of apple, pear, and peach trees flourish, but the vast deposits of coal, oil, and natural gas are what have come to dominate the area's economy. Farmington sits at the edge of the Navajo Reservation, and the dusty town of Shiprock is squarely within it. Both are more interested in serving their residents than attracting tourists.

Southwest of the town of Shiprock, its namesake—a 7,178-foot jagged rock monolith—dominates the semi-desert landscape. **Shiprock** begins as an apparition, fuzzily coming into view. But once you've spotted it, this core of an extinct volcano commands your attention, a massive form rising from a dusty plain. Navajos call the mystical rock Tse Bida'hi (the "winged rock") and many tribal legends surround it. Nineteenth-century soldiers thought it resembled the clipper sailing ships of the day. Numerous rock climbers have scaled it, but because two of them died trying, Shiprock has been closed to climbers since 1970.

■ BISTI/DE-NA-ZIN WILDERNESS *map page 161, B-2/3*

Nearby is the **Bisti/De-na-zin Wilderness**, which combines the fossil-rich De-na-zin washes and rock formations, the Bisti's magical mushroom-shaped spires, and the surrounding red, green, and bone-white cliffs. The eerie desolation of this moonscape (together totaling 42,000 acres) is all that remains of what once was a shallow sea bordered by swamps and forests and inhabited by dinosaurs. Some 75 million years ago, duckbill and horned dinosaurs sloshed along the seashore, huge conifers towered above a jungle of ferns and palms, and salamanders, snails, worms, sharks, and crocodiles choked the waterways. Eons of wind and water have carved the sandstone and shale formations.

Today, snakes and lizards scurry across the hard, dry rocks, which are absent of any vegetation—a far cry from the days when their outsized ancestors dominated the wet wilderness. The presence of billions of tons of coal underneath the surface of the Bisti poses the constant threat that this magical, unspoiled land could be destroyed one day by open-pit mining. *505-599-8900.*

Known to the Navajo as Tse Bida'hi (Winged Rock), Shiprock rises 1,178 feet from the desert floor.

■ **GALLUP** *map page 161, A-4*

Gallup, one of the foremost trading centers for Native American arts and crafts, calls itself the Heart of Indian Country, and for good reason: the town is 25 miles southeast of Window Rock, Arizona, capital of the Navajo Nation; 98 miles southwest of Chaco Canyon, home of the ancient Anasazi; and 38 miles north of Zuni Pueblo. Most of the Indians you see along the streets of Gallup have come in from the nearby Navajo Reservation to shop and to sell their wares (and sometimes to have a few drinks, as the sale of liquor is prohibited on the reservation).

At one time, this gritty little town was the epitome of the Wild West. Its first building was the Blue Goose Saloon, constructed in the 1860s near a stagecoach stop. After coal was discovered north of Gallup in the late 1870s, immigrant miners from across Europe, including Slavs, Austrians, and Italians, converged on the town, digging hard in the sooty mines (which closed in 1950). After the Santa Fe Railroad reached the community in 1881, mining camps sprang up a few miles outside of town, appearing much like today's suburbs.

HARVEY GIRLS

When the railroad snaked its way into New Mexico in the late 1800s, connecting the southwestern frontier with the eastern United States, little thought was given to the comfort of the passengers who would be riding the iron horse. Towns, if you can call them that, consisted of a few canvas tents and flimsy wooden shacks. One would be designated as the depot, while another wooden shack served as a very basic dining hall for train passengers. Inside, they ate greasy meat, canned beans, rancid bacon, and eggs preserved in lime and shipped from the East Coast. Worst of all, passengers had 20 minutes to gulp down this unsavory repast before they reboarded, resuming a jolting journey at 20 mph across the dusty desert. To avoid this unpleasant eating ritual, seasoned travelers either headed for a saloon, which was amply supplied and more comfortable than the dining shack, or they brought along apples, bread, and cheese, hoping such provisions would last throughout their trip. Often, they didn't. This inadequacy failed to concern railroad executives, but one young entrepreneur knew customers deserved better and would pay for food they could digest.

Fred Harvey was born in London. After emigrating to New York City at 15, he spent years working in restaurants. He knew the value of quality food and service and he was convinced that a network of classy restaurants along a rail line was not just a good idea, but a great one. In 1878, he convinced officials at the Atchison, Topeka and Santa Fe Railway to give it a shot. That was all he needed, and soon Harvey and his Harvey Houses brought a refinement to the Santa Fe Railway unsurpassed by other rail lines.

In New Mexico, 16 Harvey Houses graced the tracks. Usually they were two-story brick buildings with dining rooms on the main floor and staff living quarters upstairs. Situated in isolated communities such as Clovis, Deming, Belen, Vaughn, and Raton, these welcome whistle-stops served also as social centers for area residents. In addition, six of the railroad's showpiece hotels lined the tracks in New Mexico: the Montezuma and Castañeda in Las Vegas, El Ortiz in Lamy, the Alvarado in Albuquerque, and El Navajo in Gallup. Santa Fe's La Fonda, while not on the railroad tracks, was a Harvey hotel popular with passengers stopping at Lamy. (The Alvarado, El Ortiz, and El Navajo have since been demolished.)

Unlike the Spanish or Mission Revival style of most of the Harvey Houses, El Navajo opened in 1923 as a tribute to the American Indian. The furniture of this elegant restaurant and hotel was upholstered in Navajo weaving designs, and Navajo sand paintings adorned the walls.

Many of the women who worked for the chain received their training at El Navajo. Midwesterners between the ages of 18 and 30, most from poor families, left Missouri towns and Kansas farms and headed west, not so much for the adventure as for the much-needed job. Although their duties were strictly to serve customers, these women never were referred to as waitresses; rather, they were known proudly as Harvey Girls. Immaculately attired, they served a four-course meal in less than 30 minutes, usually three times a day, to rail passengers.

Rules were rigid: no makeup, no jewelry, hair pulled away from the face atop the head. They wore starched black-and-white skirts, white aprons, high-collared shirts, black shoes and stockings, and hairnets. Introduced in 1883, this uniform changed little during the next 50 years. If they spilled anything on their precisely pressed uniforms, no matter how small a spot it left, they were instructed to change into a fresh outfit. And they were forbidden to marry while under contract with Fred Harvey.

Regardless of where they were sent—the windswept plains of Vaughn, the heart of Indian country at Gallup, or the bustling state capital of Santa Fe—most of the women loved the West. Many married rail workers or fellow Harvey House employees and raised families in their adopted towns.

A Harvey Girl in the lunchroom at El Ortiz, a Harvey House hotel in Lamy, 1910–12.

Within two years of the railroad's arrival, 22 saloons (including the Bucket of Blood) and two dance halls were competing with the Blue Goose. David Gallup was paymaster of the railroad, which ended at this western outpost; and come payday, workers would say they were going to Gallup's to collect their wages. The name stuck.

During those early years, prostitution and gambling were in an exuberant (if illegal) state of availability. Soldiers, lumberjacks, cowboys, railroad workers, and miners were regular customers. In 1895, a bevy of respectable East Coast women arrived at Gallup to work for a Harvey House restaurant; some said their presence improved the town's reputation. Many of these women married and settled in Gallup, turning the wild outpost into a quiet family town.

Beginning in the 1930s, Hollywood directors descended upon Gallup to use its unspoiled red-rock canyons and majestic piñon-covered mesas as backdrops for Westerns starring such luminaries as Joel McCrea, Wallace Beery, Ronald Reagan, and Kirk Douglas. To house them in style, R. E. Griffith, brother of the director D. W. Griffith, built the **El Rancho Hotel** in 1937. The door to this oversized two-story ranch house opens onto a brick-floored lobby, where guests can sit and marvel at the deer heads, Navajo rugs, and Indian and Western art tacked to the walls. A gallery of autographed movie star photographs lines a second-floor balcony, and rooms are named after some of the stars who've slept in them—including Betty Grable, Burt Lancaster, and Lee Marvin. *1000 E. U.S. 66; 800-543-6351.*

Route 66 bisected Gallup in 1926, and many of the shops and tourist courts that sprang up to entice a new world of motorists are still in business. A showpiece from that era, the **El Morro Theatre**, has been refurbished to its original 1928 Spanish Colonial Revival–style grandeur, with Spanish Baroque plaster carving and bright polychromatic painting. Locals come here for second-run Hollywood movies, as well as dance performances. *207 West Coal Avenue; 505-722-7469.*

Gallup's most popular event is the five-day **Inter-Tribal Indian Ceremonial**, held annually in August. Begun in 1922, when it was a strictly local affair, the show now attracts Native American dancers, craftsmen, and cowboys from throughout North America. Members of the different tribes flaunt their finery—ornate turquoise necklaces, feathered headdresses, buffalo masks—in the parades that wind through downtown on Thursday evening and Friday and Saturday

Navajo weaver Nellie Mae Davis cradles her grandson.

Navajo weavers outside a hogan on Navajo tribal lands.

mornings, and professional cowboys from around the country compete in the All-Indian Rodeo, held east of town at Red Rock State Park (where there's plenty of Indian frybread, or Navajo tacos—frybread covered with mutton, cheese, lettuce, and tomatoes). Indian crafts range from traditional Navajo blankets, silver jewelry, and beadwork to modern sculpture and painting. During the fair, the town's population of 20,000 doubles, and lodging is virtually unobtainable; make reservations several months in advance. *505-863-3896.*

A marvelous way to travel through New Mexico is on the *Southwest Chief,* the Amtrak train that travels daily between Los Angeles and Chicago. A Navajo tour guide boards the train in Albuquerque and during the two-and-a-half-hour ride to

Gallup imparts some of the tribe's lore to interested passengers. As the silver train rumbles past vermilion mesas, the guide may point to a traditional Navajo hogan and explain why it is built facing east. "The philosophical reason is because we believe that all good things in life come from the east, where the sun rises in the morning," he says. There is also a practical purpose: "Obviously, if you've got the sun shining at your door in the morning, it's going to warm your house up a little faster." *Amtrak; 800-USA-RAIL.*

If you're curious about Navajo weaving, you might want to attend the monthly **Crownpoint rug auction**, where bidding is lively and the artisans are on hand to discuss their work. Typically the auction takes place at the Crownpoint Elementary School on the third Friday of the month. *505-786-7386.*

■ ZUNI PUEBLO *map page 161, A-5*

The radiant desert sunsets that have been attracting people to New Mexico for years proved to be the undoing of 16th-century Zuni Indians living at Hawikuh, a settlement 12 miles south of the present-day pueblo. It was here that in 1539 Fray Marcos de Niza caught a glimpse at sunset of the walls of the pueblo's dwellings turning gold in the waning light. The man of God thought he saw gold-plated walls and envisioned treasure-laden streets, and when he returned to Mexico, he passed on his account. The next year, the Zuni Indians of Hawikuh found Francisco Vásquez de Coronado on their doorstep.

Although the Zunis grudgingly accepted the Spanish presence, they never fully embraced the Christianity that was forced upon them, occasionally burning mission churches and killing priests. To this day, Christianity takes a back seat to their own ancient religion. The Zunis maintain an elaborate ceremonial organization, which entails various esoteric cults, such as those of the rainmaker, kachina, beast, and war gods. Sacred Zuni fetishes, including quartz crystals, turtle-shell rattles, and seashells, are used by the priest in charge of each cult to carry out his duty. Because the Zunis believe the sun is the source of life, the most revered man in the tribe is the Sun Priest, who oversees solstice ceremonies.

The Zunis took part in the Pueblo Revolt of 1680, but they feared the certain retaliation of the Spanish. After the rebellion, they took refuge on Corn Mountain, a majestic mile-long multicolored sandstone mesa that stands 3 miles southeast of the present-day pueblo. Alongside a shallow wash where the mesa makes a slight dip, they built three-story rock houses. They remained here, farming the lowlands,

BRIDGING TWO NAVAJO WORLDS

From behind him in the medicine hogan, Officer Jim Chee could hear the chanting of the First Dancers as they put on their ceremonial paint. Chee was interested. He had picked a spot from which he could see through the hogan doorway and watch the personifiers preparing themselves. They were eight middle-aged men from around the Naschitti Chapter House in New Mexico, far to the east of Agnes Tsosie's place below Tesihim Butte. They had painted their right hands first, then their faces from the forehead downward, and then their bodies, making themselves ready to represent the Holy People of Navajo mythology, the yei, the powerful spirits. This Night Chant ceremonial was one that Chee hoped to learn himself someday. Yeibichai, his people called it, naming it the Talking God, the maternal grandfather of all the spirits. The performance was nine days long and involved five complicated sand paintings and scores of songs. Learning it would take a long, long time, as would finding a hataalii willing to take him on as a student. When the time came for that, he would have to take leave from the Navajo Tribal Police. But that was somewhere in the distant future. Now his job was watching for the Flaky Man from Washington. Henry Highhawk was the name on the federal warrant.

—Tony Hillerman, *Talking God*, 1989

for 12 years, until Diego de Vargas reclaimed the territory for Spain. Then they left the mountain and settled where the pueblo is today.

Zuni craftsmen are famous for their extraordinarily beautiful jewelry, in particular silver pieces inlaid with turquoise, shell, and jet, and for making animal fetishes out of carved minerals, glass, and stones, embellished with gemstones. The placement of tiny gemstones (most often turquoise), close together in intricate patterns set in silver, is called "Zuni needlepoint."

Zuni Pueblo has 11,000 members, making it the largest in New Mexico. It appears much like any other small New Mexican town, with a maze of low, flat-roofed houses, small vegetable patches, and dusty unpaved streets. A few craft shops are mixed in among stores and businesses.

Tribal permission is required if you wish to visit two nearby places of interest—the crumbling ruins at Hawikuh and the unexcavated Village of the Great Kivas, 18 miles north of Zuni. *Zuni Pueblo; 505-782-4481.*

■ THE WAY TO GRANTS *map page 161, B/C-5/6*

Indians from Zuni and Acoma Pueblos knew their way across the massive lava flow—the remains of five major eruptions from nearby volcanoes—between their villages south of the present-day town of Grants. (As recently as 700 years ago, rivers of molten rock, accompanied by flying cinders, oozed across the sandstone and limestone valley. Indian legends tell of rivers of "fire rock.") Carrying loads of precious salt and turquoise, under an intensely blue sky, the natives walked the jagged landscape, filling wide gaps in the hardened lava with boulders to create bridges, and erecting cairns on the sharp rock so they wouldn't lose their way across the unrelenting terrain.

Early Spanish and American travelers rarely ventured across the hardened lava. Leading their horses around it, they called the 114,000-acre lava-rock valley El Malpais ("the badlands"). In 1988, the federal government recognized its unique geological features and established **El Malpais National Monument and Conservation Area.** *El Malpais Information Center (NPS) is 23 miles south of Grants on NM 53; 505-783-4774.*

The volcanoes that once spewed blistering hot lava still brood above the scene. **Bandera Crater** can be seen at the end of a half-mile-long trail carpeted in soft cinder. Peering down 800 feet into the extinct volcano, it's reassuring to know that it last erupted about a million years ago. All that remains are rust-colored scree walls with an occasional ponderosa pine stretching for the sun. Nearby, a sturdy wooden staircase leads 75 feet below the jagged surface of broken basalt to the opening of an **ice cave,** part of a lava tube formed when the surface of molten lava pouring from the volcano cooled and hardened, while the lava within continued to flow. Afterward, moisture seeped through the cracked and porous basalt and froze in the cold cave. A blast of chilly air emanates from the opening, which is coated with thick layers of ice—mossy green with algae thousands of years old. Icicles dangle from the ceiling, and steady droplets of water drip from them into a blue-green pool. This brisk, 31-degree Fahrenheit air discourages lengthy visits. *Bandera Crater/Ice Caves, 25 miles southwest of Grants on NM 53; 505-783-4303 or 888-423-2283.*

The ancient Indian trade route, which NM 53 roughly follows, also passes by a massive 200-foot-high sandstone mesa visible for miles, atop which sit two Zuni pueblos, one unexcavated and one with partial walls showing. It's been preserved as **El Morro** ("the bluff") **National Monument.** At the base of the pale cliff is a

SHALAKO DANCE AT ZUNI PUEBLO

As the short winter day gives way to evening, residents at Zuni Pueblo excitedly anticipate the final celebration of their ceremonial year. Huddled in doorways, wrapped snugly in wool blankets against the chill of the fading light, the Zunis occasionally glance to the south. They are awaiting the arrival of the Shalakos: six 10-foot-tall messengers of the Rain Gods who will spend the night blessing six houses built in their honor during the previous year and offering prayers for the tribe's fertility, longevity, prosperity, and happiness.

The Shalako ceremony is a reenactment of the creation of the Zuni people and their migration to the place destined to be their home. It is the most elaborate of any pueblo ritual, beginning at dusk and lasting through the night.

The ceremony always takes place in late November or early December, and preparations begin shortly after the Zuni New Year, early in January—almost 11 months in advance. Tribal leaders select the dancers, and families accept responsibility for building or remodeling the six houses. In addition to the half-dozen Shalako houses, two others are built each year: one for the Council of the Gods and one for the Mudheads, 10 dancers who wear knobby, adobe-colored masks and paint their bodies with pinkish clay, creating the effect of distorted creatures.

Shalako Day begins with women baking bread in beehive-shaped *hornos* and stirring great pots of chile and beans that will serve the guests. They also grind corn into sacred meal that the messengers will use to bless shrines and the Shalako houses.

In mid-afternoon the Fire God makes his appearance: a boy between the ages of 10 and 14, identified by numerous turquoise necklaces and a black mask painted with yellow, blue, red, and white dots. He, his ceremonial Godfather, and the four-member Council of Gods, representing the four compass points, visit the sacred pueblo shrines, performing prayers and rituals at each one.

At dusk the Shalakos slowly walk over the top of a hill on the south side of the Zuni River. Two horns and wooden eyes jut from their spectacular, if somewhat awkward, turquoise masks, which are adorned with wooden beaks and a profusion of feathers: eagle feathers for the headpiece and downy feathers that run from the ends of the horns down the back. These imposing bird-like creatures are robed in white embroidered clothing, with a massive ruff fashioned from glossy raven feathers.

As they proceed to their sacred shrine, occasional clacks can be heard as their beaks snap together. Well after dark and after cold temperatures have numbed onlookers' feet, the Shalakos follow a special footpath to the river and pick their way across. Members of the crowd fall in behind each of the Shalakos, following the dancer to the house that has been prepared for him.

Solemnly, the Shalako plants prayer plumes inside the threshold and deposits seeds in baskets at an altar at the end of the room, below which is an excavation signifying the womb from which the Zuni people emerged at their creation. The Shalako mask is placed in front of the altar, and numerous rituals follow, including a feast for invited Indians, during which the Shalako takes a little food from each bowl passed to him and wraps it in *piki*—a paper-thin bread made from blue corn. He also walks to the river to make sacrificial offerings to tribal ancestors.

Shortly after midnight, men gather about a large drum in a corner of each Shalako house and begin a rhythmic pounding that continues until sunrise. The Shalako dancer again puts on the feathered mask and begins moving in time to the beat. He gracefully dips and sways, and swoops from one end of the room to the other, often clacking his protruding beak. The dance is interrupted only when an understudy assumes the beat, giving the main dancer a break.

During the night, the Mudheads travel in pairs to each Shalako house, singing and providing comic relief, often taunting the towering Shalako dancers. In the morning, the Shalakos return to their ancestral homes across the river, leaving behind enough blessings and good will to sustain the Zunis for another year.

Shalako dancers at Zuni Pueblo in 1897.

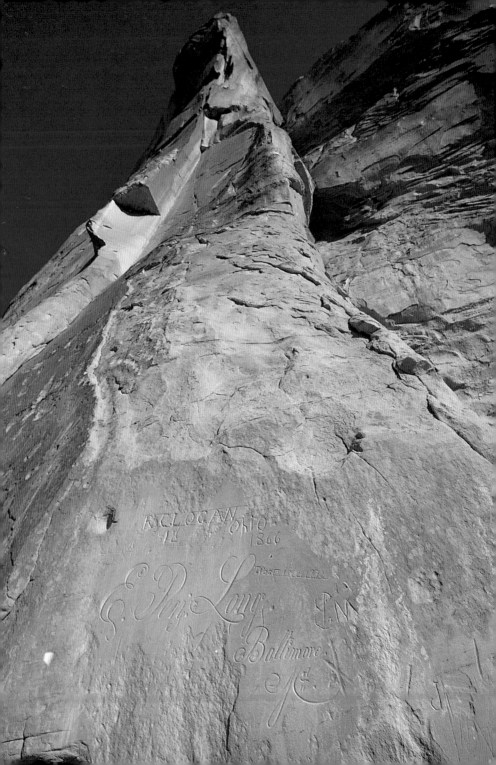

natural basin filled with water, replenished by summer rains and winter snows. A natural rest stop for nearly a thousand years, it has not escaped the temptation of travelers to leave their marks on the nearby sandstone surface. Indian petroglyphs were first, followed by signatures and messages written by Spanish explorers and later Anglo settlers. Two years before Jamestown, Virginia, was founded in 1607, Juan de Oñate left an inscription, which translates as: "Passed by here the Governor Don Juan de Oñate, from the discovery of the Sea of the South on the 16th of April 1605." (The "Sea of the South" was the Gulf of California.) When Diego de Vargas was on his way to reclaim Zuni territory after the Pueblo Revolt, he too left his mark: "Here was the General Don Diego de Vargas who conquered for our Holy Faith, and for the Royal Crown, all of New Mexico at his own expense, year of 1692." Through the centuries, explorers, traders, soldiers, surveyors, and settlers carved messages as they passed by. Thus the name **Inscription Rock** seems most appropriate.

El Morro National Monument's fine visitors center, with a museum of ancient tools and pottery, is open year-round. *On NM 53 between Gallup and Zuni; 505-783-4226.*

■ GRANTS   *map page 161, C-5*

Set on a flat plain in the protective shadows of the towering Mount Taylor, an 11,301-foot ancient volcano, Grants is a busted mining town trying to revive itself. One main street pretty much takes care of the sights in this dusty community, named after the three Grant brothers—Angus, Lewis, and John—who won a contract to build the section of the Atlantic and Pacific Railroad between Isleta Pueblo and Needles, California. The town's entire economic history, in fact, has been one of boom and bust. It first boomed in 1881 as a camp for railroad workers. With the completion of the tracks, the town's population dwindled. But then, the construction of Bluewater Dam on the nearby Rio San Jose caused Grants to bloom as an agricultural community. By 1941, Grants farmers were producing millions of pounds of carrots a years—lush-topped ones, the kind Easterners craved. When their competitors began encasing carrots in colorful cellophane wrapping, local farmers didn't follow suit and demand dropped.

Spanish explorers, settlers, and wayfarers of every sort left graffiti at El Morro.

A Laguna Tale

We children were always warned not to harm frogs or toads, the beloved children of the rain clouds, because terrible floods would occur. I remember in the summer the old folks used to stick big bolls of cotton on the outside of their screen doors as bait to keep the flies from going in the house when the door was opened. The old folks staunchly resisted the killing of flies because once, long, long ago, when human beings were in a great deal of trouble, a Green Bottle Fly carried the desperate messages of human beings to the Mother Creator in the Fourth World, below this one. Human beings had outraged the Mother Creator by neglecting the Mother Corn altar while they dabbled in sorcery and magic. The Mother Creator disappeared, and with her disappeared the rain clouds, and the plants and animals too. The people began to starve, and they had no way of reaching the Mother Creator down below. Green Bottle Fly took the message to the Mother Creator, and the people were saved. To show their gratitude, the old folks refused to kill any flies.

—Leslie Marmon Silko, *Yellow Woman and a Beauty of the Spirit,* 1996

The town's next wave of prosperity began in 1950, when Paddy Martinez, a Navajo sheep rancher, found an unusual-looking yellow rock at the base of Haystack Mountain, adjacent to one of his pastures. Convinced it was uranium, he rode into Grants and showed it to a merchant friend, who scoffed at the idea it could be valuable ore. Martinez staked a mining claim anyway, thus setting the stage for another Grants comeback. For the next 30 years, it was sustained by the uranium industry, although Paddy himself never became a miner. He rented the land around Haystack Mountain to the Santa Fe Railroad, which paid him a monthly sum, moved to the shores of nearby Bluewater Lake, and continued to graze sheep.

By the early 1980s, the demand for uranium had dropped. The last Grants-area mine closed in January 1990, but not before boosters had opened the **New Mexico Museum of Mining.** There, visitors can visit a simulated uranium mine, complete with an elevator that imitates a 900-foot descent into the earth. *100 North Iron Street; 505-287-4802 or 800-748-2142.*

■ LAGUNA PUEBLO *map page 161, D-6*

About 27 miles east of Grants, Laguna—the largest of the six villages that make up Laguna Pueblo—comes into view along I-40. It was named for a nearby lake that has since become a meadow. Although the area has been occupied since 3,000 B.C., the pueblo was established in its modern form in 1699 by the Spanish governor Pedro Rodriguez Cubero. Later that year, builders completed the San José de Laguna Church, the last of the early mission churches to be established in New Mexico.

Today, the imposing stone church still stands on a hill overlooking simple pueblo dwellings. Its ornate and colorfully painted pine altar, carved by Indian craftsmen, is flanked by paintings of St. Barbara and St. John Nepomucene, and an animal hide attached to the ceiling is colored with Indian symbols of the rainbow, sun, moon, and stars.

The pueblo has proven its facility for adapting to the modern world. In the 1870s, pueblo residents—influenced by nearby Anglo settlers who married into the tribe—adopted a tribal constitution modeled after the U.S. Constitution. And in recent years, the pueblo has been successful in business.

■ ACOMA PUEBLO *map page 161, D-6*

At the same time the Chaco civilization was at its peak, residents at Acoma were building adobe and rock homes high atop the 357-foot Rock of Acuco, a multicolored sandstone mesa rising from a sandy plain southeast of present-day Grants. Some historians estimate Acoma Pueblo has been occupied since 1075, making it the oldest continuously inhabited city in the country.

The Acomas say their ancestors arrived in 600 from Mesa Verde, in what today is southern Colorado, looking for a mesa that Iatiku, mother of all Indians, told them resembled the tip of an ear of corn. When they found the Enchanted Mesa, they built a rock-walled village atop it, with only one route leading up its precipitous cliffs. Legend has it that one day, when almost everyone in the tribe was tending fields on the plains below, a violent storm moved in, obliterating the path to the top. A young girl and her grandmother were stranded there, and rather than starve, they leapt to their deaths. Grief-stricken, and with access to the summit now denied them, the tribe moved to the nearby Acuco Mesa.

Some historians believe the early dwellers chose to build atop Acuco for the protection it afforded them from marauding tribes. The solitary citadel served the tribe well in 1540, when Spaniards, on their relentless search for the Seven Cities of Cibola, mistakenly thought they saw those riches reflected in the pueblo's mica window panes. Though their attempt to scale the mountain was unsuccessful, the soldiers killed a hundred Acoma men.

Acoma residents successfully held off intruders until 1598, when the pueblo voluntarily submitted to the Spanish. This peaceful acquiescence was short-lived, however; that same year, the Indians killed Juan de Zaldivar and 12 soldiers who were seeking cornmeal. Unfortunately, Zaldivar was a nephew of Juan de Oñate, Spanish governor of New Mexico. Seventy men quickly avenged Zaldivar's death, killing at least 100 Acoma men and kidnapping 60 young Indian girls to sell in Mexico as slaves. They also severed a foot of each of the remaining Indian men.

With the Indians decisively subdued, the Spanish soon were overseeing construction of the San Esteban del Rey Mission, completed in 1640. Forty-foot-long roof beams were cut in the mountains 30 miles south and carried on men's backs up the rugged slopes of the mesa. Today, the mission's stark, white-washed walls contrast with a wooden altar painted in bright reds, blues, yellows, and greens. Each year, prior to San Esteban's feast day, the walls are freshly painted, using paint mixed from ground pink and white sandstones quarried at nearby mesas and applied with traditional yucca and sheepskin brushes.

At one time, several thousand Indians lived in multistory rock-walled dwellings crowded onto the 70-acre mesa. Each dawn, with a brilliant sun illuminating a distant snowcapped peak (now called Mount Taylor), they would have descended a steep staircase carved from the soft rock and set about their various occupations—gathering wood from nearby woodlands and tending to their fields. Every night they would have climbed the steep mountain staircase back to the village.

Today, about 13 Acoma families reside at the pueblo, which has never had running water or electricity. All of life's essentials, even dirt for the cemetery, must still be hauled up from below. Occasionally, one may see an antenna rising above the ancient dwellings, attached to a generator-driven television that keeps the inhabitants informed of world events. Most of the tribal members live in the nearby villages of Acomita, McCartys, Laguna, or Paraje, where they can bathe in hot water from a spigot and are closer to schools and work.

San Esteban del Rey Mission, Acoma.

The only way outsiders can see the mesa-top village is on a guided walking tour, which departs regularly from a visitors center at the base of the mountain. You ascend in a van on a narrow road constructed in 1941 by movie producer Walter Wanger in order to shoot scenes for the film *Sundown,* starring Gene Tierney. (For the film, set designers imported fake trees and real ostriches to make the dusty pueblo resemble an African village.) A tribal member acts as a guide, leading guests into the mission church and its cemetery, then through the narrow streets that wind among the rock and adobe buildings. Around every corner, artisans display for sale the tribe's precise thin-shelled pottery, painted with black, white, and orange pigments taken from sandstone and rich mountain soil.

After the hour-long tour, you can return to the visitors center taking the path the original inhabitants of Acoma would have taken. The ancient rock stairway descends the mountain along narrow, often steep, passages, using natural steps that have been worn smooth and handholds carved by years of use into the weathered sandstone walls. *505-552-6604 or 800-747-0181.*

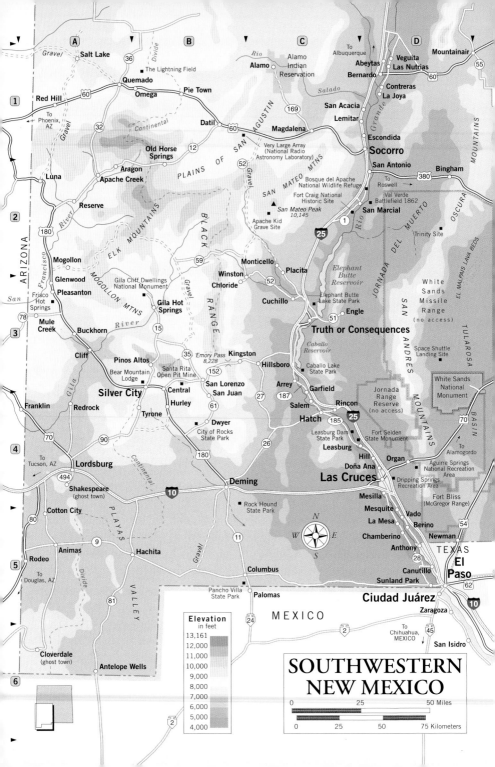

SOUTHWESTERN
N E W   M E X I C O

From the aquamarine waters of Elephant Butte Lake and the cactus prairie near Lordsburg to the pine-clad mountains of Silver City, the landscape of south-western New Mexico reflects a vibrant diversity. The bone-dry desert is relieved by the Rio Grande, which wends its way through the region, creating wetlands for migratory birds and providing sustenance to fields of onion, cotton, and chiles. Pale green hillsides dotted with piñon and juniper rise to the dense woods of the Gila National Forest, once the home of the Mimbres Indians and still the home of mountain lions and black bears. You can drive for miles with-out seeing another car, and if you do, it'll probably be a pickup truck with a gun rack in the cab.

Like a hazy mirage, rugged mountain ranges rise up from the flat, desolate landscape, where wide expanses of desert grasses mix with the crooked branches of mesquite trees. Vast stretches of cracked earth covered with clumps of grass are relieved by isolated ranches and barbed-wire fences that extend in long lines against the hills.

Along NM 9, which dips close to the Mexican border, immigrants illegally slip across the open range in the dark of night. Water flows steadily in irrigation ditches along NM 187, which passes cotton fields displaying their unmistakable white bolls. Just across the road, a dark-green carpet of chile fields provides a stunning contrast. In the fall, the chile's pungent odor assaults your olfactory nerves to remind you that winter is just around the corner.

The past, too, is never far away. Here you'll find the remains of ancient Indian cliff dwellings, the crumbling ruins of 19th-century forts, and the tattered shacks of once-thriving mining camps.

In recent years, the quiet, slower-paced lifestyles of ranching and farming, along with a mild climate, have been attracting retirees. Nowhere else in the state are motorists more apt to lift a hand across a steering wheel as a greeting in pass-ing, or sales clerks more likely to inquire where you are heading. Many towns are so small that every stranger who stops is noticed.

■ History

As far back as 5,000 years ago, the ancestors of the Mogollon Indians learned how to cultivate corn and squash from their southern neighbors in Mexico. By 300 B.C., they were shaping pottery and living in pit houses dug 4 feet underground and covered with timber and dirt. Some four to five centuries later, they moved into large caves along the Gila River, where they continued to grow vegetables, or built freestanding masonry dwellings deep in the mountains. One branch of Mogollons, the Mimbres, developed exquisite black-on-white pottery painted with designs ranging from geometric patterns to stylized reptiles. These fragile pots are usually found at gravesites with a hole punctured in the bottom—it was through this hole that the pot's spirit, thought to be part of its maker, was released.

The Mogollon culture had peaked by A.D. 500, but the Indians continued to hunt and farm in the mountains and valleys of southwestern New Mexico until the early 1300s, when they left the Gila to resettle along the Rio Grande and other drainage areas. One of their cave settlements has been preserved at the Gila Cliff Dwellings National Monument, 44 miles north of Silver City.

■ Apaches and Geronimo

By the early 1300s, bands of roaming Apaches had entered the region. As the men hunted deer and bison, the women gathered berries, roots, and seeds. Historians tend to lump the southern Apaches into two main groups: the Mescaleros, who lived in animal-skin tepees, and the Chiricahuas, who erected grass-and-brush huts called wickiups. Girls wound their hair around two willow hoops over the ears, while some older women adopted the style of Plains Indians and wore long braids. They sewed deerskin robes and animal-skin moccasins, which could be pulled up to the knee for warmth or folded down to protect against thorns and rocks.

Of the Mescaleros, the late C. L. Sonnichsen, author of numerous books about the culture and folklore of the Southwest, wrote:

> They owned nothing and everything. They did as they pleased and bowed to no man. Their women were chaste. Their leaders kept their promises. They were mighty warriors who depended on success in raiding for wealth and honor. To their families they were kind and gentle, but they could be unbelievably cruel to their enemies—fierce and revengeful when they felt that they had been betrayed.

In the 16th century, Spanish explorers looking for gold passed through southwestern New Mexico on their way north. At that time, several groups of Pueblo Indians were living in earthen homes along the southern Rio Grande, and they probably were both alarmed and amused by the armored conquistadors and their cumbersome entourages. After abandoning their quest for gold, the Spanish concentrated on colonizing what today is northern New Mexico. As a result, southwestern New Mexico was well traveled but rarely settled. Towns such as Socorro and Mesilla served as stations on El Camino Real, a 1,500-mile trade route that connected Mexico City with the provincial capital of Santa Fe.

The great Apache warrior Geronimo, in 1885.

Entire families made this arduous journey, carrying household goods and chickens in carts and herding cattle and churro sheep. As more settlers headed to Santa Fe, they began to notice the fertile fields of the Mesilla Valley. But the noisy caravans also were noticed by the Apaches, who resisted the Spaniards from the outset, staging attacks, stealing water, food, and animals, and sometimes taking captives.

One Apache warrior in particular carried a hatred for the intrusive Spanish with him his entire life. Born a member of the Bedonkohe Apache band sometime in the late 1820s, he was named Goyahkla, but later was known as Geronimo. As a child, before he even saw a Spaniard, Geronimo heard stories of campaigns in which Apaches were taken as slaves or killed outright. When the Apaches retaliated, the Spanish turned other tribes against them.

At age 17, Geronimo was designated a warrior, which gave him the right to accompany his tribe into battle. He spent 60 years traversing the wooded canyons of southwestern New Mexico and the desolate cactus plains that spilled into Arizona and Mexico, alternately living peacefully and fighting for his people. By the mid-1850s, he had lost two wives and four children to the Spanish.

As early as 1855, the U. S. government was coercing Indians to sign treaties giving away their land. Geronimo didn't trust the white man's word, nor did he care to live on a reservation. As U.S. soldiers gradually reduced his domain, however, capturing and sending Indians to reservations, Geronimo realized that his days of freedom were numbered and began negotiating with the American officers. During this time he tried unsuccessfully to live on the San Carlos Reservation in Arizona. Finally, on September 5, 1886, the aging warrior surrendered to Brig. Gen. Nelson Miles at Skeleton Canyon, on a rugged raiding route between Mexico and the Arizona mountains. "We placed a large stone on the blanket before us. Our treaty was made by this stone and it was to last until the stone should crumble to dust; so we made the treaty and bound each other with an oath," Geronimo said.

General Miles promised the great warrior cattle, horses, mules, and farming tools, along with a house and a large tract of land covered with timber, water, and grass. Geronimo was also guaranteed a reunion with members of his tribe already in the government's custody. Instead, he and a few other warriors were sent by train to Florida, where they spent the next eight years either incarcerated or working for the federal government in Florida and Alabama. Some died of tuberculosis. Finally, in 1894, they were reunited with their families and relocated to Fort Sill, Oklahoma, where they were given houses, land, and animals. The defeated warrior died in 1909 after falling off a horse.

■ SETTLEMENT AND THE RAILROAD

After the Treaty of Guadalupe-Hidalgo of 1848 ended the Mexican-American War and designated the Rio Grande as the boundary between the two countries, peaceful settlement of the region began. In 1854, the United States signed the Gadsden Purchase and for $10 million bought from Mexico all land west of the Rio Grande. The town of Mesilla, on the Rio Grande, now flew the U.S. flag, and it boomed: mule trains, stagecoaches, and miners en route to the silver and copper mines of the Gila Mountains stopped for supplies. Mesilla, which today sits on the eastern side of the river because of a flood-caused change of course in 1863, was also an important way station on the Butterfield Trail, a 2,800-mile stagecoach route established in 1850 to transport passengers and mail twice weekly from Tipton, Missouri, to San Francisco.

After the Mexican-American War, the U.S. government concentrated its energies on the Apaches, who continued to attack stagecoaches and wagon trains.

Uncertainty as to what the Indians might do added a sharp edge of fear to all journeys through this wild territory. Most often the warriors took firearms, food, supplies, livestock, and horses, but sometimes they killed their victims as well. One stagecoach driver, Bigfoot Wallace, was once forced to walk 80 miles to town after the Apaches purloined his mules. On another occasion, he came limping into El Paso with his stage stuck full of arrows.

In an effort to calm travelers' nerves, the federal government erected numerous forts in the region during the 1860s and '70s. The remains of one, Fort Selden, built 12 miles north of Las Cruces in 1865, have been preserved as a state monument, even though its soldiers saw little action during its 25 years of service.

In the 1880s, the Southern Pacific Railroad made its way eastward into New Mexico, and Lordsburg and Deming sprang up as railroad camps. In 1881, the Atchison, Topeka & Santa Fe Railroad came southward through New Mexico to join the Southern Pacific at Deming, forming the nation's second transcontinental railroad route. Mesilla, which had been the region's largest city, declined when the railroad bypassed it, locating its depot at the county seat of Las Cruces instead. There, alongside traditional single-story adobes, Victorian homes with screened-in

Troops at Fort Selden stand ready to guard settlers against marauding Indians, ca. 1886.

Stagecoach leaving Silver City for Georgetown, 1885.
(opposite) Panning for gold remains a quixotic Southwestern hobby.

porches were built for "lungers"—tuberculosis patients—who came west for New Mexico's clear dry air. Now able to ride in comfort and safety, they arrived in far greater numbers, and many stayed on after their recuperation.

The discovery of silver, gold, copper, iron, lead, and zinc in the mountains southwest of Socorro already had attracted miners, who set up rudimentary camps near their claims. In 1871, Silver City was established and soon became a place where rowdy miners swapped stories, ordered supplies, and enjoyed an occasional home-cooked meal. With the arrival of a spur that linked the mining camp to the Deming station, miners no longer had to travel as far to haul in supplies and ship valuable ores. Speculators and businessmen of a type not inclined to endure dusty, bumpy stagecoach rides now began crowding onto trains headed to the fledgling mining towns. Meanwhile, farmers and ranchers took a new look at the arable land along the Rio Grande, which became appealing once the threat of Apache attacks was removed. With passengers now protected inside rail cars, the forts were no longer needed; all were abandoned by the end of the century.

BILLY THE KID

Barefoot and bareheaded, Billy the Kid thought he was among friends in the darkened Fort Sumner bedroom of Pete Maxwell when he asked who was sitting at the foot of his friend's bed. That hesitation, on a summer evening in 1881, cost him his life. Sheriff Pat Garrett answered the question with two bullets, the first entering just above the outlaw's heart. Henry McCarty, AKA Henry Antrim, AKA William Bonney, was dead, but not his legend.

McCarty, as the Kid was first known, was born in the Irish slums of Brooklyn in 1859. He made his way west with his older brother Joe and his mother, Catherine McCarty, who suffered from tuberculosis. In 1873, she married William Antrim at the First Presbyterian Church in Santa Fe, and they moved the family to Silver City, where Antrim went about seeking his elusive fortune in the silver mines.

One of Henry's schoolteachers there recalled him as "a scrawny little fellow with delicate hands (he supposedly loved to play the piano) and an artistic nature, always willing to help with the chores around the schoolhouse."

Catherine Antrim died when Henry was 14, and he started hanging out with George Shaffer, a young friend who liked to drink and steal. One night they made off with a bundle of clothing from a local Chinese laundry, and Henry was caught "holding the bag." While in jail, he wriggled his wiry body up a chimney to freedom. At 15, he headed for Arizona where he shot his first man on record and didn't stick around to plead self-defense.

Back in New Mexico, Henry, now a seasoned outlaw, changed his name to William Bonney. His baby face and beanpole body secured him the nickname "the Kid." Wavy brown hair accented his 5-foot 7-inch, 135-pound frame. Innumerable books have been written about Billy, frequently painting him as a half-crazed, ruthless, bratty teenage killer; in reality, he was charming, cheerful, loyal, and generous. He didn't smoke or drink, refused to consort with prostitutes, and dressed neatly in dark colors—except for an occasional Mexican sombrero. His downfall was a hair-trigger temper that could be set off without warning.

Shortly before the outbreak of the Lincoln County War, Bonney was hired to work on a ranch owned by John Tunstall, a young Englishman who sought to undermine the economic stronghold of Lincoln merchants and cattle ranchers James Dolan and Lawrence Murphy.

After Tunstall was murdered—the killing that set off the conflict—the young Bonney vowed, "I'll get some of them before I die." As a member of the Regulators, a group of men that formed to avenge Tunstall's death, he did just that. Bonney played a role in the killing of three men he believed were Tunstall's murderers, and he was blamed for shooting Sheriff William Brady, who previously had mistreated some of the outlaw's friends. It was for Brady's murder that Bonney was convicted in a run-down adobe Mesilla courtroom in April 1881 and returned to Lincoln to be hanged.

Shackled and handcuffed, Bonney awaited his fate in an upstairs room adjacent to the sheriff's office in the Lincoln County Courthouse, guarded closely by deputies Bob Olinger and James Bell. One evening while Olinger took five other prisoners across the street to eat at the Wortley Hotel, the Kid found himself alone with Bell. He asked Bell to escort him to the privy. As they returned, Bell carelessly lagged behind, which gave Bonney a chance to beat the deputy to the top of the stairs, shackles and all. Hiding behind a corner, Bonney quickly twisted his skinny hands from the handcuffs. When Bell topped the staircase, Bonney viciously swung the loose cuff across the deputy's head, cutting open two gashes across his scalp. Bleeding and slightly stunned, Bell was no match for the agile outlaw, who wrestled away the deputy's holstered revolver. As Bell retreated down the stairs, Bonney shot him dead.

The Kid quickly grabbed a loaded shotgun from Olinger's office and ran to a corner window. Olinger, who had rushed across the street when he heard the shots, opened the courthouse gate and looked up into the barrel of his own shotgun pointing at him from an upstairs window. Bonney didn't hesitate to fire, shredding Olinger's upper body with the buckshot the lawman had loaded earlier in the day.

No one in the terror-stricken town dared approach Bonney as a friend saddled up a horse for him. According to Robert Utley's account in *Billy the Kid, a Short and Violent Life,* Bonney smashed Olinger's shotgun across the railing of the courthouse porch and hurled its pieces at the dead lawman, who had despised and verbally abused the desperado.

His bold and fearless flight from Lincoln solidified Bonney's standing as the territory's leading fugitive. The *Las Vegas Optic,* a daily newspaper, editorialized, "With a heart untouched to pity by misfortune and with a character possessing the attributes of the damned, he has reveled in brutal murder and gloried in his shame."

After his escape, Bonney was sheltered and fed by his many friends throughout the region. One of these was Pete Maxwell, whose father had renovated the barracks of Fort Sumner as his home. Spending the night at the old fort, Bonney was heading to Maxwell's kitchen to cut a slab of meat for a midnight snack when he entered his friend's bedroom to ask about a couple of strangers outside. Inside was a third visitor, Sheriff Pat Garrett, who had come to inquire about the Kid's whereabouts—and by chance found his prey.

■ OUTLAWS AND LAWMEN

During this era, legends were born. Billy the Kid, known as Henry McCarty to his Silver City classmates, lived in the mining district with his mother, brother, and stepfather in the early 1870s. One story has it that this famous outlaw killed his first man in a barroom brawl when he was 12 years old. Whether or not that is true, the seeds of his legend germinated during the Lincoln County War, a struggle for supremacy among cattle barons that broke out in 1878 in what was then the biggest county in the territory. His death at the age of 21 in a Fort Sumner bedroom in 1881 only added to the legend, elevating it to a near mythic level, where it continued to blossom as the years passed.

The arrival of the railroad hadn't eliminated the need for lawmen, and in the person of Elfego Baca, Socorro had one of the flashiest. In 1884, at the age of 19, Baca traveled 137 miles from his home in Socorro to Frisco (now Reserve) to stump for a candidate for sheriff. While he was trying to win votes for his friend, an inebriated Texas cowboy began harassing residents and shooting up the town. Since Baca was the closest thing to a lawman in town at that moment, he appointed himself deputy sheriff and arrested the perpetrator, only to find himself surrounded by 80 agitated cowboys who demanded their friend's release. Baca refused and barricaded himself inside a low-slung *jacal,* a small hut constructed of poles spaced at least two inches apart and connected by mud plaster. During the next 36 hours, more than 4,000 shots were fired at the jacal. A total of 367 bullets riddled the small front door, hitting nearly everything inside, including a plaster-of-paris reproduction of a saint, known as Nuestra Señora Santa Ana. The self-appointed sheriff was untouched, though he killed four of the Texans. Baca gave up the fight when a real deputy arrived from Socorro. He was subsequently tried and acquitted, and eventually served as mayor of Socorro, deputy U.S. marshal, county clerk, school superintendent, and, after earning a law degree, as the no-nonsense sheriff of Socorro County. His survival skills are remembered every June on the final day of the Hilton Open, a pro-am golf tournament, when the Elfego Baca Shoot challenges golfers to tee off from the top of 7,500-foot Socorro Peak, then scramble down the mountain after their balls until they arrive at the golf course at the New Mexico Institute of Mining and Technology. It usually takes about 15 shots to win the hole. *For information, call First State Bank, Socorro; 505-835-8211.*

■ Dams and Onions

By the early 1900s, farmers along the Rio Grande were beginning to tire of the muddy waterway's irregular behavior. One year, the river would flood its banks, only to dry up the next. Wanting reliability, they encouraged construction of a dam that would store water in the wet years and release it during the dry ones. Surveys began in 1903; Elephant Butte Dam was completed in 1916, forming a lake behind it that would be an oasis for recreational boaters, fishermen, and anyone else seeking relief from the relentless summer sun. A second lake was formed when Caballo Dam was completed in 1938 to create a secondary storage reservoir 11 miles south. The already fertile farmland downstream became even more abundant, and its fields soon brimmed with white cotton bolls, green and red chile peppers, and shady pecan orchards.

Today, NM 187 and NM 185 pass through the hamlets of Arrey, Hatch, and Radium Springs, beside which neat rows of crops spread to the river and nearby hills. You can tell the season by the smell in the air: if it's the sharp aroma of ripe onions, it must be summer; the unmistakable scent of chiles means it's fall. Similarly, when tufts of wayward cotton bolls stick to roadside signs and litter the highway, winter is nigh.

■ Socorro *map page 186, D-1*

Socorro, which means help or aid in Spanish, was named by Juan de Oñate, New Mexico's first governor, in thanks for food and water that the Indians there provided his entourage one desperate afternoon in 1598 when they had just staggered out of the near waterless desert of the Jornada del Muerto. This is a quiet, dusty town, but it has a small historic district, which you can begin to explore at the tree-shaded plaza, unromantically named **Kittrel Park** in memory of the dentist who first planted trees and grass there in the 1880s. In the center are a gazebo and black cast-iron benches where you can listen to the songs of robins and finches.

The brick-solid **Hilton Block**, anchored by the Hilton Drugstore, was founded by a relative of Conrad Hilton. (Nobody seems to know which one.) No operas have ever been performed at the nearby **J.N. Garcia Opera House** (110 Abeyta Avenue), but the renovated 1886 building has been the site of concerts, masked balls, school programs, and college basketball games. The two towers you see north of the plaza mark the **San Miguel Mission** (403 El Camino Real), first built in the early 1600s, but mostly destroyed during the Pueblo Revolt of 1680; the current church replaced it on the same spot.

The **Val Verde Hotel** (203 East Manzanares; 505-835-3380), built in 1919 to serve passengers on the Santa Fe Railroad, was abandoned in the 1960s and reopened in the late 1980s. Although the Val Verde Steakhouse on the main floor is open to the public, the hotel rooms are rented exclusively to students from the **New Mexico Institute of Mining and Technology**. Founded in 1946 to train mining engineers, New Mexico Tech has since expanded to include research projects in petroleum mining and explosives technology. Its mountain-top laboratory is the only one in the United States dedicated to studying the physical dynamics of thunderclouds. The institute's **Mineralogical Museum** (505-835-5420) houses a collection of more than 10,000 specimens, including bison vertebrae, giant ground sloth fossils, turquoise, quartz, and lesser-known gems such as yellow zippeite and charcoal gray goethite. Although the exhibit is geared mostly toward aficionados, it has giant mammoth fossils and a case of fluorescent minerals from around the world of interest to all. Some specimens are for sale.

■ **VERY LARGE ARRAY**   *map page 186, B-1*
West of Socorro, U.S. 60 traverses the windswept Plains of San Agustin. Past the old shipping center of Magdalena, giant white satellite dishes mysteriously sprout from the horizon, part of a 27-antenna network that makes up the National Radio Astronomy Laboratory, better known as the **Very Large Array**, the world's most powerful radio telescope. Each antenna is 82 feet in diameter and weighs 235 tons, and they move about on railroad tracks. A visitors center is open daily; a self-guided tour takes visitors past exhibits that illustrate how radios and the telescope work, and how they came to be. If you continue the tour outside, you'll walk past one of the giant dishes. *From U.S. 60, turn south on NM 52, then west on the VLA access road.*

■ **SOUTH OF SOCORRO**   *map page 186, C/D-2*
The sleepy community of **San Antonio** sits on a drainage ditch along the Rio Grande. As a youth, Conrad Hilton worked as a bellboy in his father's hotel here, but travelers should know the town for the **Owl Bar,** reputed to serve the finest green chile cheeseburger hereabouts. The well-worn hardwood bar that runs the length of the front room was salvaged from the nearby Hilton after it burned down in the 1940s. According to owner Rowena Baca, a group of Civilian Conservation Corps workers volunteered to walk the massive bar to its current location for a unique fee: burgers and beer. The move took two days. *US 380. 505-835-9946.*

The dish-shaped antennas that make up the Very Large Array are laid out in the shape of a Y and connected to form a radio telescope.

Thousands of sandhill cranes, pure white snow geese, and ducks fly overhead along NM 1, which winds south past fields of wheat, corn, and millet—a lavish dinner table for the birds who spend their winters at the nearby **Bosque del Apache National Wildlife Refuge.** The refuge was established in 1939 to provide a winter home for the graceful whooping crane, then threatened with extinction— but repeated efforts to establish a stable migrating flock have failed, and none can be seen at the refuge nowadays. Nonetheless, more than 3,000 ducks, hundreds of Canada geese, and scores of wading birds such as herons and egrets take over the wetlands each summer. Bird-watching is best at dawn from October to February, when the snow geese depart in a breathtakingly beautiful—and cacophonous— cloud for a day of feasting at the nearby fields. *505-835-1828.*

Wide open spaces rimmed by gentle mountain ranges make for prime cattle country.

■ TRUTH OR CONSEQUENCES *map page 186, C-3*

In 1950, when NBC producer Ralph Edwards put out the word he was looking for a town willing to name itself after his offbeat radio (and later television) show, cattleman Burton Roach took up the challenge. As a state senator and president of the Chamber of Commerce of Hot Springs, New Mexico, Roach thought a name-change might be the way to distinguish *his* hot springs from all the other hot springs and get some free advertising in the bargain.

The town's citizens voted on the idea, and the town took the show's name, *Truth or Consequences,* for its own. As promised, Edwards brought his production staff and show crew to New Mexico for the first live, coast-to-coast broadcast from its new namesake—airing the program (no joke) on April Fools Day, 1950. Thereafter, Edwards returned every May for 50 years to emcee the **Ralph Edwards Fiesta,** and although he is no longer able to participate, the celebration is still held annually. Edwards also has his own room at the **Geronimo Springs Museum,** where photos and memorabilia from the program line the walls. *211 Main Street; 505-894-6600.*

Perhaps it was this brilliant marketing strategy, or more likely the steaming hot mineral springs beneath the town and the oases in nearby **Elephant Butte** and **Caballo Reservoirs,** but T or C, as the town is called, has become a haven for retirees. Long before Hot Springs was established, Indians soaked aching muscles in the soothing waters after a long day's ride. Today, the soothing waters are available at six mineral baths lined up on or near Broadway at the southern end of town. They are all that remains of the bathhouses built in the 1930s to serve the tourist court motels, and each retains a rustic charm and personality of its own.

In the early 1980s it occurred to entrepreneurial landowners outside T or C that the moderate, dry climate might be perfect for wine grapes. They weren't the first to think of the idea. In 1662, a century before the first grapes were planted in California, Franciscan priests were producing naturally fermented wine for their masses from mission grapes grown in southern New Mexico. For a sample of local cabernets and chardonnays, call for an appointment, then drive 30 minutes east of town to the abandoned rail shipping point of Engle, where you'll find the vineyard and winery of **Chateau Sassenage**. *505-894-7244.*

■ **NEARBY GHOST TOWNS** *map page 186, B/C-2/3*

Several once-thriving mining and commercial centers are scattered in the vicinity of Truth or Consequences, their busy streets now deserted, their bustling mercantile stores now reduced to wooden skeletons. Northwest of town, NM 52 passes through **Cuchillo** (Spanish for "knife"), a Hispanic hamlet tucked into an abrupt outcropping. During the gold rush days of the 1860s, prospectors and suppliers changed horses here, and stagecoaches let their passengers off to stretch their legs.

The mining district of **Winston** sits amid a broad meadow of pale green and yellow grasses, surrounded by gently rising hillsides dotted with piñon pines. Silver was the lure here in the 1880s, attracting prospectors. Today, cattle graze in the valley, and tall weeds and grass prosper between the false-fronted and mostly abandoned wooden buildings.

Beyond this almost nonexistent town, the road turns to gravel, ending 2 miles farther on at **Chloride**. In 1879, Henry Pye, a muleskinner and prospector, discovered veins of silver chloride in a nearby rock outcropping. He established a claim, but a few months later, before he could enjoy the wealth he had envisioned, he was killed in an Apache raid. The boom that followed drew hundreds of miners who built a picturesque settlement of adobe and wooden homes in the range's wrinkled foothills. Today, many original buildings remain, most of them abandoned. A few hardy residents have restored some of the structures and built new ones.

At the southern end of the Black Range and southwest of T or C, NM 152 crosses rugged mountains, winding among steep, pine-covered slopes. But first, it bisects the old mining district of **Hillsboro**, its tin roofs hidden underneath giant cottonwoods. Once a gold- and silver-mining boomtown and Sierra County seat, Hillsboro turned into a ranching center after the minerals were depleted. Today, novelty shops, art galleries, and antique stores line the main street. Eccentric artists, solitary writers, and slow-moving retirees share quiet days and evenings under the stars with rough-riding ranchers and diehard miners. Every Labor Day weekend, the village comes alive during the **Hillsboro Apple Festival,** when the sidewalks are lined with arts and crafts booths, food stalls, and apples harvested from nearby orchards. *505-895-5686.*

Nine miles deeper into the mountains, **Kingston** is the last stop before NM 152 climbs over 8,228-foot Emory Pass on its way to the Mimbres Valley. During a heyday that began in 1880, 7,500 fortune hunters flocked to the pine-covered slopes of Kingston, which surrendered more than $10 million worth of silver in less than 15 years. For a short time the town boomed. Twenty-two saloons lined the broad sidewalk on the main street, and the 19th-century musical comedy star Lillian Russell performed at the town's theater. Kingston had no church until a hat was passed in the saloons one night to raise money for one. Today, 30 resourceful people remain—writers, retirees, and other longtime residents who continue to hold regular meetings of the Spit and Whittle Club. They say they love the clean air and, on cold days, the sweet smell of burning piñon.

■ LAS CRUCES *map page 186, D-4*

Framed by the lush banks of the Rio Grande and the dry, rugged Organ Mountains (named for their resemblance to pipe organs), Las Cruces sits in the heart of the Mesilla Valley. When New Mexico was being settled, the wagons of Spanish colonists that passed this way were frequently ambushed by Apaches. In 1787, the bodies of several oxcart caravan drivers were found and crosses were erected on their graves. Forty-three years later, a party of 30 travelers from Taos met the same fate and more crosses were raised. What began as an eerie graveyard known as La Placita de las Cruces ("The Place of the Crosses"), has grown to become the second-largest city in New Mexico.

Moreno Drug Company, Las Cruces, ca. 1910.

In the mid-1800s, colonists began putting down roots. They lived in jacales, made by placing poles vertically in a ground trench, lashing the poles together, and coating them with mud plaster to form walls that could be whitewashed. Vigas and *latillas* supported dirt roofs. Adobe bricks were used in later homes, brick copings topped parapets, square wooden columns supported porches. Many of these houses are still visible in the Mesquite Street area—Las Cruces's oldest neighborhood—stuccoed in pastel pink, green, blue, and shades of brown that range from tawny to deep chocolate.

After the Santa Fe Railroad reached Las Cruces in 1881, farmlands between the Mesquite district and the depot made room for new homes that reflected the styles of the town's new East Coast residents—hip box, Queen Anne, bungalow—along with some patterned after the traditional adobe style. A few pre-railroad farmhouses survive in the **Alameda-Depot Historic District**, which is worth exploring on foot.

South of town, the College of Las Cruces opened in 1880 and within a decade had grown into the New Mexico College of Agriculture and Mechanic Arts, which later would become **New Mexico State University**. The second-largest university in the state, it is noted for its agricultural research, especially the cultivation of chiles. Of the 200 known varieties of chile peppers, 30 are grown and studied in fields irrigated by the Rio Grande. Researchers continually work to develop milder hybrids so that people with sensitive palates—most of whom seem to reside east of the Mississippi—can enjoy their unique spiciness. The grassy campus, with its red-tiled roofs topping tan stucco buildings, stretches across 6,250 acres and includes grazing pastures, one of the largest computer centers in the Southwest, and one of only three full-time planetary observatories in the country. Clyde Tombaugh, discoverer of the planet Pluto, was professor emeritus at NMSU until his death in 1997.

The **University Art Gallery** (505-646-2545) annually hosts as many as a dozen exhibitions of contemporary art, both of national importance and faculty shows. Shows at the **New Mexico State University Museum** (505-646-3739) focus on the historical Southwest and northern Mexico. Also on campus is the **American Southwest Theatre Company** (505-646-4515), where professor emeritus and Tony award–winning playwright Mark Medoff has introduced a number of his works.

The **New Mexico Farm and Ranch Heritage Museum** occupies 47 acres to the east of the university. A working ranch and farm, complete with sheep, bunnies, and cows, help tell the 300-year story of New Mexico agriculture. *4100 Dripping Springs Road; 505-522-4100.*

ADOBE 101

In southwestern New Mexico, building an adobe home is an intense rite of passage which requires, in its purest form, no previous construction experience. . . . Adobe is a cunning mixture of clay and sand. Too much clay and the brick cracks while drying, too little and it lacks strength. We tested the proportions of our soil by throwing handfuls of dirt into a jar of water, shaking vigorously, and watching the layers settle. Amazingly, our land appeared to be a huge dehydrated adobe mix—add water, stir, and pour. This we did, every day, ten hours a day, for three weeks. It was hard work, but not unpleasant. Transformation! The ground formed into squares that we set on their sides to dry and then gingerly stacked. On one good day, eighty wet-looking bricks lay in soldierly rows before us. On most days, there were only sixty or fifty. We ended up with thirteen hundred adobes: a hundred less than we thought we should have, a hundred more than we would actually need.

—Sharman Apt Russell, *Songs of the Fluteplayer,* 1991

Just past the university's golf course, Dripping Springs Road leads to **Dripping Springs Recreation Area,** where a trickle of water seeping from the volcanic rock forms a few refreshing pools. For years, this desert oasis in the Organ Mountains was known mostly to Las Cruces residents, who were generously permitted to use it by the A.B. Cox family, who owned a cattle ranch there. In 1988, the family sold the 2,852-acre spread of cactus-laden foothills and rugged rock outcroppings, and it now belongs to the Bureau of Land Management. The main ranch house has become a visitors center, and maintained trails wend through ocotillo, cholla, and prickly-pear cactus.

One of the trails—a 1.5-mile uphill path—leads to the ruins of a resort built on the property in the 1870s by Col. Eugene Van Patten, who called his 16-room building with dining hall and large ballroom Van Patten's Mountain Camp. Later known as Dripping Springs Resort, it attracted such notables as Pat Garrett and Pancho Villa. Van Patten went bankrupt in 1917 and sold the resort to a doctor who turned it into a tuberculosis sanatorium. After a few more changes of ownership, the Cox family acquired it in 1958.

A trail from the visitors center leads to La Cueva, a 10-foot-tall cave that was inhabited as long ago as 5000 B.C., probably as a shelter for early hunters in pursuit of rabbit, antelope, deer, and bighorn sheep. Today, there's a picnic area near La

Cueva. Although the ranch is open to the public daily, preservation of the fragile environment remains of primary concern. Of nine threatened and endangered plant species found on the ranch, five are native to the Organ Mountains. In addition, seven endangered birds and two mammals are at home here, as well as two extremely rare mollusks: the earred terrestrial snail and Organ Mountain snail. BLM employees lead interpretive tours with advance notice.

To reach the ranch, take University Boulevard east off I-25, heading toward the mountains. When the pavement ends, you are on Dripping Springs Road. Most of the 10-mile trip is on gravel, and it takes about 30 minutes. *505-522-1219.*

Las Cruces's major employer is **White Sands Missile Range**, a 4,000-square-mile expanse of lonely desert that follows the eastern edge of the Organ and San Andres mountain ranges. Nearly 9,000 residents cross San Agustin Pass every day to punch time clocks on a tree-shaded campus at its base. In 1942, the U.S. military established the Alamogordo Bombing Range as a weapons testing site; eventually the test area was enlarged to include 2.7 million acres of tall grassland, displacing hundreds of ranchers and their families. In 1945, the northern part of the range (by then called the White Sands Proving Ground) was a convenient place to detonate the world's first atomic bomb, which had been developed farther to the north at Los Alamos. When, toward the end of the war, the scientists that had developed Germany's V-2 rocket defected to the United States, they and White Sands were pressed into service for development and testing of the first generation of the rockets that eventually landed an American on the moon. The range's current name, White Sands Missile Range, reflects an expanded mission: testing rockets, missiles, and payloads for the space shuttle program. To protect travelers from wayward rockets along U.S. 70, which cuts through the range, roadblocks are erected during firings. *For a recording of scheduled road closures, call 505-678-1178.*

■ **MESILLA** *map page 186, D-4*

Mesilla lost both population and prestige to Las Cruces in the great railroad rush of the 1880s; in recompense, the sleepy town retained its 19th-century character. From miles away, the white crosses atop two steeples of the **San Albino Church** can be seen towering above the tree-shaded town. This block-long brick church anchors the northern end of a quiet central plaza. Black wrought-iron benches with wooden seats are a perfect place to watch the afternoon sun transform the mud-brown walls of shops and galleries into hues of soft yellow and rose red and

Frank L. Oliver's Mercantile Store, Mesilla, ca. 1890.

muse about the days when the plaza bustled with stagecoaches in for repair at the Butterfield station and when cowboys impressed each other over shots of whiskey with tales of herding cattle on the untamed range. The Confederate flag flapped above the plaza for a year between 1861 and 1862, and 20 years later, in a stuffy nearby courtroom, a shackled Billy the Kid was sentenced to die for the murder of Lincoln County Sheriff William Brady. And don't forget: for a time Mesilla was the capital of the Territory of Arizona.

Today, the Butterfield station's blacksmith shop, saddle shop, and horse stables have been turned into the dining rooms of **La Posta de Mesilla** (2410 Calle de San Albino; 505-524-3524), a superb Mexican restaurant where waterfalls burble and parrots babble. Across the street, the **William Bonney Gallery** (2060 Calle de Parian; 505-526-8275), once the jail that housed Billy the Kid, displays bronze sculptures and Native American pottery and baskets. The courthouse where Billy was sentenced to hang is now the **Billy the Kid Gift Shop** (2385 Calle de Guadalupe; 505-523-5561). The **Fountain Theatre** (2469 Calle de Guadalupe; 505-524-8287)—built in 1905 and named for Albert Jennings Fountain, a flamboyant member of an old Mesilla family—is New Mexico's oldest movie house, in continuous operation since its opening.

■ THE VALLEY *map page 186, D-4/5*

South of Mesilla, with the jagged peaks of the Organ Mountains a distant backdrop, NM 28 follows the bends of the Rio Grande, passing beneath a three-mile-long canopy created by thick groves of pecan trees. This pecan orchard, **Stahmann Farms,** has 3,850 acres of trees, making it one of the largest in the world. Samples are available at the Stahmann store. *22505 South NM 28; 505-525-3470.*

Throughout the area, deeply dug irrigation ditches filled with swiftly flowing water feed wide expanses of deep-green chile fields, white-tufted cotton plants, and pale green heads of lettuce. Mixed in with these lush crops is **La Viña Winery.** Stop in for a glass of chardonnay or zinfandel at its tasting room, set among the grapevines. *4201 South NM 28, La Union; 505-882-7632.*

Farmers who tend these fields live in small hamlets with names like **San Miguel, Chamberino,** and **La Mesa.** They meet to share a beer and discuss local politics at **Chope's Bar and Cafe** (16145 NM 28; 505-233-3420) in La Mesa. As the conversation heats up, so does the green chile that smothers plates of enchiladas and burritos served here. This chile is for palates accustomed to fire. If yours isn't, expect to leave with a runny nose and perspiring brow.

■ DEMING *map page 186, B-4*

Deming is a railroad town named after Mary Ann Deming, who just happened to be married to Charles Crocker, a California silver baron and one of the promoters of the Southern Pacific Railroad, which in 1881 met the Atchison, Topeka & Santa Fe Railroad at this spot among creosote bush and cholla cactus north of the Little Florida Mountains. He named the resulting ramshackle gathering of tents and shanties after his wife.

The boisterous railroad camp has grown into a quiet, tidy, tree-lined town unsullied by heavy industry or much auto traffic and proud of its clean air and pure water from the Mimbres River, which passes through underground. Outside town, cows and steers chew on patches of desert grass that have sprouted between mesquite trees and yuccas, fields of waving milo, and the white pods of cotton plants that flourish in the intense sun.

According to some people, the best thing about Deming is the **Deming Duck Race,** which began in 1980 when Steve Marlowe, a realtor, and Harold Cousland, editor of the *Deming Headlight,* were bemoaning the tedium of small-town life. Marlowe asked Cousland whether duck races might liven things up—knowing full well that there weren't any ducks flying around their hot, dry, landlocked home-town. Cousland considered Marlowe's idea daffy, but liked it, and the first Great American Duck Race was announced.

Through the years, the wacky event has gone from a joke to the town's most popular annual attraction, typically drawing up to 20,000 spectators during four days in late August. More than 800 webbed entrants compete for $1,300 in prize money. Duck trainers are said to warn their fowl, "Be a winner, or be dinner." *888-345-1125.*

A more sober attraction, the **Deming Luna Mimbres Museum,** is housed in the old National Guard Armory. One room displays more than 500 lovingly cos-tumed dolls; another holds a collection of intricately stitched quilts dating back to 1847. A chuck wagon conjures up the traveling kitchens of roundup days, and Mimbres pottery, arrowheads, and baskets represent the tribes that once roamed the region. *301 South Silver Avenue; 505-546-2382.*

Southeast of town, the relentless sun beats down on the Little Florida Mountains, reflecting specimens of cloudy agate, blood-red jasper, shiny black per-lite, and smoky quartz. Here, in **Rockhound State Park**, people wander through the yuccas, beavertail, and barrel cacti, searching for precious geodes. In an unusual twist, they are encouraged to take their finds home. *NM 497; 505-546-6182.*

The raid on Columbus by Pancho Villa in 1916 was the only land invasion of the United States in the 20th century.

■ COLUMBUS *map page 186, C-5*

This sleepy border town hasn't been the same since the early morning hours of March 9, 1916, when Pancho Villa led a band of Mexican revolutionaries in an attack on it and burned most of it to the ground. Eighteen Americans were killed—some residents, others soldiers stationed at Camp Furlong. The following day, U.S. Army Gen. John J. Pershing headed across the border into Mexico, leading 10,000 soldiers through a desolate desert covered with thorny cactus and parched mountains. Although trucks and motorcycles provided support for soldiers on horseback, and eight Curtis JN-3 biplanes (known as Jennys) of the First Aero Squadron took to the sky, the deep sand and mud in northern Mexico's roadless expanse overtaxed the vehicles, and the biplanes didn't have enough power to clear Mexico's 12,000-foot mountains. Pershing spent most of a year vainly chasing Villa through Mexico, returning to Columbus on February 5, 1917.

Pancho Villa at his headquarters in Ciudad Juárez, 1914.

Despite the devastation wrought by Villa, the citizens of Columbus have named a state park after him, figuring, one assumes, that a Pershing State Park wouldn't draw as many visitors as **Pancho Villa State Park**. They could be right: the park, alongside the ruins of Camp Furlong, is the community's main attraction. Campsites are carved out of a dense mass of orange-tipped ocotillo, knee-high beavertails, century plants, mesquite bushes, yuccas, and yellow-budded cholla. No fewer than 5,000 varieties of cactus and wildflowers are crowded into this botanical paradise. *505-531-2711.*

■ LORDSBURG *map page 186, A-4*

Named for a Southern Pacific engineer, Lordsburg is mainly a gas-up-and-stretch stop, but 3 miles southwest of town a collection of tin-roofed adobe buildings is worth a longer look. Hidden among a group of small hills covered in mesquite, yucca, greasewood, and beavertail cactus, the old town site of **Shakespeare** has gone through numerous incarnations: first as a watering hole for Apache Indians, then as a stop on the Butterfield Trail, then as a boisterous mining boomtown.

Shakespeare grew from a stopover into a destination in 1870 after W. D. Brown, a dropout from a government survey party, discovered some promising-looking ore in the nearby Pyramid Mountains. Tents and adobe shacks shot up overnight across the stark brown landscape. Some time after the silver boom died down, two scruffy miners showed a bag of uncut stones to California banker William Ralston, who paid them $600,000 for their claim in the same mountains. Reports of a diamond strike began to circulate, and within a few weeks, more than 3,000 prospectors converged on Shakespeare. More tents and buildings went up, until the main street was lined with seven saloons, a barbershop, stores, restaurants, boarding houses, a Chinese laundry, and an assay office. Nobody found any diamonds, but nobody seemed to care. There was no church, no newspaper, and no law; free-for-all fights and murder were commonplace. The diamond strike was soon determined to be a swindle: the mountainside purported to contain the rich deposit had been salted with a few appropriately placed diamonds. Within days, Shakespeare was nearly empty.

A bumpy dirt road cuts through greasewood and yuccas to what's left of the town. In 1997, it suffered a devastating fire that destroyed a number of buildings, most notably the old general store, which doubled as a museum. A hay barn, blacksmith shop, and general store have been rebuilt. Tours are conducted on the

second weekend of each month or by appointment. *On NM 494, 2.5 miles south of Lordsburg; 505-542-9034.*

Straddling the Continental Divide in New Mexico's boot heel are the tall grass-lands of the **Gray Ranch,** whose preservation was assured when the Nature Conservancy purchased the 500-square-mile spread in 1990. At one time owned by California mining and livestock baron George Hearst (father of publishing magnate William Randolph), the ranch is home to nearly 100 rare and endangered plant and animal species, including the ridgenosed rattlesnake, Sanborn's long-nosed bat, the white-sided jackrabbit, and night-blooming cereus, a spiny-stemmed bush with delicate white blooms that come out at night. In 1994, the richly endowed spread was transferred to the Animas Foundation, which continues the Nature Conservancy's preservation work. Although it is not open to the public, the ranch has a reputation as one of the nation's most significant areas of biological study.

■ **SILVER CITY**   *map page 186, B-3*

One prospector who traveled to Shakespeare to check out its famous silver strike took a quick look at the distinctive ore, scratched his head, and headed back north to Pinos Altos, a gold-mining burg in the foothills of what today is the Gila National Forest. John Bullard knew where there was plenty more of the valuable silver: right outside his home. After word got around, the pine-covered hills were soon covered with makeshift tents and shacks, and the area became known as Silver City. Saloons, restaurants, billiard halls, meat markets, and—inevitably—banks popped up on the dirt streets, along with the offices of doctors, lawyers, dressmakers, and tailors. Smooth-talking gamblers in wide-rimmed black hats warmed seats in gambling houses. Bow-legged cowboys swaggered up to bars, demanding shots of mescal. Silver City's new residents apparently were eager to know of the larger world, for by the end of 1882 six newspapers were being published in the mining district.

Prior to the arrival of the railroad, which reached Silver City in 1881, 12- and 14-horse teams hauled ore from the Mogollon Mountains to town, where it was shipped by stage and wagon train. Stacks of gold and silver bricks stood outside freight offices. Incredibly, the temptation to pinch one or two proved stronger than the threat of the noose: public hangings were frequent.

The hanging room in the ghost town of Shakespeare.

Unlike civic officials in most of the boomtowns of the day, Silver City's lawmakers had the foresight to prohibit frame buildings within the town's limits, hoping to forestall the possibility of fires. As a result, most of the original town has survived. Brick and adobe buildings, which mix Victorian architecture with the flat-roofed vernacular style, line almost every street. A white picket fence surrounds the two-story H.B. Ailman House, now the **Silver City Museum** (312 West Broadway; 505-538-5921) and a good place to start a stroll. Stop inside for a historical walking tour brochure.

An example of the town's resourcefulness is **Big Ditch Park,** a 55-foot-deep trench that once was its Main Street. As miners sought their fortunes, they loosened the soil of Silver City's hills, causing massive flooding when heavy rains came between 1895 and 1903. Walls of water as high as 12 feet raged through town, gutting Main Street to the bedrock. In 1980, the city turned it into a park.

Like so many other towns in New Mexico, Silver City lays its own claim to Billy the Kid. You can follow the outlaw's brief presence in the mining district by viewing the site of his boyhood home (since torn down); the Star Hotel, where he worked as a waiter; his mother's grave; and the site of the jail from which he made his first escape.

■ **OUTSIDE SILVER CITY** *map page 186, B-3/4*
Unlike many early mining districts that fizzled after the ore played out, Silver City's mines are still producing, though copper has replaced silver as the primary metal. Thirteen miles east of Silver City is the **Santa Rita Open Pit Mine**—which used to be the village of Santa Rita until it was engulfed by a massive open-pit copper operation. From an observation deck, you can peer into the 1,000-foot-deep mine, which stretches more than a mile across.

Southeast of Silver City off NM 61 is an island of house-size boulders on the burnt-sienna prairie. This jumble of Tertiary tuff, which flowed from an erupting volcano a million years ago, has been turned into **City of Rocks State Park**, with picnic tables and campsites wedged among the boulders. The only sound in this wide plain comes from the wind, which regularly whistles through ocotillo, cholla, and yucca cacti. Mountain ranges line the horizon in every direction. *505-536-2800.*

Celebrating Mexican Independence Day, Silver City, ca. 1900.

Three miles north of Silver City, amid a flat expanse of piñons and junipers, sits a commanding two-story Pueblo Revival bed-and-breakfast inn that caters to naturalists. The **Bear Mountain Lodge**, which backs up to the Gila Wilderness, was the vision of Myra McCormick, who in 1959 began welcoming visitors to the inn she had built with her husband. Upon her death 40 years later, the 160-acre guest ranch became the property of the Nature Conservancy. Now extensively renovated, the lodge is a deluxe destination for nature lovers. A resident naturalist leads short daily hikes around the property as well as longer excursions. *505-538-2538; 877-620-2327.*

Pinos Altos, 7 miles north of town, hasn't fared as well as Silver City. But the cozy hamlet, named for the surrounding tall pines, has done well at preserving its frontier past. A walk along the dirt streets of town takes you past the **Pinos Altos Ice Cream Parlor**, housed in the old Norton Store. The creaky wooden floors of the **Buckhorn Saloon** (32 Main Street; 505-538-9911) don't seem to bother Indian Joe, a life-sized doll that sits at one end of the bar, day and night. Some of the best steaks to be eaten in these parts are served in the adjacent brick-walled dining room.

■ GILA NATIONAL FOREST

■ GILA CLIFF DWELLINGS NATIONAL MONUMENT
map page 186, B-3

Heading north from Pinos Altos, NM 15 enters the 3-million-acre Gila National Forest and, contained within it, the 438,360-acre Gila Wilderness, established by Congress and the U.S. Forest Service in 1924 as the country's first designated wilderness area. After crossing the Gila River and Gila Hot Springs the road ends at the **Gila Cliff Dwellings National Monument,** where a one-mile loop trail takes you up and through 42 rock-walled rooms built into the side of a volcanic cliff. (You can climb ladders to explore the dark interiors.)

The well-protected dwellings look much as they did when the Mogollon Indians lived in them 700 years ago. The Indians hunted deer, cultivated vegetables and tobacco on nearby mesas and along the West Fork of the Gila River, and gathered wild berries and nuts in the nearby forest. No one knows why they left their cliffside homes in the early 1300s, but many think they joined other Pueblo Indians to the north and south. *Off NM 15, 44 miles north of Silver City; 505-536-9461.*

■ GLENWOOD *map page 186, A-3*

Northwest of Silver City, U.S. 180 passes through a few small ranching communities. Glenwood has the most to offer—a few motels, a bar, and the **Catwalk,** a 200-foot-long steel walkway anchored to the rock wall of Whitewater Canyon above the rushing waters of Whitewater Creek. In the 1880s, a group of miners built a 3-mile-long wooden pipeline to carry water from the upper reaches of the creek to their mill and mining camp at the mouth of the canyon. This provided them with a reliable water source, because too often the plentiful water of the creek would dry up by the time it reached their settlement. The pipeline did need repairs from time to time, however, and where it dangled high above the creek, they could only be made by walking on the tube, thus the name "catwalk."

Long after the mill closed in 1913, a trail was completed along the same route, and a steel catwalk was added along this most precarious stretch to create a secure hiking path. The metal platform hugs the rock face 25 feet above the creek, alongside hybrid oaks, sycamores, alders, and lichen-covered boulders. When it returns to ground, the trail meets up with others that weave through the Gila National Forest, where Rocky Mountain bighorn sheep and mule deer roam the slopes.

The Mogollon Indian ruins at Gila Cliff Dwellings National Monument.

■ MOGOLLON *map page 186, A-2*

A few miles past Glenwood along U.S. 180 is the turnoff to Mogollon (pro-nounced MUH-gee-own), an old mining town wedged into a narrow canyon. In the bustling days of 1890, it boasted 20 saloons and 2,000 residents, including Ben Lilly, one of the West's most adept mountain lion hunters. Lilly charged ranchers $50 for each dead mountain lion he brought them; he bagged 110 during his career. Mines in the Mogollon area produced millions of dollars worth of gold and silver before closing at the outbreak of World War II.

A walk through this rustic village takes you past a clock that always reads four o'clock, the hour the last shift ended in the mines. Today a handful of hardy people live year-round in the weather-beaten hamlet along Silver Creek, joined in the summer by about three dozen others, mostly shopkeepers who cater to vacationers heading into the Gila Wilderness. The road (NM 159) leading to town is only nine miles long, but it takes a good 30 minutes to negotiate its steep incline and sharp curves. Past Mogollon, it turns to gravel as it approaches the wilderness area.

Farther up U.S. 180, NM 12 turns off toward the ranching centers of Reserve, Aragon, and Horse Springs, passing through the ancient home of the Mimbres Indians. These people lived throughout the Gila National Forest and down in the Mimbres Valley, southeast of Silver City. What distinguished them from their Mogollon relatives was their pottery, decorated in geometric designs and surreal animal figures. Many of these pots, typically found at grave sites, have been dug up on ranches throughout the Tularosa Mountains near Reserve and Aragon. The Mimbreños abandoned their homes in the 12th century, long before their distant Mogollon relatives left the Gila River. You won't see the remains of any Mimbres dwellings in the valley; none have been preserved. To view the nation's largest per-manent exhibit of Mimbres pottery, head back to Silver City and visit the **Western New Mexico University Museum** (1000 West College Avenue; 505-538-6386).

■ THE LIGHTNING FIELD *map page 186, B-1*

In the middle of a high-desert sagebrush plain 30 miles northeast of Quemado, a grid of 400 stainless steel poles rises to the sky, looking like a giant bed of nails. The poles are spaced in rows 220 feet apart, covering an area that measures 1 mile by 1 kilometer. They stand between 15 and 26 feet high, so that if a giant piece of glass were placed atop them, it would lie flat. This precisely calculated art installa-tion, called *The Lightning Field,* is by Walter De Maria, an internationally known artist who spent five years searching for just the right spot.

No cattle roam this 3,400-acre plateau, which stands at an elevation of 7,200 feet; not many people, either. But between May and October, six guests at a time are permitted to visit, each paying a minimum of $110 ($135 in July and August) to spend the night in a homesteader's cabin on the land and share a hot meal.

Most important, they share the experience that De Maria envisioned when he conceived the field in the early 1970s. Considering the land itself a major part of the work, he looked for isolation, terrain as flat as possible, and high lightning activity, and combed remote areas of California, Nevada, Utah, Arizona, and Texas before deciding on this site 11.5 miles east of the Continental Divide. Completed in 1977, the project was commissioned and is maintained by the Dia Art Foundation, a New York–based nonprofit organization that promotes large-scale art projects.

The Lightning Field—400 poles of extraordinary landscape sculpture.

During thunderstorms, which occur most often in July and August, the poles become lightning rods and perform spectacular light shows. But most of the time the pointed steel shafts stand silent. That fits with De Maria's vision that the light be as important as the lightning. Early in the morning and at sunset, the poles are transformed into radiant rods as they reflect the soft rays of the sun. When the sun is overhead, they fade from sight.

Despite the esoteric nature of this installation, about 300 people visit it each year—making advance reservations a must. Their comments vary. Some claim it is a religious experience, others say it's an utter waste of time. *P.O. Box 2993, Corrales, NM 87048; 505-898-3335.*

S O U T H E A S T E R N
N E W   M E X I C O

Southeastern New Mexico seems to stretch on forever, the edges of its vast plains meeting spacious skies at a seemingly endless horizon. A few lofty mountain ranges interrupt the occasionally monotonous emptiness, across which figures both notable and notorious have sallied forth. The most famous of them, baby-faced outlaw Billy the Kid, roamed the region's piñon-covered hills, grama-grass plains, and heavily forested mountains, charming women and gunning down men until he himself was shot with his boots off. Later notables have included Smokey Bear, a tiny black bear cub who became the nation's symbol of the fight against forest fires; Peter Hurd, who captured on canvas the people, orchards, and fields of the pastoral Hondo Valley; and Norman Petty, who launched the careers of many rock-and-rollers in his Clovis music studio.

On the eastern plains, at the border, the state seems indistinguishable from its influential neighbor, though New Mexicans there bristle when their area is referred to as "Little Texas." Nevertheless, Texas-type, stretched-out terrain and the long lazy drawl that goes with it carry across the state line into the feedlots at Clovis and the oil wells at Hobbs. Sleek black pumps rhythmically bob up and down beside sheep and cattle who nonchalantly munch on grass. A strong wind sweeps across boundless fields of peanuts, white cotton bolls, tall corn stalks, and sweet-smelling onions. Between this high tableland and the mountains that rise grandly from the cactus plains, the Pecos River flows.

The cool pine-scented mountains of the Lincoln National Forest run the length of the region. From them rises solitary Sierra Blanca—the tallest peak in the Sacramento range, with an altitude of nearly 12,000 feet. At the southern end, the Carlsbad Caverns extend more than 800 feet below a cactus-covered ridge, an underground world of colossal limestone sculptures.

On the western fringes of the mountains, the Tularosa Basin—a vast expanse of harsh Chihuahuan desert—extends west to east from the rugged San Andres and Organ Mountains to the Sacramento Mountains. Within this flat-bottomed bowl is the world's largest surface deposit of fine gypsum granules, preserved in part as

Yucca is one of the few plants adapted to life in the gypsum dune field preserved as White Sands National Monument.

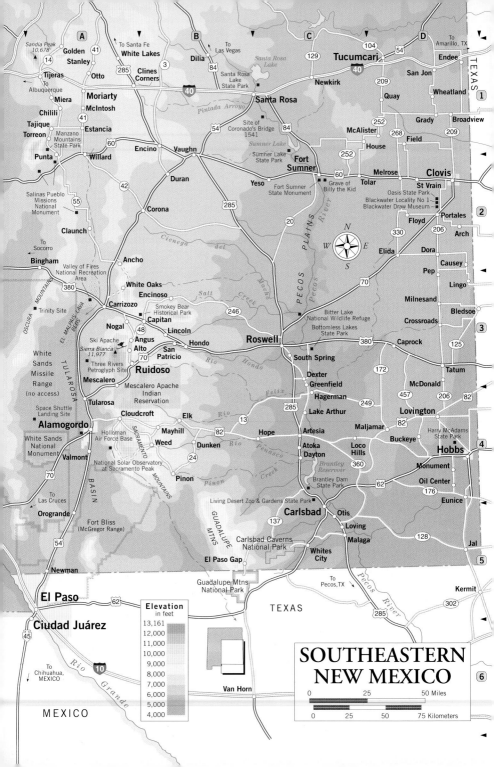

SOUTHEASTERN NEW MEXICO

Elevation
in feet

13,161
12,000
11,000
10,000
9,000
8,000
7,000
6,000
5,000
4,000

0   25   50 Miles

0   25   50   75 Kilometers

White Sands National Monument. These windswept dunes escaped the federal government's grasp in the 1940s when the military appropriated much of the surrounding range to develop weapons. The atomic bomb was first tested here, and today 2.7 million acres of this spiny cactus desert make up the top-secret defense installation of White Sands Missile Range.

■ HISTORY

Cool wetlands and forests covered much of southeastern New Mexico when the state's first inhabitants arrived from the north. By about 12,000 years ago, the Clovis culture was stalking now-extinct forms of antelope, dire wolves, and bison through the grasslands, eating the meat and crafting warm clothing from the hides.

Mescalero Apaches arrived sometime after A.D. 1200, hunting deer and bison and harvesting berries, roots, seeds, and cacti in the forests and on the plains west of the Pecos River and east of the Rio Grande. A favorite treat was mescal, the heart of the agave cactus, which they roasted and ate. Women wove agave fibers into baskets.

These roving Indians did not welcome the arrival of European settlers, and for more than 200 years they made the newcomers' lives miserable, raiding their food supplies and stealing cattle and sheep. Later, Comanche and Kiowa Indians came to the region and joined the Apaches in keeping the settlers on edge. During and after the Civil War, Brig. Gen. James Carlton was assigned to put a halt to the attacks. In 1862, his men rounded up 400 Mescalero Apaches and confined them at the Bosque Redondo Reservation, which had been carved out along the Pecos River. Two years later, Indian scout Kit Carson burned the fields and homes of Navajo Indians in eastern Arizona and western New Mexico, forcing their surrender. Gaunt and humbled, 8,500 Navajos then embarked on the "Long Walk," a forced march more than 300 miles long across cactus plains, rivers, and hardened lava flows to the reservation, where Fort Sumner had been built. There they lived unhappily alongside the Apaches, their traditional enemies.

Carlton later set out to make farmers of these nomadic tribesmen, but the plan was a fiasco from the start. Parasites ravaged the crops and alkaline water infected the Indians with dysentery. The general finally admitted defeat, and in 1868 the Navajos were given 3.5 million acres straddling the Arizona–New Mexico border (additional acquisitions increased their reservation to 17 million acres, the largest in the United States). In 1873, the Mescaleros received 460,177 acres of timbered slopes and pastures in the Sacramento Mountains, and a year later, the Comanches also made their peace with the military.

Once the free-roaming Indians were confined to reservations, more settlers arrived and established large sheep and cattle operations. In the late 1800s, the Santa Fe Railroad stretched across the region, passing through the Estancia Valley. Three more lines entered the state from the south. In the early 1900s, a steady stream of homesteaders settled on the eastern plains, farming 160-acre plots. In Roosevelt County, the population more than tripled between 1904 and 1910.

During World War II, the U.S. military established numerous Air Force bases across the creosote desert. In 1942, bases were opened at Clovis, Alamogordo, and Roswell—small towns widely separated, where new aircraft could be tested. (Only one, Walker Air Force Base at Roswell, is now closed.) As weapons became more sophisticated, federal officials sought a safe place to test new ones, and ranches in the Tularosa Basin were turned into White Sands Proving Ground. It was here, in 1945, that the world's first atomic bomb was detonated. Today, rockets regularly shoot skyward at what has become White Sands Missile Range, and sleek Stealth fighters swoop across the cholla and yucca-filled desert.

Tens of thousands of pounds of wool produced in the Roswell area went to market in 1909.

■ TULAROSA BASIN *map page 222, A-3/4/5*

This 100-mile desert valley flanked by two mountain ranges has been the home of Mogollon Indians, Spanish colonists, and railroad and ranch families. Today, much of the area is controlled by the military—at the top-secret White Sands Missile Range, Holloman Air Force Base, and McGregor Range.

■ WHITE SANDS *map page 222, A-3/4*

To make way for these extensive military installations, begun as weapons testing grounds during World War II, local ranchers patriotically agreed to relinquish their land. Initially, 150 families were displaced, and more followed as additional land was condemned to expand the installations.

One place that escaped the military development was a span of glimmering white desert dunes created by erosion of the Permian rocks of the San Andres Mountains. **White Sands National Monument** spreads across 230 square miles of windswept dunes; its grains may look like ocean sand, but are actually fine granules of gypsum rather than silica. Only half of these rolling hills, which reach heights of 50 feet, are included in the monument, which is surrounded on the north, west, and south by the White Sands Missile Range (Holloman Air Force Base is to the east). The sweet fresh smell of gypsum permeates the air, and the fine-grained sand swirls about picnic shelters; the undulating expanse of white is interrupted only by an occasional yucca cactus shooting skyward. On and around the dunes, animal species have adapted to blend in protectively with the gypsum: there are white mice, white lizards, and light-colored insects. This soft, silent, ghostly world of grit seems like an oasis in the surrounding harsh desert. When the moon is full, the glistening sands reflect an eerie glow into the night, and the effect is quite unearthly. Guided walks take place daily from Memorial Day to Labor Day; during that period, the dunes are open until 11 P.M. on full-moon nights. *White Sands National Monument Headquarters, 15 miles southwest of Alamogordo on U.S. 70; 505-479-6124.*

The huge **White Sands Missile Range** is off-limits to the public, but U.S. 70, a major highway, runs through it, connecting Alamogordo and Las Cruces. From time to time, travelers on this road are stopped at one of the regular roadblocks erected during missile firings. In 1982, one group of bystanders witnessed the graceful landing of the Space Shuttle *Columbia,* when bad weather prevented it from landing in California and it descended onto the range's hard-packed sand at Northrop Strip.

But very few people were on hand in the early morning hours of July 16, 1945, when the first atomic bomb exploded near the upper edge of this sparsely populated rangeland, just west of the Oscura Mountains. The explosion, equal to 18,600 tons of TNT, created a blinding flash of light, vaporized the soil beneath it, and sent a billowing cloud 40,000 feet skyward. A shock wave shattered windows in Silver City, 120 miles away, and early-rising Albuquerque residents noticed a flash on the southern horizon and felt the shock waves. The massive nuclear explosion left a crater 400 yards in diameter and 8 feet deep, and intense heat fused sand in the crater into a glasslike substance the color of jade. This material was called Trinitite after Trinity, the top-secret site's code name. Until 1953, **Trinity Site** was off-limits due to dangerously high levels of radiation left behind by the blast. A lava-rock obelisk now stands at the site, which is open to visitors two days a year: the first Saturdays of April and October. *Take Exit 139 on I-25 (U.S. 380 to San Antonio). After 12 miles, you'll come upon the Stallion Gate entrance to White Sands Missile Range; 505-437-6120 or 800-826-0294.*

On the opposite side of the Oscura Mountains, another spectacular eruption that preceded the atomic bomb by nearly a millennium left behind a 44-mile-long lava flow that in some places is 5 miles wide and 70 feet deep. Indian legends tell of a volcanic eruption that caused a valley of fire 5 miles west of present-day Carrizozo. Because the cracked black rock carpet isn't much good as rangeland or farmland, the state made it into a state park and called it, appropriately, **Valley of Fires.** Remarkably, cholla, sotol, prickly pear, and gray-green saltbush sprout from between the dark rocks. *Valley of Fires National Recreation Area, U.S. 380 west of Carrizozo; 505-648-2241.*

■ **ALAMOGORDO AND VICINITY** *map page 222, A-4*
In 1897, Charles Eddy, a rancher who became a major railroad developer, received financing to construct the El Paso and Northeastern Railroad, which was to run from El Paso to Tucumcari, passing along the edge of the Sacramento Mountains. Within a year, he had purchased Alamo Ranch from cattleman Oliver Lee, and put it to use as a division point on the rail line; it later grew into the town of Alamogordo (which means "fat cottonwood"). For years, the settlement was a trading center for ranchers, farmers, and the lumber industry.

(opposite) A peace protest at ground zero, Trinity Site. (following pages) Walking at sunset in White Sands National Monument.

But it wasn't until World War II brought the bomb to cattle country that the town began to establish its modern-day identity as a major military training and testing center. Nearby, missiles are launched and space-shuttle payload experiments are conducted at White Sands Missile Range; just outside of town, pilots learn to fly Stealth jets at Holloman Air Force Base.

In 1954, Col. John Stapp, a Holloman flight surgeon, became the fastest man in the world when he tested a rocket sled that blasted across the desert at 632 mph. Strapped into the one-ton contraption, which was powered by nine rockets with a total thrust of 40,000 pounds, Stapp suffered two black eyes, burns from the straps, and bruises from bits of sand that whipped past his body.

The sled today is on display at the **New Mexico Museum of Space History**, a complex that includes the **International Space Hall of Fame**, a five-story mirrored gold cube set against the foothills of the Sacramento Mountains. Inside the

A flying object at the New Mexico Museum of Space History.

cube (built at a cost of $2 million), visitors can try their hand at the controls of Space Station 2001, learn how an RL-10 rocket engine works, or envision themselves behind the controls of the lunar rover, gathering moon rocks. Also part of the museum is the **Tombaugh IMAX Dome Theater and Planetarium**, named after astronomer Clyde W. Tombaugh, who discovered the planet Pluto in 1930. Regularly changing films are shown on a four-story wraparound screen that gives you the feeling you're an astronaut on a space shuttle mission or a member of the historic Lewis and Clark expedition. At times when movies aren't being screened, a special projector re-creates views of the heavens from any vantage point on Earth on any night of the year. The **John P. Stapp Air and Space Park** holds a Nike Ajax missile, an X-7A test vehicle, and other missiles and rockets. *At the end of NM 2001, Alamogordo; 505-437-2840 or 877-333-6589.*

Lest you lose your head in the clouds of progress, the annual **Rattlesnake Round-up** in April will remind you to watch where you walk. Local wranglers trap up to 1,500 rattlers, mostly western diamondbacks, from the nearby desert to be sold for meat to a Colorado restaurant. But before they are turned into dinner, wallets, and boots, the snakes are displayed at the gathering. One year, a teenager willingly crawled into a sleeping bag with about 50 rattlers and lived to tell the tale.

About 10 miles south of Alamogordo, just before the mountains give way once and for all to dry, cracked, cactus-covered earth, is **Oliver Lee Memorial State Park**, a 180-acre oasis tucked away in Dog Canyon, at the base of the Sacramento Mountains. Apaches lived here long ago, enjoying the seeps and springs of the lush canyon and the protection of its steep rock walls. They also lured soldiers up the dead-end gully to ambush them. *505-437-8284.*

South of the park the desert sprawls out and once again becomes the property of the U.S. government. McGregor Range, yet another missile testing ground, stretches across 1.1 million acres to Fort Bliss, an army base in El Paso, Texas. Like its neighbor White Sands, the McGregor Range displaced about 200 ranchers when it was created in 1954—but one crusty character for years resisted attempts by the government, both peaceful and otherwise, to remove him from his home. "I am not afraid of missiles," said 82-year-old John Prather. "I've raised mules all my life." By 1957, the Army admitted defeat and permitted the stubborn rancher to live out his life at his home in the middle of the missile range. He was buried there in 1965. Prather's principles inspired Edward Abbey's 1962 novel, *Fire on the Mountain.*

A Form of Paradise

We were riding north from El Paso in my grandfather's pickup truck, bound for the village of Baker and the old man's ranch. This was in early June: the glare of the desert sun, glancing off the steel hood of the truck, stung my eyes with such intensity that I had to close them now and then for relief. . . .

When my eyes stopped aching I could open them again, raise my head and watch the highway and fence and telephone line, all geometrically straight and parallel, rolling forever toward us. Heat waves shimmered over the asphalt, giving the road far ahead a transparent, liquid look, an illusion which receded before us as fast as we approached.

Staring ahead, I saw a vulture rise from the flattened carcass of a rabbit on the pavement and hover nearby while we passed over his lunch. Beyond the black bird with his white-trimmed wings soared the western sky, the immense and violet sky flowing over alkali flats and dunes of sand and gypsum toward the mountains that stood like chains of islands, like a convoy of purple ships, along the horizon.

Those mountains—they seemed at once both close by and impossibly remote, an easy walk away and yet beyond the limits of the imagination. Between us lay the clear and empty wilderness of scattered mesquite trees and creosote shrubs and streambeds where water ran as seldom as the rain came down. Each summer for three years I had come to New Mexico; each time I gazed upon the moon-dead landscape and asked myself: what is out there? And each time I concluded: something is out there—maybe everything. To me the desert looked like a form of Paradise. And it always will.

—Edward Abbey, *Fire on the Mountain*, 1962

■ CLOUDCROFT *map page 222, A-4*

Cloudcroft was founded after the El Paso and Northeastern Railroad Company ran out of timber for cross ties during construction of a rail route connecting El Paso with Tucumcari. The only logical solution to the problem was to build a spur into the Sacramento Mountains, where wood was plentiful. Because of its steep, winding route, which rose 6,000 feet in a distance of 27 miles, this branch line, the Alamogordo and Sacramento Mountain Railway, became known as the Cloud Climbing Railroad. Completed in 1900, it was in operation until the late 1940s, when it hauled its last load of timber down the track.

But timber was not the only payload. There were also passengers. In 1899, a Victorian log retreat was constructed at the 9,200-foot mountaintop. It burned down in 1909 and was replaced in 1911 by **The Lodge,** a spectacular inn built of stucco in a Renaissance Revival style. The Lodge attracted the celebrated likes of Pancho Villa, Clark Gable, and Judy Garland; today, visitors seeking relief from sizzling El Paso summers can treat themselves to a first-class experience in the cool of this year-round resort, which has one of the highest golf courses in the world. The fairways are well-maintained and the setting is bucolic—although occasionally a bear will lope across a green just as you are trying to concentrate on your stroke. Inside, guests can belly up to a massive bullet-ridden mahogany bar that was shipped to Cloudcroft from one of Al Capone's haunts in Cicero, Illinois. The inn's restaurant is named after a resident ghost—redheaded Rebecca, a flirtatious chambermaid who was killed by a jealous lover in the 1930s. Borrow the brass skeleton key from the desk and climb a stairway to the copper-domed observatory for a panoramic view of shimmering White Sands National Monument. At night, the four-story tower, where guests once watched for approaching trains, is a great place to gaze at a dark sky brilliant with stars. *800-395-6343.*

On the subject of stargazing, the **National Solar Observatory at Sacramento Peak,** one of the world's largest such observatories, is in Sunspot, about 18 miles south of Cloudcroft. The observatory's sophisticated telescopes, one of which rises 13 stories, enable scientists to study the sun's gaseous outer envelope and sunspots. (Down the road from the observatory, amateur astronomer Alan Hale first caught a glimpse of what became one of the most-watched celestial shows of the 20th century, Comet Hale-Bopp.) Check out the armillary sphere and sundial at the visitors center. The observatory is open to the public year-round during the daytime; in the summer, guided tours are offered on weekends. *On NM 6563, 18 miles south of Cloudcroft; 505-434-7000.*

The friendly, rustic village of Cloudcroft caters to tourists. In the summer, something is going on nearly every weekend, from arts and crafts fairs to music festivals. But the natural beauty of 215,000 acres of the Lincoln National Forest—with the fresh smell of tall pines, a profound quiet, and spectacular views of the white swath of gypsum sands laid out below in the Tularosa Basin—is enough to make a visit worthwhile.

Southeast of Cloudcroft, the national forest continues along a ribbon of mountains that eventually provides Texas with Guadalupe Peak, its highest at an altitude of 8,749 feet. In New Mexico, the rugged Guadalupe Mountains also provide relief from an otherwise monotonous horizon, most dramatically at the 80-foot-high Sitting Bull Falls, west of Carlsbad. Across the border in Texas, the mountains are part of Guadalupe Mountains National Park, which includes desert lowlands, lush canyons, and forested hillsides.

■ **TULAROSA** *map page 222, A-4*
A welcome break in the dry basin is found at Tularosa, a peaceful, tree-shaded hamlet of simple well-tended adobe homes, some of which date from 1863. In that year, about a hundred Hispanic farming families from the Mesilla Valley, which had been washed out by floods along the Rio Grande, decided to move north to the Rio Tularosa. Buildings on many of the town's original 49 blocks have been restored or are undergoing renovation, and reveal finely crafted ornate facades, intricate wood carving, and pressed-tin trim. There is a calming ambiance to Tularosa, which, like Carrizozo to the north, took its name from a reed—a reddish one that grows on the banks of the Rio Tularosa. Irrigation ditches that were dug when the village was settled continue to carry water to tall cottonwoods and orchards of pecan, apple, quince, peach, and cherry trees.

Tularosa, however, is best known as the "City of Roses." Here people take their rosebushes seriously, and they certainly have their opinions—about when and how to prune, what fertilizer is best, which blooms are most beautiful, and which are most fragrant. During the first weekend of May, as red, pink, yellow, and white roses bloom throughout town, Tularosa residents celebrate the annual Rose Festival. A queen is crowned and rides in state, surrounded by the thorny blooms, in the Rose Festival parade.

Off U.S. 54 in Three Rivers Canyon is the **Three Rivers Petroglyph Site**, where more than 21,000 carvings have been preserved on an assortment of rock outcroppings along a ridge overlooking the Tularosa Basin. A 1,400-yard winding path leads past etchings of stylized bighorn sheep, lizards, birds, and trees, along with handprints, sunbursts, and a variety of geometric designs. Archaeologists have determined that the Jornada branch of the Mogollon culture deserves credit for the artwork. The artists, possibly sitting at this site while serving as lookouts, lived in several villages along the Three Rivers drainage about 1,100 years ago. By 1400, the culture had moved north, probably because of drought. One of these abandoned villages has been partially excavated and reconstructed. *505-525-4300.*

■ **CARRIZOZO** *map page 222, A-3*

At the intersection of U.S. 380 and U.S. 54 is the friendly community of Carrizozo. Folks here can be thankful that land prices in the nearby gold-mining boomtown of White Oaks were running high in 1899, when the El Paso and Northeastern Railroad was deciding on the location of its terminus. Because land was less expensive at this tree-shaded spot at the base of the Sacramento Mountains, the terminus was built here, and Carrizozo grew up beside it. A reed native to the surrounding plain and nearby foothills, *carrizo*, provided the town with a name. (Legend has it that a ranch foreman embellished the name with an extra "zo"—a misspelling of the Spanish suffix *so,* which indicates abundance.) Carrizozo prospered, while its erstwhile competitor, White Oaks, which produced about $3.1 million in gold between 1879 and 1940, is now a ghost town.

As the popularity of rail travel diminished, so did the economic life of Carrizozo, but it carries on as the seat of Lincoln County. Residents have opened up a few gift shops in hopes that tourists heading up to the mountains will stop to enjoy the peaceful pace of their little town.

■ **SMOKEY BEAR** *map page 222, A/B-3*

Farther east on U.S. 380 is Capitan, a village that didn't used to have much to brag about, especially after a devastating forest fire destroyed 17,000 acres in the Capitan Mountains in 1950. But in the blaze's smoldering aftermath, firefighters discovered a badly singed black bear cub clinging to the side of a charred pine tree. The frightened cub was named "Hotfoot," because of his severely burned feet, and was treated at the nearby Flatley Ranch, after which game warden Ray Bell flew him to a veterinary hospital in Santa Fe. Hotfoot soon was renamed Smokey, and Bell later kept the cub in his home, where he ran roughshod over the family's other household pets. Once healed, Smokey was flown to Washington, D.C., where he lived out his life at the National Zoo.

For the U.S. Forest Service, which had invented the character of "Smokey Bear" ("Only *you* can prevent forest fires!") six years earlier, the rescued bear cub proved to be one good thing to come of the Capitan fire: a real-life bear now brought life to the fire-prevention campaign. When Smokey died in 1976, he was replaced by Smokey II, also from the Capitan Mountains. Capitan's townsfolk have created the **Smokey Bear Museum** (102 Smokey Bear Boulevard; 505-354-2298), a log structure housing scrapbooks documenting Smokey's discovery and subsequent

The original Smokey Bear, a cub found after a forest fire.

celebrity. Films of the famous bear are shown at the nearby **Smokey Bear Historical Park** (118 Smokey Bear Boulevard; 505-354-2748), where a trail leads to Smokey's grave. Down the street there's the Smokey Bear Motel, which houses the Smokey Bear Restaurant, which dishes up the Smokey Bear Burger.

■ **RUIDOSO** *map page 222, A-3*
Ruidoso is a popular destination for Texans hoping to cool off in the hot summer months or to ski the Sierra Blanca slopes in the winter. Originally named Dowlin's Mill, for Capt. Paul Dowlin of the New Mexico Volunteers, a Union regiment, the town's name was changed in 1885 to Ruidoso, which means "noisy," for the babbling river that runs through it. Dowlin's mill still stands and is a favorite tourist stop, housing a gift and bookshop. The mill itself, still operational, grinds flour and cornmeal for sale.

By the turn of the century, cabins had cozied up to the banks of the Rio Ruidoso, concealed among the tall pines of the White Mountains. The town had become, and continues to be, a summer resort for flatlanders seeking relief from the sweltering heat of southern New Mexico and West Texas. You can fish for trout in nearby streams, hike mountain trails, and savor the pine-scented air—and when not browsing in the tourist shops that line the main street, you can amble down the road to the racetrack at **Ruidoso Downs** and raise your blood pressure betting on the quarter horses. Every Labor Day, these horses compete for $2 million in the **All American Futurity,** the world's richest quarter-horse race. The **Hubbard Museum of the West** houses a Pony Express saddle, carriages, and wagons, and the 10,000-piece collection of horse-related items assembled by Anne Stradling, who began collecting at the age of seven. *841 NM 70 West, in Ruidoso Downs; 505-378-4142.*

In 1997, the $22 million **Spencer Theater for the Performing Arts** in nearby Alto began hosting a year-round program of world-class traveling productions, from musical concerts to plays. The intimate 514-seat hall, with a crystal lobby that juts from the building like a cut diamond, was designed by Antoine Predock, one of New Mexico's premier architects, and it displays a blown-glass installation by Dale Chihuly. *Airport Highway 220, Alto; 505-336-4800 or 888-818-7872.*

■ MESCALERO APACHES *map page 222, A/B-3/4*
Next to Ruidoso is the **Mescalero Apache Indian Reservation.** The Mescaleros didn't take well to their incarceration at Bosque Redondo in 1862, but they have adjusted quite well to the tenets of capitalism, becoming one of the most financially successful tribes in the country. In addition to running a timber operation and a fish hatchery that supplies trout to a number of pueblo lakes, the Mescaleros operate **Ski Apache** on the flanks of the nearly 12,000-foot Sierra Blanca. With a vertical drop of 1,800 feet, the resort has eight chairlifts and the state's only gondola to whisk skiers up the mountain.

The tribe's flagship enterprise, **Inn of the Mountain Gods**, sits in the shadow of the massive peak, alongside Lake Mescalero. The inn, along with the adjacent **Casino Apache**, will take on an even swankier appearance following an extensive renovation in 2004. Golf, tennis, and horseback riding programs are available. *505-464-5141 or 800-545-9011.*

Back up on U.S. 380 is **Fort Stanton**, built in 1855 to protect settlers from the Mescaleros. By 1896, the fort had been decommissioned, and two years later it was turned into a U.S. Marine Hospital for tuberculosis patients. From 1966 to 1995, the whitewashed buildings served as a state-run school for the mentally disabled. Most recently, a few buildings have been used as a probation and substance-abuse rehabilitation facility for parolees.

■ LINCOLN *map page 222, B-3*

Along the Rio Bonito, in a narrow valley at the edge of the Capitan Mountains, is the town of Lincoln, settled in 1849 by a small group of Hispanic farmers. Mescalero Apaches chased them out three times, but the feisty settlers kept returning. The village was known as Las Placitas del Rio Bonito until 1869, when the townsfolk renamed it after Abraham Lincoln.

Prime cattle country surrounded the town, and it became an important ranching center. As Lincoln prospered, more people wanted a piece of the business it generated, and they were willing to fight for it. One struggle escalated into a notorious period of violence, the Lincoln County War, which began in 1878.

The conflict started when Alexander McSween and John Tunstall opened a mercantile store to compete with an already established shopkeeper, Lawrence Murphy. Murphy, who didn't much appreciate the spirit of competition, attempted to crush the two by filing a lawsuit against McSween pertaining to a previous matter involving insurance. A month after a guilty verdict was handed down, Tunstall, McSween's financial backer, was shot to death on the road to his ranch. The same gunmen who killed Tunstall then were deputized by Sheriff William Brady and sent to search for his killers, whom they obviously had no intention of finding.

Meanwhile, Tunstall's friends, some of whom had witnessed his murder and were outraged by the lack of justice, formed a faction called "the Regulators" to avenge his death. It wasn't long before they managed to shoot and kill Sheriff Brady and three of Tunstall's murderers. Pretty soon, everyone in town had taken sides: you were either a McSween man or a Murphy man. More gunfights followed, culminating in the Five-Day Battle of July 1878. As McSween's men holed up inside his home, one of Murphy's supporters set the house on fire. McSween was killed while trying to surrender. After his death, the Regulators fled town, but they rode around the countryside terrorizing Murphy loyalists for several more years.

One of the McSween men who was inside the house at the time it was torched, but managed to escape, was an affable, wavy-haired 19-year-old ranch hand named William Bonney. Reckless of spirit and quick with a gun, Bonney was nicknamed Billy—Billy the Kid.

Today, the tree-shaded street that cuts through Lincoln is much like it was when Billy knew it more than a hundred years ago. The biggest change is that it has been paved and displays a sign that reads U.S. 380. The entire town has been preserved

Apache dancers.

as **Lincoln State Monument** and is listed on the National Historic Register. A walking tour takes you past and through impeccably restored buildings, including the Tunstall Store, the two-story Lincoln County Courthouse (which earlier had served as the Murphy mercantile), San Juan Church, and several private homes. People do live here, but there are no schools or shops, other than a few catering to tourists. *505-653-4372 or 800-434-6320.*

The Wortley Hotel, which burned down in 1936, has been rebuilt on its original foundation. Open from May to mid-October, it has been renamed the **Pat Garrett Wortley Hotel**, and it's still known for its home cooking. It's a rare evening's entertainment that surpasses sitting in a rocking chair on the Wortley's front porch, watching the waning sunlight on nearby hillsides and listening to the nighttime quiet fall upon the town. *505-653-4300 or 877-977-8539.*

Tunstall Store in Lincoln figured in the controversy that set off the Lincoln County War.

Once a year, residents honor Billy the Kid in a folk pageant that dramatizes his last escape from the Lincoln County Courthouse. The pageant is the highlight of **Old Lincoln Days,** an event that is usually held the first weekend of August and also includes a fiddler's contest, arts and crafts fair, and a 42-mile Pony Express race that begins at the ghost town of White Oaks and ends at Lincoln. *800-263-5929.*

East of Lincoln in the **Hondo Valley,** the Rio Bonito joins the Rio Ruidoso to become the Rio Hondo. In this narrow, fertile valley, the tiny communities of San Patricio, Hondo, Tinnie, and Picacho are tucked away among corn and bean fields, as well as cherry and apple orchards. Polo is a popular pastime.

The well-known landscape painter and portraitist Peter Hurd, born in Roswell in 1904, lived with his wife, Henriette Wyeth, also a painter (of the Pennsylvania family of artists), in an adobe hacienda alongside the murmuring Rio Hondo. Their work reflects their pastoral surroundings, capturing the simple rural life in stylized landscapes and portraits of the valley's residents. Some of their paintings are on view at the **Hurd LaRinconada Gallery** located on the family ranch. You can spend a few days at the ranch, enjoying the valley's tranquility at one of a handful of designer guest houses—former ranch-hand quarters that have been tastefully refurbished. *U.S. 70 in San Patricio; 505-653-4218 or 800-658-6912.*

■ PECOS RIVER VALLEY

The Pecos River Valley was once a favorite stopover for Texas cattlemen driving their livestock north on the Goodnight-Loving Trail. Here, at the confluence of the Rio Hondo and Pecos River, there was plenty of grama grass and water enough for a thousand head. One of these Texans, John Chisum, who had blazed a trail from Paris, Texas, across the dusty reaches of North Texas into southeastern New Mexico and then up along the Pecos to Fort Sumner, liked the area so much that he built a ranch 6 miles south of present-day Roswell. His route came to be known as the Chisum Trail (not to be confused with the Chisholm Trail, another cattle route that ran between Wichita, Kansas, and the Red River in Texas).

■ ROSWELL *map page 222, C-3*

During the 1860s, a primitive trading post was established in the valley, and in 1869, a professional gambler by the name of Van Smith bought an interest in a rustic adobe hotel nearby. Before long, a town was in the making; Van Smith decided to name it after his father, Roswell. The accidental discovery in 1891 of an

The UFO Museum outside (above) and in (opposite): Was the "disk" that fell in July 1947 a weather balloon or a flying saucer? Whichever, rancher Mac Brazel found some unusual debris.

artesian water source outside town spurred irrigation efforts, which resulted in large crops of cotton, alfalfa, apples, corn, and pecans. Soon after the water was discovered, the **New Mexico Military Institute**, a combination high school and junior college, was established. In the 1930s, humorist Will Rogers paid a visit to the growing town and called it "the prettiest little town in the West."

Tree-lined Roswell has become surprisingly sophisticated, while still serving as a major shipping and trading center for ranchers. An extensive collection of the works of Peter Hurd and Henriette Wyeth hangs in the **Roswell Museum and Art Center**, whose eclectic collection also includes paintings by Georgia O'Keeffe, Marsden Hartley, and Stuart Davis. Not content with art alone, the museum also has re-created the workshop of Dr. Robert Goddard, the rocket pioneer who spent 11 years in Roswell perfecting his liquid propulsion system and who, almost single-handedly, advanced the science of rocketry through experiments conducted in a rancher's field. *11th and Main Streets; 505-624-6744.*

In recent years, Roswell has gained international status for the role it has played (or, for skeptics, has *not* played) in UFO history. The **International UFO Museum and Research Center** in Roswell is dedicated to UFO phenomena, in particular a mysterious 1947 crash on a ranch northwest of Roswell. Early reports of the crash,

known as the Roswell Incident, told of a spaceship and three alien bodies. Military personnel quickly stepped in to describe the wreckage as a crashed weather balloon with no passengers. *114 North Main; 505-625-9495 or 800-822-3545.*

The **Roswell UFO Festival,** held in early July, commemorates the crash and attracts earthly aliens from around the globe. Visitors can participate in Alien Rock and Bowl at the local bowling lanes, attend the UFO Electric Light Parade, buy out-of-this-world gewgaws, and discuss the latest UFO theories.

On the town's outskirts, supernatural pursuits give way to natural attractions. Sailboats and windsurfers share the cool azure waters at **Bottomless Lakes State Park** (505-624-6058); and Canada geese, sandhill cranes, ducks, and herons rest their wings at **Bitter Lake National Wildlife Refuge** (505-622-6755).

■ ARTESIA AND VICINITY *map page 222, C-4*

Eight miles north of Artesia, in a cotton belt unimpressive for its natural beauty, is the hamlet of Lake Arthur. The town enjoyed a moment of fame in 1977, when an image of Jesus Christ appeared on a flour tortilla made by Maria Rubio as she was preparing burritos for her husband's lunch. The tortilla has never been eaten. Instead, it is now honored inside a shrine in the Rubio backyard, and visitors come from all over to view the miracle.

Heading south, the smell of petroleum will probably hit your nostrils—an unmistakable indication you have arrived at Artesia, a small town most noted for its rich underground oil and natural gas reserves. The odor comes from the Navajo Refining Company, the town's largest employer. Black pump jacks line the level horizon, and mesmerizing oil-well rockers gently sway back and forth. Natural gas wells are marked by intricate arrangements of pipes, valves, and gauges called "Christmas trees." Residents say if you live here long enough, it gets so you don't even smell the oil.

■ CARLSBAD CAVERNS NATIONAL PARK *map page 222, C-5*

One of the largest cave systems in the world, Carlsbad Caverns comprises a 3-mile maze of rooms the size of concert halls, whose floors and ceilings are blanketed with house-size stalagmites and stalactites. Filling these massive vaults are grandiose formations laced with delicate tracery. A paved path descends through a black opening in a limestone ridge into the eerily lit bowels of the earth, leading you past dripping, pale-green limestone walls and into rooms that seem as extraterrestrial as anything talked about in Roswell. The names of the most spectacular formations reflect the lifelike shapes millions of years of limestone deposits have created: Whale's Mouth, King's Palace, Hall of Giants, Queen's Chamber Draperies. The Big Room, aptly if unimaginatively named for an expanse that could hold 14 Astrodomes, makes you feel as insignificant as an ant on a sidewalk. Its ceiling curves 256 feet above the floor. The temperature of 56 degrees F never varies.

The sound of slowly dripping water is never far away. Neither are the thousands of Mexican free-tail bats that spend their days clinging to the moist ceiling of the caves. Fortunately for visitors, the 300,000-member colony bunches together in an area away from the tour route. Between May and November, a thick black cloud of them swirls up from the subterranean cool every evening at dusk at a rate of 5,000 to 10,000 a minute. Then they're off to a summer's night of feasting on flying insects.

The concealed caves went unnoticed until 1901, when a young cowboy, James White, spotted what looked like a cloud of smoke spiraling upward near the foothills of the Guadalupe Mountains. The cloud turned out to be the bats heading off for the night. Using a rope ladder, White descended into the damp caverns and saw for the first time what thousands of people now see each year. By 1930 his discovery had become a national park.

If you're yearning for an adventure similar to White's, you can visit **Slaughter Canyon Cave,** which is away from the main caverns and open for guided flashlight tours. While you don't need a rope ladder, sturdy shoes and endurance are required to hike the strenuous 1-mile trail uphill to the cave's entrance, where you can imagine you are the first person to enter the dark interior. Flashlight beams illuminate spectacular mystical sculptures, including the Christmas tree stalagmite draped in smooth limestone deposits, one of the cave's highlights.

Each August, Carlsbad hosts its annual **Bat Flight Breakfast**, during which visitors eat scrambled eggs and sausage just as thousands of the world's only flying mammal, satiated after a night of hunting, swoop into their daytime haven of darkness. *Visitors Center is off U.S. 62/180, 7 miles up an entrance road from the park gate at White's City. A separate entrance farther south leads to Slaughter Canyon Cave. For information: 505-785-2232. For tour reservations: 800-967-2283.*

At the northwest end of town, the **Living Desert Zoo and Gardens State Park,** a preserve for plants and animals native to the Chihuahuan Desert, is a great alternative for people who prefer not to set foot inside a dank, dark cave. The preserve

is laid out among prickly pear, yucca, cholla, sotol, and agave cactus plants in the Ocotillo Hills overlooking Carlsbad. Here caged mountain lions pace back and forth among boulders; Mexican hawks perch atop branches; rattlesnakes slither across the dry soil; and badgers and prairie dogs burrow below the surface. All of these animals have been brought to the park because of injuries or illness. If their injuries are too extensive, they become permanent residents; otherwise, they are treated and returned to the wild. A self-guided trail leads past the animals' homes among gypsum hills, dusty arroyos, sand dunes, and pine trees.

Each year, for four days in May, park personnel re-create a Mescalero Apache tradition: a **Mescal Roast,** at which the heart of a flowering agave (or century plant) is cooked in a special midden ring at the park and served to visitors. The taste is close to that of a sweet potato, but with a smoky molasses flavor. *Off U.S. 285; 505-887-5516.*

Littering the landscape south of town are salt beds, mined for their salt, which produces potash, an ingredient of fertilizer. At one site 25 miles southeast of Carlsbad, however, what goes into the underground chambers is far more important than what comes out. This is the Waste Isolation Pilot Plant (WIPP), a $1 billion federal facility built to house low-level nuclear waste generated by government nuclear weapons operations. Opened in 1999, WIPP was the world's first permanent repository for such wastes.

■ LLANO ESTACADO

It's been said that land doesn't get much flatter than New Mexico's eastern flank, and that's a fact. The Llano Estacado, or "Staked Plain," is an extension of the Great Plains, which stretch from Canada into Texas. In New Mexico, the grassland received its name for one of four reasons—nobody's too sure which one. It could be the multitude of tall yucca plants that sprout up from the high plateau, or the stakes early Spanish explorers pounded into the ground to tie up their horses. It could also refer to the stakes that had to be driven into the ground to give travelers a sense of direction as they traversed the vast expanse. Finally, there is the suggestion that because the literal translation of *llano estacado* is "stockaded plain," early Spanish explorers were referring to protruding mesas that rise at the northwestern edge of the plains, which they thought resembled stockades. Take your pick.

Carlsbad Caverns is the largest cave complex in the United States.

DREAMWORLD DOWN UNDER

It's useless to describe the Carlsbad Caverns. They aren't just caves; they are another world. You feel like one of Walt Disney's symphony children wandering in a dream world of unbelievable, impossible beauty. . . . You come out from a narrow passage into a big room about a hundred fifty feet across, where millions of stalactites hang from the ceiling and stalagmites rear up from the floor. This is the Fairyland, the spot that only a fool would try to describe. From here on, it is beyond imagination—a world that surely can be nothing on or of this earth.

—Ernie Pyle, *Home Country*, 1935

■ HOBBS *map page 222, D-4*

A chance meeting between two covered wagons in 1907 resulted in the settlement of Hobbs. When eastbound settler James Hobbs learned from the oncoming party of the hardships ahead at his destination of Alpine, Texas, he backtracked and put down roots just inside what today is the New Mexico border. The area is full of desert grasses, mesquite, and jackrabbits, and proved suitable for raising cattle and growing cotton. In 1928, discovery of a major oil reserve brought an onslaught of fortune hunters, and the scrubland was transformed overnight into a raucous shanty town of crude shacks, metal buildings, and tents. Spacious taverns sprang up, serving as roller-skating rinks by day and dance halls by night. The town continues as a center for the oil industry, but it has calmed down into a peaceful family community that takes pride in its two colleges.

Ranches still endure among the desert scrub; the **Lea County Cowboy Hall of Fame and Western Heritage Center** at New Mexico Junior College reflects the history of the area. In addition to artifacts, from cookware to buggies, memorabilia of those inducted into the hall of fame are on display. *NM 18; 505-392-5518.*

Because of its light winds and clear days, Hobbs attracts sailplane pilots, who glide their lightweight aircraft through the area's spacious skies. In 1983, the World Soaring Championships were held here, which spurred the creation of the Hobbs Soaring Society. Nowadays, the **Soaring Society of America** (505-392-1177) makes its home here.

■ **CLOVIS AND ENVIRONS** *map page 222, D-2*

Although in modern times the area around Clovis remained unsettled until the 1880s, prehistoric hunters roamed the region 11,000 years ago. One of their more successful hunting spots was a large pond fed by the headwaters of the Brazos River, near present-day Portales. Archaeologists believe that woolly mammoths, saber-toothed tigers, camels, and bison used the pond as a watering hole, thus providing hunters with a perfect place to trap and butcher them. Evidence of these events came to light in 1932, when a highway worker discovered spearheads and mammoth bones that had been uncovered by gusty winds that whipped across the plains during the years of the Great Drought. The pond had dried up, leaving behind a gravel pit that proved to be rich in ancient artifacts intermingled with fossils. Modern-day man named it Blackwater Draw, and the prehistoric hunter was called Clovis, after the nearby town. Today, you can take a self-guided tour along the dried-up lakebed and gravel quarries at **Blackwater Locality No. 1** (NM 467, 8 miles north of Portales; 505-356-5235), where the artifacts were found and where archaeological research is ongoing. Many of the discoveries found at the site are on display nearby at the **Blackwater Draw Museum** (U.S. 70, 7 miles northeast of Portales; 505-562-2202).

It was another watering hole that attracted early European immigrants—Portales Springs, a series of cave openings through which gushed streams of fresh water. Spanish explorers thought the caves resembled *portales,* the porches of Spanish adobe homes.

The first settler in Portales was Doak Good, a cattleman looking for a place to call his own in 1880—but it took the railroad to bring people, as well as some definition, to this endless horizon. In the early 1900s, the town of Portales was established as a construction camp for workers on the Pecos Valley and Northern Railroad. It was followed by its close neighbor to the north, Clovis, which until 1907 was known as Riley's Switch on the Santa Fe line. When rail officials chose the site as a division point for the Belen cutoff, they decided to make it a proper town. A daughter of a Santa Fe Railroad official was given the honor of finding a name. She had been studying French history at the time and was taken by Clovis, King of the Franks, who converted to Christianity in 486.

The railroad helped populate the area, and the discovery years later of the massive Ogallala aquifer turned the region into one of the state's premier agricultural belts. This underground source of water transformed the sweeping grasslands into vast fields of alfalfa, cotton, corn, wheat, and potatoes. In Clovis, cattle are fattened at some of the largest feedlots in the Southwest; these healthy bovines are sold at weekly livestock auctions to the highest bidder.

Clovis residents like to kick up their heels to the twang of country and western music, but back in the 1950s, one lonely musician took a detour from that genre. Norman Petty built a recording studio inside an ordinary-looking building at 1313 West Seventh Street. Instead of country singers, he encouraged rock-and-roll musicians to drop by and try their luck. His biggest catch was a young band leader from Lubbock, Texas, who wore dark-rimmed glasses, played an energetic piano, and sang in an exuberant voice. From 1957 until his untimely death two years later, Buddy Holly recorded most of his greatest hit records at the Clovis studio, some on his own and some with his band, the Crickets. "That'll Be the Day" was his first hit, followed by "Peggy Sue," "Every Day," and "Maybe Baby."

Following Holly's death, Petty continued to work with local musicians, the most notable being Jimmy Gilmer and the Fireballs, who enjoyed a short-lived celebrity with their hits "Sugar Shack" and "Bottle of Wine." Another popular 1950s musician Petty discovered was Buddy Knox ("Party Doll"). Roy Orbison, best known for "Pretty Woman," started with Petty, but left before recording any of his hits. Petty died in 1984.

■ **PORTALES**   *map page 222, D-2*

Portales is nutty for peanuts, growing 30 million pounds of the Valencia variety every year. For three days in October, the nutty legume is honored—as well as roasted, eaten, and displayed—at the **Peanut Valley Festival**, known here as the "Peanut Olympics" (505-635-8036). At **Eastern New Mexico University**, the Jack Williamson Science Fiction Library—named in honor of the Portales-based author

Wagons loaded with broom corn on their way to market in Clovis, 1905.

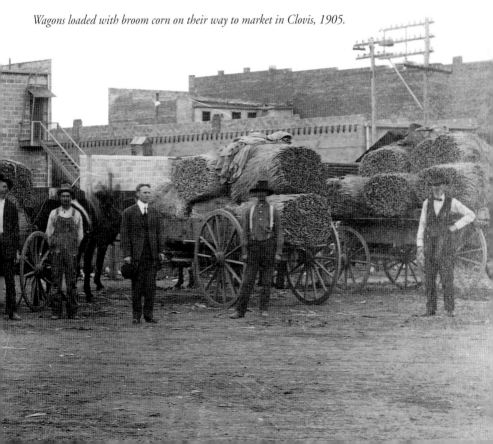

of *The Body Snatchers*—has in its collection of 17,000 volumes the original manuscripts of most of Williamson's more than 45 novels and 150 short stories.

One Portales resident, Bill Dalley, has salvaged old windmills off the prairie and erected 80 of the spinning antique apparatuses in his front yard as the **Dalley Windmill Collection.** "A lot of old ranchers tell me," he once remarked to a writer, "that if a man wants a peaceful state of mind after a hard day of roping cattle, there's nothing better than riding up to the old windmill and listening to the groan of a wheel. It's like watching fish breathe. It's all slow motion—so slow, yet powerful." *1506 South Kilgore Street; 505-356-6263.*

■ FORT SUMNER AND OLD FORT DAYS   *map page 222, C-2*
Upriver from Roswell are the crumbling ruins of Fort Sumner, site of the disastrous incarceration of Mescalero Apaches and Navajos in the 1860s. After the fort closed in 1868, some of the civilians who had moved to the fertile river valley to furnish food for the fort stayed on to grow vegetables and raise cattle. The fort is preserved as **Fort Sumner State Monument.** *505-355-2573.*

After he was killed by Sheriff Pat Garrett in 1881, Billy the Kid was buried in the Fort Sumner military cemetery, alongside two of his equally recalcitrant desperado friends, Tom O'Folliard and Charlie Bowdre. His tombstone reads: "The Boy Bandit King—He Died as He Had Lived." Because people keep trying to steal Billy's tombstone, a fence now surrounds his grave marker, located 6 miles southeast of town. Folks in Fort Sumner have formed a historical society dedicated to their folk hero and erected the **Billy the Kid Museum** in his honor. *1601 East Sumner; 505-355-2380.*

Billy-mania has also inspired the Billy the Kid Tombstone Race, one of the reasons people come to town each June for **Old Fort Days**, Fort Sumner's annual celebration of its past. Another is the Great American Cow Plop, in which a bovine is let loose to stroll in a squared-off fenced field behind a hardware store. White paint marks off 425 squares, which cost $5 each to reserve. Those who contribute watch anxiously, hoping the cow will heed nature's call on their square. This giant outdoor bingo game nets the winner $500 and raises money for the Chamber of Commerce.

A third reason to attend Old Fort Days is the rodeo. Professionals and amateurs deftly apply their skills (and lassos) at calf roping, but bull riders have the toughest job: they gingerly climb on the back of a 2,000-pound Brahma bull that isn't

Young entrepreneur at Clovis Rodeo, ca. 1940.

accustomed to carrying around anything bigger than a horsefly. It's not easy to stay seated on a heaving bull, and many cowboys don't last long. The voice that booms out of loudspeakers between events, commenting enthusiastically on the misadventures of the ring's performers, is usually as entertaining as the rodeo clowns, whose job it is to divert an angry bull bent on giving a discarded cowboy a skyward toss. In barrel racing, the only women's event, horseback riders run the length of the dirt arena, circle a barrel, then race back and out the chute, all in the blink of an eye. *505-355-7705.*

NORTHEASTERN
NEW MEXICO

In northeastern New Mexico, the peaks of the Sangre de Cristo Mountains give way to sprawling, fertile plains intersected by few waterways—the Canadian and Cimarron Rivers and the part of the Pecos that flows through the region are the largest and longest. In these parts, a whipping wind whistles through tall grama grasslands, and what seem from a distance to be brown specks on the otherwise pale green landscape resolve into cattle at close range. Simple ranch houses, whirring windmills, and the remains of long-extinct volcanoes line the horizon.

Hundreds of dinosaur footprints mark the landscape near Clayton. Chipped stone points used 10 millennia ago by Folsom Man now lie protected inside Folsom Museum. If you listen carefully, you can almost hear the creaking wheels of the heavily loaded wagons that labored along the Santa Fe Trail in the 1800s, carrying goods to and from the New Mexico frontier. When they were not interrupted by Indian raiding parties, that is: in northeastern New Mexico, the hunting grounds of the Apaches met those of the Comanches.

It was here that mountain man Lucien Maxwell became the largest single landholder in the Western Hemisphere when, in 1864, he inherited from his father-in-law a 1.7-million-acre land grant that included mountains and valuable rangeland stretching into present-day Colorado. The secluded canyons of the Sangre de Cristos proved perfect hideouts for gunfighter Clay Allison and train robber Thomas "Black Jack" Ketchum. In the late 1800s, nearly everybody who was anybody in the Wild West stayed at the St. James Hotel in the foothill town of Cimarron when passing through—Wyatt Earp, Pat Garrett, Doc Holliday, and Jesse James were frequent guests. And Oklahoma oilman Waite Phillips donated 127,395 acres of this region's forested slopes to the Boy Scouts of America, who turned a cattle ranch into Philmont Scout Ranch, a place for training their young members in camping and leadership skills.

Cattle may still outnumber people on this vast prairie, but folks in northeastern New Mexico take pride in the beauties of their region: the carefully preserved Victorian homes of Las Vegas; Santa Rosa's Blue Hole, a scuba diver's oasis in the desert; and the 6,000 statuesque elk that roam the forests of Vermejo Park, once the largest privately owned ranch in the United States and now an exclusive hunting and fishing preserve.

■ HISTORY

About 100 million years ago, when the waters of an inland sea gently lapped at what today is New Mexico's northeast corner, scores of duck-billed dinosaurs milled about near the shoreline, gorging on whatever delectable plants they could find. Some 800 fossilized footprints of these prehistoric creatures, who were 10 to 15 feet long, escaped the oozing lava that issued from a series of volcanic explosions 10,000 years ago and are now embedded in sandstone 12 miles north of Clayton. Also surviving these eruptions were prehistoric hunters, now referred to as Folsom Man, who roamed the area stalking mastodons, woolly mammoths, bison, and antelope. Many millennia later, scattered communities of Anasazi Indians grew squash, beans, and corn along the banks of the region's waterways.

By the time the gold-seeking Spanish explorer Francisco Vásquez de Coronado traipsed across the plains in 1541, these Indians were long gone. Discovering that the promise of golden riches was false, Coronado quit the environs as well, and returned empty-handed to New Spain. By the 1700s, the Jicarilla Apaches were pursuing buffalo and antelope through the region's grasslands and secluded canyons. The Comanches by then had moved into this area, and the two tribes

Lassoing the "dogies" has long been a Western art form.

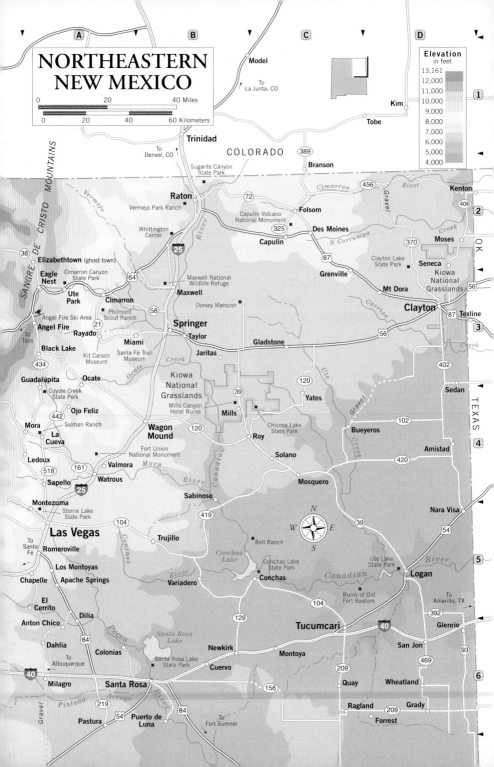

battled each other, as well as a few pockets of hardy Spanish settlers, for regional control. The settlers, who lived in small communities, had received land grants from the government of Spain. They had only to farm the land for four years to call it their own—a policy continued by the new government of Mexico after it gained independence from Spain in 1821.

■ MAXWELL LAND GRANT

The largest of the land grants was the one that came to be known as the Maxwell Land Grant, issued by Gov. Manuel Armijo in 1841 to Charles Beaubien, a French trapper, and Guadalupe Miranda of Taos, a government official. Some years later, Miranda sold out his share and returned to Mexico, his homeland; the grant took its name from Lucien Maxwell, a hunter and trapper who married Beaubien's daughter. At 1.7 million acres, it covered an area three times the size of Rhode Island, encompassing present-day Eagle Nest, Springer, and Raton and spreading into southern Colorado. After Beaubien's death in 1864, Maxwell inherited the massive landholding, which included vast amounts of minerals, timber, and some of the best pastureland in the region—upon which Maxwell introduced beet cultivation and oversaw the operation of numerous cattle and sheep ranches. Although he seemed to prefer gambling and the acquisition of elaborate furnishings for the mansion he built in Cimarron, Maxwell worked hard at developing his assets and encouraged ranchers to lease portions of his holdings. On a handshake basis, the land baron outfitted settlers with cattle, acreage, and seed to improve upon the lush grama grass that covered the lava-rock land.

Old-time cowboys break for lunch in northeastern New Mexico's Mora County.

A caravan arrives at Santa Fe, 1844.

In 1870, the sale of the Maxwell grant (by then known to contain gold deposits) to a group of British and Dutch investors set off more than a decade of fighting between settlers and the foreigners, who demanded that all squatters either buy their holdings, pay rent, or move out. During the controversy, known as the Colfax County War, farmers, ranchers, miners, and shopkeepers who had been indulged by Maxwell claimed ownership of the land upon which they had for years carved out their livings. The settlers resisted court rulings that favored the new owners, and blood occasionally was shed until 1887, when the U.S. Supreme Court once and for all confirmed the legality of the Maxwell Land Grant sale. Having acquired the British assets, the Dutch investors emerged as sole owners.

■ THE CIVIL WAR

In the 1800s, when wagon trains rolled over the Santa Fe Trail, the Comanches turned their attention from the Spanish settlers to the Anglo traders and the goods and tools they brought across the plains from Missouri. Both arms of the trade route entered New Mexico through this region: the Mountain Branch traversed southeastern Colorado before crossing the rugged Raton Pass on its way to Santa Fe, while the Cimarron Cutoff made a beeline through southwestern Kansas and northeastern New Mexico en route to the outpost capital.

The fact that New Mexico became a U.S. territory in 1848 didn't much matter at first to the Apaches and Comanches, who considered the plains their own and continued to terrorize the wagon trains along the Santa Fe Trail. The political shift had more impact after 1851, when the U.S. government built Fort Union near Watrous, where the Cimarron Cutoff and Mountain Branch joined, to protect the travelers and the area's settlers. After the Civil War broke out in 1861, the military installation was fortified for a threatened Confederate invasion that never reached that far north. A year later, a regiment from the fort helped the Colorado Volunteers turn back Rebel forces at the Battle of Glorieta Pass, 25 miles southeast of Santa Fe. This decisive victory, which is re-enacted every year 15 miles south of Santa Fe at Rancho de las Golondrinas, was the turning point in the war in the West and is referred to as the "Gettysburg of the West." The battle site, designated a National Historic Landmark, is a unit of Pecos National Historical Park.

■ **ROUGH RIDERS**

When Cuba declared war on Spain to gain its independence in 1898 and the United States went to the aid of its southern island neighbor, New Mexico Gov. Miguel Otero Jr. seized the opportunity to show the territory's loyalty to the Stars and Stripes. In response to Otero's call for volunteers, 340 qualified horsemen signed up to ride under the leadership of Lt. Col. Theodore Roosevelt. But the New Mexicans who made up about one-third of the Rough Riders unit that charged San Juan Hill did so without their horses, which had been left behind because of a lack of transport. Said one New Mexico Rough Rider, "I was born in a dugout right here in Las Vegas, raised a cowboy, enlisted expecting to do my fighting on horseback as all the boys, but landed in Cuba afoot; marched, sweated, and fought afoot; earned whatever fame afoot."

The gallantry of New Mexico's volunteers proved they supported the U.S. and not Spain—an ancestral homeland for many of them. A year later, the Rough Riders reassembled in the town of Las Vegas and once again marched behind Roosevelt—this time in a parade through town. Reunions continued into the 1960s. Fittingly, Las Vegas is the location of the Rough Riders Memorial and City Museum. *727 Grand Avenue; 505-425-8726.*

■ **LAS VEGAS** *map page 256, A-5*

Las Vegas, a well-preserved but gritty town, with the tall pine slopes of the Sangre de Cristo Mountains to the west and a carpet of grama grasslands to the east, is often confused with the well-known Nevada gambling capital. The two couldn't be more different: no neon or casinos here, only old-fashioned streetlamps that light the quiet neighborhoods of restored Victorian homes.

Las Vegas (which means "the meadows") began as a land grant in 1821, when Luis Maria Cabeza de Baca received a grant for himself and his 17 sons along the Gallinas River, a meandering stream that forms high in the mountains. (According to folklore, the river originated as a teardrop from an "eye" in the rock face of a tall peak.) Persistent attacks by Comanche Indians who considered the region their hunting domain prevented the family from ever settling the land, however.

In 1835, after wagon trains had been rolling by the site on the Santa Fe Trail for 14 years, a group of 34 Spanish colonists established the town of Las Vegas and quickly set about planting beans and other crops. They also grazed sheep in nearby meadows and built simple dirt-roofed homes of adobe bricks. Men and boys worked long hours tending their herds, while the women cooked, spun thread, wove cloth, sewed clothing and bedding, and fashioned beautiful lacework and embroidery. Residents purchased tools and ribbons from caravans that regularly passed through. The town also served as a major way station on the Santa Fe Railroad, which arrived in 1879.

Even early on, Las Vegas residents looked to construction materials other than adobe. **Our Lady of Sorrows Church** was the largest stone structure in New Mexico when it was built, between 1862 and 1870, of randomly fit blocks of Anton Chico sandstone. But it was the wave of settlers who arrived by train that actively scorned the indigenous adobe homes, preferring instead the building styles popular in the Midwest. As a result, Las Vegas is an architectural treasure trove, with 900 of its structures on the National Register of Historic Buildings.

West of the Gallinas River is the original town site, built around a traditional tree-shaded plaza with a turquoise-trimmed gazebo in its center. The finely restored **Plaza Hotel**, an Italianate showpiece when it was built in 1882, anchors the northwestern corner of the block. In the early 1900s, the hotel often served as the center of operations for movies filmed in the area. By 1915 the unspoiled appearance of Las Vegas had attracted film star Tom Mix, who acted in such westerns as *Never Again, The Girl and the Mail Bag,* and *The Tenderfoot's Triumph.* It also hosted meetings of the "One Lung Club," for easterners sent West by their doctors to recover from tuberculosis in the dry mountain air. *230 Plaza; 505-425-3591 or 800-328-1882.*

Las Vegas neighborhoods east of the river look as if they were plucked from the Midwest or New England. Homes here display Victorian gables, Italianate bay windows, and Tudor half-timbers; well-kept lawns complement restored turn-of-the-century multistory homes surrounded by precisely placed trees and shrubs. The **Carnegie Library,** built in 1903 and modeled after Thomas Jefferson's home, Monticello, is the focal point of a block of shady elms and deep green grass. It's hard to believe that hundreds of miles of prairie spread out just east of town.

■ MONTEZUMA *map page 256, A-5*

A winding road, NM 65, follows the Gallinas River into the mountains, entering the timbered Pecos Wilderness west of Las Vegas and passing by a few villages. One of these is Montezuma, the location of the area's most spectacular late 19th-century structure, known today as **Montezuma Castle**. This massive 343-room edifice was built as a spa in 1888 by the Santa Fe Railroad to take advantage of the hot springs nearby. A 5-mile spur led to the multistoried wooden building with numerous turrets and balconies. For a decade, this splendid hotel was the crown jewel of the rail line, providing hospitality to such customers as Ulysses S. Grant, Rutherford Hayes, Kaiser Wilhelm, and Japanese emperor Hirohito. Guests rode horses in the nearby mountains, fished for trout in the Gallinas River, played poker in oak-paneled card rooms, and soaked in the thermal baths, which reached temperatures of 110 degrees Fahrenheit. By the middle of the 20th century, however, the spa was no longer fashionable and was sold to the Catholic Church, which used it as a seminary for Mexican priests until 1972. Vandals and vagrants had the run of the place until 1981, when the Armand Hammer Foundation turned the 110-acre complex into the **United World College of the American West**, a 2-year institution for international students 16 to 19 years old. The castle showed signs of its years of neglect until a complete renovation in 2001 restored it to its original grandeur. Nearby on the campus is the **Dwan Light Sanctuary,** a building designed as a place of contemplation and reflection for people of all beliefs, where 12 large prisms cast fantastic spectral rays of light across the whitewashed walls. It's best to call ahead before visiting either the castle or the sanctuary. *505-454-4200.*

From Montezuma, NM 65 continues through rugged mountains, ending at the base of the 10,000-foot **Hermit's Peak**, named after onetime resident recluse Giovanni Maria Agostini, who had been born of noble parents in Italy but chose to spend most of his life wandering around Europe and the Americas. In 1863, seeking solitude, he took up residence in a cave just below the peak's eastern summit. Men from Las Vegas built him a small cabin, and there he carved religious emblems that he exchanged in town for cornmeal he could make into mush. Four years later, feeling restless, he moved on to southern New Mexico, where he was found dead in the Organ Mountains in 1869, age 68, a dagger in his back.

■ NORTH OF LAS VEGAS

Driving north for 25 miles on NM 518, you'll come to **Salman Ranch**, a 19th-century homestead that today is a raspberry farm. Between August and October, you can buy fresh berries at the farm's store or cool off with a raspberry sundae. *505-387-2900.*

The pointed lettuce-green leaves of an occasional yucca cactus interrupt the undulating prairie, whose grasses take on rust and yellow hues as I-25 traces the path of the Santa Fe Trail. At Watrous, today a roadside hamlet with fewer than 100 residents, the Mountain and Cimarron branches of the Santa Fe Trail merged in the shade of leafy cottonwoods alongside the waters of the Mora River.

■ FORT UNION NATIONAL MONUMENT *map page 256, A-4*

At the end of NM 161, the crumbling ruins of Fort Union rise like a mirage from the pastel-green prairie. These partial walls are all that remain of the largest 19th-century U.S. military installation in the Southwest, which from 1851 until 1891 protected settlers and travelers on the Santa Fe Trail and served as a major military supply station. Preserved as a national monument, the fort is a reminder of the days when travel wasn't particularly convenient—or safe.

A flagstone walkway passes by what once served as officers' quarters. Brick fireplaces and chimneys that tower above deteriorating walls have somehow survived the relentless wind that steadily whistles through the ruins. With the press of a button, the fort's re-creation of a bugle call interrupts the silence of the prairie. Press another, and the voice of an officer's wife complains to her husband about a leaky

(opposite) Dwan Light Sanctuary, at the United World College of the American West.

roof, or a sergeant barks out orders to his men. Close your eyes, and the fort's store-houses, offices, barracks, and corrals take shape, with soldiers executing drills on the parade ground. Open them, and the soft snapping of grasshoppers is all that permeates the stillness. *505-425-8025.*

■ **WAGON MOUND** *map page 256, A/B-4*
Heading north on I-25, traffic is sparse and cattle amble along their grama-grass dining table. Over a rise, a few volcanic mesas jut skyward. One, which resembles a covered wagon, was the last great landmark on the journey westward across the plains. When a ranching town was established on the mesa's flanks in 1850, it originally took the name Santa Clara, then changed it nine years later to the more literally descriptive Wagon Mound.

A drive through this sleepy hamlet today provides a glimpse of simple tin-roofed adobe architecture. A dog may lie sleepily in the middle of the street, expecting cars to go around him. Nowadays, the highlight of the year for the town's 310 residents is **Bean Day**—the same holiday other Americans call Labor Day. This harvest celebration began in 1910, when pinto beans were a big crop for area farmers. Even though beans aren't grown here anymore, residents gather for bicycle and sack races and a parade in the morning; a free noon meal of barbecued beef, pinto beans, and coleslaw; and a rodeo and evening dance. Information on Bean Day is available from the Wagon Mound City Hall. *505-666-2408.*

■ **SPRINGER AND VICINITY** *map page 256, A/B-3*
In the late 1800s, the quiet ranching centers of Springer and Maxwell grew up alongside railroad tracks and riverbanks: Springer on the Cimarron River, Maxwell on the Canadian. In Springer, the main attraction is the **Santa Fe Trail Museum**, in the old Colfax County Courthouse. Artifacts range from Springer High School portraits to a Santa Fe Trail–era covered wagon. *606 Maxwell Avenue; 505-483-5554.*

About 30 miles east of Springer, north of U.S. 56, the imposing **Dorsey Mansion** sits tucked into the base of Chico Hill, overlooking a sprawling grama grass plain. This odd-looking log-and-sandstone house, with its Gothic-like turret, was the creation of Stephen Dorsey, a U.S. senator from Arkansas who fulfilled his elaborate vision of a ranch house by building this pretentious mansion in stages between 1880 and 1886 and making it the site of lavish all-night parties. Its indoor plumbing (a luxury in those days), billiard rooms, lily "pond" (with three islands), well-stocked wine cellar, and purebred English bulls were the talk of the region. When no one is on duty the gate is locked, so call ahead to arrange a tour. *505-375-2222.*

Southeast of Springer in the late 1800s, Melvin Mills, an overachieving lawyer and rancher turned agriculturalist, planted 14,000 trees—apple, peach, pear, cherry, plum, walnut, almond, and chestnut—and cultivated melons, tomatoes, grapes, and cabbages along a 10-mile-long ribbon of shoreline in the Canadian River Canyon. Undaunted by thousand-foot-tall canyon walls and a steep gravel road leading to the braided riverbed, Mills blasted underground irrigation channels and constructed cisterns, a cider press, bunkhouses, and a stone mansion on the river plain. He hauled his crops to Springer, where they were shipped to Harvey Houses along the Santa Fe Railroad. The Mills Canyon Hotel, which Mills also built, was a popular vacation spot and served a stagecoach line that crossed the canyon here. In 1904, Mills's efforts were washed away in a disastrous flood that sent raging waters through the canyon. All that remains are the hotel's partial stone walls and a few scraggly fruit trees.

West of Springer on NM 21, at **Philmont Scout Ranch**, ash gray mule deer, stately elk, black bears, a herd of buffalo, and more than 250 head of Hereford cattle share the pine and spruce-covered slopes with the thousands of Boy Scouts who practice survival skills here every summer. NM 21 follows the Mountain Branch of the Santa Fe Trail and skirts the edge of the ranch, which was established in the 1920s by Waite Phillips, a founder of Phillips Petroleum, and donated to the Boy Scouts of America for use as a wilderness camp beginning in 1938. Through later acquisitions, the ranch now encompasses 137,493 acres along the Cimarron Range of the Sangre de Cristo Mountains.

At Philmont headquarters, red tin roofs top tan stucco buildings, pristine in their manicured setting of close-cropped grass and gravel roads. Here in 1926 and 1927, Phillips, an Oklahoma oilman, built **Villa Philmonte,** the lavish two-story Mediterranean-style home where his family spent its summers. Bear and cougar skins draping the walls and a custom-made piano and a shower with seven shower-heads are evidence of the oilman's prosperity. Daily tours are given throughout the summer. Across the road, the **Philmont Museum/Seton Memorial Library** honors Ernest Thompson Seton, an author, artist, naturalist, and the first chief scout of the Boy Scouts. The stucco building houses Seton's collection of 3,000 paintings of birds, rabbits, and buffalo, along with his personal library. Seton spent many years in New Mexico at his own ranch, Seton Village, just east of Santa Fe. *505-376-2281.*

Seven miles south of the ranch's headquarters, at its southeastern boundary, is the spot where, in 1845, Kit Carson built a flat-roofed adobe house and cultivated a 15-acre garden along the banks of Rayado Creek. Four years later, Lucien Maxwell (of the Maxwell Land Grant) joined the Indian scout along the creek, but by 1857 Carson's busy schedule fighting Indians and Maxwell's desire to move into the town of Cimarron forced the men to give up the ranching operation.

Today at Rayado, young guides dressed in 19th-century clothing lead tours at the **Kit Carson Museum**, a reconstruction of the mountain man's home, and share tales of frontier life along the Santa Fe Trail during that era. The exhibits include a bed that reportedly was too soft for Carson: after two nights on it, he spread his buffalo robes on a hard adobe bench in the corner and slept there instead. *505-376-2281.*

■ CIMARRON *map page 256, A-3*

The town of Cimarron took shape along the shady banks of the blue-green Cimarron River in 1841. The sheltered settlement, which began as a principal stop on a branch of the Santa Fe Trail, soon became a major gathering spot for ranchers, miners, and gunslingers. After Lucien Maxwell relocated the headquarters of his immense land-grant holdings to Cimarron in 1857, the town's popularity grew. It received another boost in 1864 when Maxwell completed a three-story adobe mansion that occupied a city block. Inside were rooms for billiards, gambling, and dancing, as well as a rear section for prostitutes. Every night large sums of money exchanged hands during games of faro, roulette, monte, poker, and dice. Chauvinism was the order of the day: the house had separate women's and men's sides. At Cimarron's height, 15 saloons, four hotels, a post office, and a newspaper office lined the streets. Jesse James, Thomas "Black Jack" Ketchum, and Billy the Kid were frequent visitors. Hunters, trappers, and gold prospectors used the town as a jumping-off point for their excursions into the nearby mountains.

Cimarron—which means "wild" or "untamed" in Spanish—lived up to its name. Angry gamblers who didn't like a card they were dealt often picked fights. Gunslingers who tipped one too many shots of whiskey liked to show off by shooting holes in the ceiling. Disputes were settled in the dirt streets and only the victor walked away. The *Las Vegas Gazette* once reported, "Everything is quiet in Cimarron. Nobody has been killed for three days."

Cowboys Tom Day and Simon Arreola saddle up for a day on the range.

Having weathered a turbulent past, Cimarron has quieted down and today remains a ranching center. A walk through the original town site takes in its first well, in which a rusty bucket hangs from an untouched new rope; the iron bars of a stone-walled jail built in the 1870s; and small adobe homes with swings and friendly dogs in the yard. A four-story stone gristmill built by Maxwell in 1864 is now the **Old Mill Museum** (505-376-2417), displaying antique surgical equipment, documents of the Maxwell Land Grant, and original place settings and silverware from the (now restored) St. James Hotel, across the street.

■ St. James Hotel

One of the most popular gathering spots in the New Mexico Territory during the late 1800s was the St. James Hotel. Originally a saloon, it was built in 1873 by Henri Lambert, a Frenchman who had served as personal chef to President Abraham Lincoln and Gen. Ulysses S. Grant. For the remainder of the century, until the Santa Fe Railroad lured travelers to the growing metropolis of Raton, the St. James played host to some of the most ornery bad guys around, the likes of Thomas "Black Jack" Ketchum, not to mention the 26 unfortunate fellows who left the place feet first, the victims of gunfights. A regular guest was Jesse James, who usually stayed in a room at the end of the hall on the first floor and signed the guest book R.H. Howard (the book is on view in the lobby). Many of the Old West's good guys, including Pat Garrett and David Crockett (a nephew of the famous frontiersman), also slept in the hotel's comfortable beds. It was here that Buffalo Bill Cody and Annie Oakley planned Bill's Wild West Show, Zane Grey wrote *Fighting Caravans,* and Frederic Remington stayed between sketching trips to the nearby piñon hills.

High-backed Victorian couches and chairs enhance the lobby of the restored St. James. Deep-brown bureaus line the walls as they did a century ago. Linen covers tabletops in the dining room, which was the original barroom. Despite a decor that evokes subtle elegance, a look upward reveals about 20 bullet holes still visible in the pressed tin ceiling. When it was installed in 1903, after more than 400 bullets had riddled the previous one, three layers of oak floorboards were laid in the room above to protect guests—who most likely were thankful, considering the additional punctures.

When Jesse James stayed at the St. James Hotel, he registered under an alias, R.H. Howard.

NAME.	RESIDENCE.	Time.	Room.	REMARKS.

Sunday, August 28 1881

Name	Residence		Room	Remarks
C. W. Williams	Ocate		8	
E. A Milward	do		8	
L. I. Brumley	do		8	
Roberto Nevarez	do		8	
Luciano Gallegos	Mora		8	
J. F. Robison			8	
M. B. Stockton	Raton		8	100
G. W. Geer	Raton		8	
James Lynch	Elizabethtown	Supper		Paid
John E. Codlin	E. town	Supper		Paid

Monday, August 29 1881

Name	Residence	Remarks		
Ramon Flores	Ocate	D 3 days		
Pablo Marec	Ocate	D 2 Paid 1881		
F. M. Darling	Capulin	D pd Paid		
John Pearson	wife Willow Gulch	D pd		
Mrs. J. Bowman	Springer	D		
Greenwood	Hard Scrabble			
Thos. Knott	Hard Scrabble	D		
Jose Francisco Lucero		D Paid		
Juan C. Lucero		D Paid		
John Leacey	L. P. Springer	New		
R. H. Howar	Cimarron			
John M. Kellar	Sweet Water	D days p		
Frank Maryland	Ute Creek	D pd		
Henry Babust	Camavon	8 b		

Red-orange carpeted hallways lead to 14 rooms furnished with antique beds, dressers, and couches. A nameplate on each door identifies the room with one of its famous regulars. Near the end of the second-story hall, a potted plant blocks the entrance to Room 18, in which no one sleeps—except a ghost who refuses to check out. Some claim the ghost is the restless spirit of James Wright, a gambler killed while trying to claim the hotel as his winnings in a poker game. A second ghost said to drift through the second-floor hallway is that of Mary Lambert, owner Henri's first wife. A rush of strong perfume is a sign she is around. Additional spirits come and go, adding to the ambiance. *17th Street and Collison Avenue; 505-376-2664.*

As it heads west, US 64 winds through the twisting gorge of the Cimarron Canyon, where sandstone faces meet the road and tall ponderosa pines line the gently flowing waters of the Cimarron River. This spectacular passage through the mountains emerges at the northern end of Eagle Nest Lake, in the magnificently spacious Moreno Valley.

■ RATON   *map page 256, B-2*

In 1866, a 32-year-old frontiersman began digging and blasting a well-graded wagon road across the rugged 7,622-foot Raton Pass. Once he had completed the road, "Uncle" Dick Wootton stretched a heavy chain across it and began charging travelers a toll—$1.50 for each wagon, although Indians went for free.

Eight miles south of the pass, travelers stopped for water and feed at Willow Springs Ranch. In 1880, after the Santa Fe Railroad laid tracks alongside Wootton's path, a division point was established at the ranch, which was renamed Raton. Within a year, the new village at Raton had 3,000 residents. Attracted by the area's luxuriant rangeland and rich coal deposits, folks called it the "Pittsburgh of the West." Early citizens lived in boxcars parked on sidings next to the railroad. As the years passed, brick and stone buildings were erected to accommodate stores, restaurants, hotels, and a newspaper office.

A row of 20th-century-style fast-food restaurants and gas stations attests to the town's ongoing role as a major stopover for travelers crossing Raton Pass into Colorado. Downtown, however, about 70 historic buildings squeeze compactly into a five-block district, beckoning visitors with an attractive variety of architectural designs, from the Spanish Mission Revival style of the Santa Fe depot to the terra cotta–trimmed windows of the Raton Realty Building and the Corinthian pilasters of the Roth Building. Most spectacular is the 480-seat **Shuler Theater,** with its rococo interior. When completed in 1915, the ornate building held an opera house, a fire station, and city offices under its roof. Elaborate woodwork, gold-trimmed box seats, and a high ceiling painted to resemble a cloud-filled sky decorate the theater, which remains a venue for cultural events, including musicals, concerts, school band concerts, and dance recitals. Walk-in visitors are always welcome. *131 North Second Street; 505-445-4746.*

Ten miles south of downtown on U.S. 64, the National Rifle Association operates the **Whittington Center,** the most comprehensive shooting facility in the United States. Set on 33,000 acres dotted with piñon and junipers, it contains 14 shooting ranges and hosts annual national championship events. Public tours are available daily. *505-445-3615.*

Six miles northeast of town on NM 526, **Sugarite Canyon State Park** sits between two mesas along the banks of Chicorico Creek. Three mountain lakes are stocked with rainbow trout, and hiking trails lead onto Little Horse Mesa and through the ruins of an early-20th-century coal mining camp. *505-445-5607.*

Forty-five miles to the west of Raton is **Vermejo Park Ranch**, a private hunting and fishing resort that sprawls across nearly 588,000 acres. Once part of the Maxwell Land Grant, the ranch has been through a succession of owners and is now a working bison ranch owned by former media giant Ted Turner. In summertime, this private paradise for outdoorsmen accommodates fishermen who come in search of rainbow, brown, brook, and cutthroat trout in 21 of the ranch's clear blue lakes. In the fall, hunters scout for deer, elk, antelope, and bear. *505-445-3097.*

■ CAPULIN VOLCANO NATIONAL MONUMENT *map page 256, C-2*
Sweeping upward from a yellow-grass prairie about 30 miles east of Raton is a gently rounded forested mound—the remains of a once-violent volcano responsible for much of the lava rock that caps the terrain in northeastern New Mexico. The last time the volcano erupted was 10,000 years ago, when red-hot lava, cinders, ash, and rock debris shot skyward and fell back upon the crater, piling up to create the 1,000-foot-tall conical mound.

The volcano is preserved as a national monument, and a paved 2-mile road spirals to its summit. Two short trails begin at a parking lot: one follows the rim, providing a panorama that takes in the snowcapped peaks of the Sangre de Cristo Mountains, distant volcanic hills and mesas, and sprawling rangeland that reaches

to the horizon. The second trail descends into the center of the volcano, partially filled with pumice that has slid down its sides. Lupine, penstemon, golden pea, and bright yellow sunflowers dot the slopes, and the lilting songs of grosbeaks, goldfinches, and bluebirds fill the air. *On NM 325, 3 miles north of Capulin and U.S. 64/87; 505-278-2201.*

Capulin's fiery eruptions were probably witnessed by Folsom Man, who hunted bison, camels, musk oxen, and giant sloths throughout the area some 10 millennia ago. The early culture's presence remained unknown until 1908, when George McJunkin, a cowboy and former slave, discovered some stone spear points among large bleached bones in an arroyo near the tiny community of Folsom, a shipping point on the Colorado and Southern Railroad. In 1926, after years of persistent pestering, McJunkin finally convinced skeptical archaeologists to inspect the site. They determined that the bones belonged to an extinct strain of giant bison and that the spear points had been chipped by one of the state's earliest inhabitants. Some of the spear points are displayed at the **Folsom Museum,** which is open from Memorial Day through Labor Day. *Main Street, Folsom; 505-278-2122 (summer), 505-278-3616 (winter).*

■ CLAYTON AND VICINITY   *map page 256, D-3*

Two volcanic mounds have served as a landmark since the early 1700s, when Comanche Indian Chief Orejas de Conejo (Rabbit Ears) roamed the state's northeastern grasslands. After the chief was killed in battle and buried on the largest peak, the mountains were named after him. In 1717, the knobby hills north of Clayton were the site of one of the bloodiest battles of the Spanish-Comanche War, when a volunteer army of 500 Spaniards surprised the Indians, took 700 of them prisoner and killed hundreds of others. In the 1800s, Rabbit Ears Mountain served as a major landmark on the Cimarron Cutoff of the Santa Fe Trail, which passed nearby. Ruts still can be seen, and six famous watering holes along the trade route can be reached within one 50-minute drive of town.

Since 1887, when Clayton was established by the Colorado and Southern Railroad, rail cars have been hauling fat cattle to market from the area's abundant grazing land. Named for U.S. Sen. Stephen Dorsey's son, the town is remembered

The rococo interior of Raton's Shuler Theater is distinguished by elaborate woodwork, gold-trimmed box seats, and a high ceiling painted to resemble a cloud-filled sky.

for the celebrated hanging of Thomas "Black Jack" Ketchum in 1901. Along with his brother, Sam, and two other partners, the Texas-born outlaw with dark, beady eyes and a habit of wearing black murdered a few men and robbed a few trains, mostly in New Mexico. Abandoned by his gang because of his uncontrollable temper, Ketchum attempted to rob the same train he and his partners had held up three years earlier. Unfortunately for the outlaw, this time the train's conductor, Frank Harrington, was armed with a shotgun, which he fired into Ketchum's heart (or so he thought). The outlaw fell with a shattered arm and escaped, only to be apprehended the next day. He lived, but lost his right arm.

The next spring, after being convicted of train robbery, a crime punishable by hanging, Ketchum was prepared to meet his maker in Clayton, which was abuzz with newspaper reporters and spectators who bought tickets to the event. Ketchum remained calm as officers slipped the noose around his neck, but Sheriff Salome Garcia was so nervous he missed the rope with his hatchet. The second attempt was a clean cut; the trap door fell open and Ketchum fell through. His body quivered, then collapsed onto the ground. The outlaw was dead, but not by hanging: his head had been jerked off his body. A local doctor adeptly sewed it back on so Ketchum could be properly buried. No mourners accompanied the plain pine coffin to the cemetery east of town, but flowers occasionally adorn the frequently visited grave.

Few trees shade the flat streets of Clayton, which bills itself as the carbon dioxide capital of the world. Bravo Dome, the world's largest and purest concentration of natural carbon dioxide, is embedded in sandstone 50 miles southwest of town. On the surface cows dominate, and thousands can be seen contentedly eating the grama grass. Tawny antelope and quail often share the feast.

Clusters of brown bovines dot the pale-green prairie that stretches in all directions throughout the eastern plains, interrupted only by tiny communities with names like Bueyeros, Amistad, Mosquero, Roy, and Nara Visa. One of these small towns, **Logan,** is experiencing an influx of retirees attracted to the refreshing and well-stocked waters of nearby Ute Lake. In town, a faded mural depicting events in the history of New Mexico graces a 25-foot-long outside wall of the Casa Blanca Motel. The colorful if aging work of art was painted by Manuel Acosta, a former pupil of Peter Hurd—a famous portraitist who was born in Roswell and produced most of his work at his home in the Hondo Valley.

■ TUCUMCARI *map page 256, C-5*

Situated at the edge of the Llano Estacado, near the base of the flat-topped Tucumcari Mountain, the tree-lined community of Tucumcari got its start in 1901 as a construction camp on the Rock Island Railroad. Known briefly as Six-Shooter Siding, the settlement attracted homesteaders who tried for years to coax crops from the sandy soil. In 1908, when the railroad decided to turn the camp into a division point, a more respectable name was called for, and was appropriated from that of the nearby mountain, which reportedly had served as a Comanche lookout in years past. Most likely, Tucumcari is a derivation of the Comanche *tukamukaru,* which means to lie in wait for someone or something to approach.

When Route 66 sliced through the center of town in the mid 20th century, the strip known as Tucumcari Boulevard filled with tourist courts, cafés, and gift shops. Today, the boulevard is still the place to find most of the town's 28 motels (comprising about 1,500 rooms—or so billboards hundreds of miles away on I-40 claim). One tourist court, the **Blue Swallow Motel** (815 East Tucumcari Boulevard; 505-461-9849), has endured and still welcomes overnight guests. A neon bird flies over the motel, where you can park your car in a garage adjacent to your room. Accommodations are basic, but comfortable, and you will have the distinction of staying on Route 66. The **Tucumcari Historical Museum** (416 South Adams Street; 505-461-4201), in a two-story brick building, has in its collection Folsom spear points, mammoth's teeth, antique bottles, petrified wood, a pre-1900 windmill, a covered wagon, and old saddles.

During summer months, many of the cars and trucks that pass through Tucumcari are heading to **Conchas Lake State Park**, 32 miles northwest of town. The clear, blue-green waters of this desert oasis on the Canadian River provide irrigation for area farmers and cool relief to swimmers. Water-skiers dip and lean as they slice through the calm water, and fishermen cast lines from boats and the rocky shoreline. *On NM 104; 505-868-2270.*

Northwest of Tucumcari and south of Mosquero sprawl the 300,000 acres of **Bell Ranch,** one of the last places in the West where cowboys still round up cattle on horseback and chuck wagons still bounce and rattle to branding operations in far-flung corners. Its name comes from the bell-shaped mountain on the property, the image of which also figures in the brand.

In 1824, when Bell Ranch founder Pablo Montoya obtained a Mexican land grant for this choice pasture land, the holding stretched across 655,000 acres. Montoya had been mayor of Santa Fe, but left his governmental duties to become a *comanchero,* trading with Comanches throughout the northeastern plains. As he roamed, he kept an eye out for land with good grass and ample water, a place where he and his seven children could raise cattle and spread out.

While the Bell changed hands a few times over the years, it remained intact until 1947, when it was divided into six sections and sold. The largest parcel, 130,000 acres including the brand and the ranch's headquarters, with adobe structures built by Montoya, was bought in 1970 by William Lane, an Illinois businessman, who not only promised to keep it "a real working ranch for the production of fine cattle," but also added 176,000 more acres of the original grant. His family maintains his vision. Bell Ranch cowboys still ride the mesas and canyons, in chaps worn for more than their rugged looks, hat brims stained with hard-earned sweat. (They also offer occasional trail rides, but for groups of at least 20 riders.)

Designated in 1970 as both National and State Historic sites, ranch headquarters, including the White House, the original ranch house, are 10 miles north of the village of Conchas. *505-868-2966.*

■ SANTA ROSA *map page 256, B-6*

In 1865, when Don Celso Baca traveled around the state as an officer in Col. Kit Carson's First Regiment of New Mexico Volunteers, he noticed a fertile plain wedged between the Pecos River and El Rito Creek. There, Baca built a *hacienda,* set up a cattle operation that grew into one of the area's largest, and in 1879 constructed an adobe chapel nearby to honor his mother. The tiny chapel was dedicated to Santa Rosa de Lima, the first canonized saint of the New World.

When 4,000 workers converged on the site in 1901 to build tracks to connect the Rock Island Railroad with the Southern Pacific, the emerging town took its name from the chapel. After rail workers moved on to their next assignment, farming and ranching sustained the community until Route 66 was paved through its center.

In sleepy Santa Rosa, travelers on I-40 will find an assortment of cafés and motels. But it also has gained a reputation among scuba divers, who travel hundreds of miles to immerse themselves in the **Blue Hole**, a 90-foot-deep artesian

TAPPING THE EARTH'S SPIRIT

For Ultima, even the plant had a spirit, and before I dug she made me speak to the plant and tell it why we pulled it from its home in the earth. "You that grow well here in the arroyo by the dampness of the river, we lift you to make good medicine," Ultima intoned softly and I found myself repeating after her. Then I would carefully dig out the plant, taking care not to let the steel of the shovel touch the tender roots. Of all the plants we gathered none was endowed with so much magic as the yerba del manso. It could cure burns, sores, piles, colic in babies, bleeding dysentery and even rheumatism. I knew this plant from long ago because my mother, who was not a curandera, often used it.

—Rudolfo Anaya, *Bless Me Ultima,* 1972.

well carved in the sharp limestone. The bell-shaped pool of crystal-clear water is fed by a subterranean river that supplies 3,000 gallons per minute and is inhabited by goldfish, catfish, and snails. The diving den maintains a constant temperature of 60 degrees Fahrenheit, enabling year-round use (505-472-3370). Nine miles north of town, the still waters of **Santa Rosa Lake**, in Santa Rosa Lake State Park (NM 91; 505-472-3110), beckon windsurfers, water skiers, swimmers, and fishermen in search of prize walleye.

Possibly, Francisco Vásquez de Coronado camped at Puerto de Luna as he traveled across northeastern New Mexico en route to the imaginary city of gold. Ten miles south of Santa Rosa on NM 91, Puerto de Luna sits on a bend of the Pecos River where his men probably built a bridge. A wonderful insight into this village and Santa Rosa is found in *Bless Me, Ultima,* a novel by Rudolfo Anaya, who grew up in the area. This tale of growing up on the *llano* in the 1940s abounds with descriptions of the river, the spring-fed lakes, and the faith by which people lived.

Pueblo Pottery of New Mexico

Pueblo Indians have been making pots for utilitarian use and for sale or barter for 1,300 years. The practice of making them for barter declined toward the middle of the 19th century, when the opening of the Santa Fe Trail flooded the region with imported goods. But with the coming of the railroad in the 1880s and the arrival of appreciative visitors, Pueblo potters realized the commercial potential of their pottery and entered a new period of improvement and exploration. These pots from Zuni and Laguna Pueblos were made during this period.

Zuni polychrome, 1890

Zuni Pueblo, south of Gallup, near the Arizona border, was visited by conquistador Francisco Vásquez de Coronado in 1540.

Zuni polychrome fetish, 1920

Laguna Pueblo, in central New Mexico between Albuquerque and Grants, has a long pottery tradition.

Laguna polychrome, 1910

Acoma pots in black and white

Acoma pottery has long been valued by collectors. Hand-drawn, intricate, geometric designs, as the one on the left above by S. Chino, are typical. The clays used by the different pueblos come from sources nearby, and Acoma clay is especially white.

Acoma Pueblo is high on a mesa west of Albuquerque.

Santa Clara Pueblo has produced many famous pottery families, among them the Gutierrez, Tafoya, and Naranjo. This pot by Anita Suazo is typical of the carved pottery of Santa Clara.

Santa Clara Pueblo is on NM 30 between Santa Fe and Taos.

Santa Clara pot with bear claw design

San Ildefonso jar, 1910   *San Ildefonso pot, Maria Martinez*

The polychrome pot above was typical of San Ildefonso Pueblo pottery until Maria and Julian Martinez began to make their famous black-on-black pottery designs. Their work is now world-famous, and it often commands more than $5,000 per piece. Many members of the extended Martinez family have also become exceedingly famous.

The Jemez Pueblo pot to the left is typical of the modern, sophisticated work found in galleries in Santa Fe.

Jemez Pueblo is in the Jemez Mountains north of Albuquerque.

Jemez polychrome pot

Jemez pot

The beautifully crafted, three-inch, black-on-red pot to the left was made by C. G. Loretto of Jemez Pueblo.

Figurines have long been a part of Cochiti Pueblo ceramics. Storyteller dolls, first made famous by Helen Cordero, are favorites. The male storyteller doll to the right was fashioned by Ada Suina, who puts coat after coat of slip on her figurines to achieve subtlety and gloss.

Cochiti Pueblo storyteller doll

The figurine in the shape of a turtle at right was made by Helen Cordero. Cochiti Pueblo is between Albuquerque and Santa Fe, adjacent to Cochiti Lake.

Cochiti turtle figurine

P R A C T I C A L
I N F O R M A T I O N

■ Area Code and Time Zone

All New Mexico answers to the 505 area code. The state is in the Mountain time zone.

■ Metric Conversions

1 foot = .305 meters   1 mile = 1.6 kilometers   1 pound = .45 kilograms
Centigrade = Fahrenheit temperature minus 32, divided by 1.8

■ Climate

| CITY | ELEVATION | AVERAGE TEMPERATURE | | | AVERAGE ANNUAL | |
		July High/Low	January High/Low	Extremes High/Low	Rain	Snow
Albuquerque	5,311'	92 65	47 24	107 -17	7.8"	11"
Carlsbad	3,120'	96 68	59 31	115 -7	12.4"	5"
Chaco Canyon	6,175'	91 55	43 12	102 -38	8.5"	19"
Cimarron	6,540'	83 55	47 19	99 -35	15.3"	33"
Santa Fe	7,200'	85 56	42 18	99 -18	13.8"	29"

The sun shines on New Mexico at least 75 percent of the year, making it a great place to visit anytime. Because of altitudes that range from 3,000 feet to 13,000 feet, temperatures vary widely, from 98 degrees Fahrenheit in Deming to 70 degrees in Chama in summer, and from 65 in Roswell to 32 in Taos in winter. Consistent dry air prevents either extreme from being too unpleasant.

Precipitation also varies. It's not unusual for the northern mountains to get 300 inches of snow in winter, compared to one inch annually in the southern desert. Rain is usually in the form of afternoon thunderstorms, which can cause dangerous flash floods. From mid-June through mid-September, campers should not pitch tents along streambeds and should stay on high ground until storms have passed.

The combination of high altitude and intense sun requires the use of sunscreen every day. Dressing in layers is recommended any time of the year.

■ GETTING THERE AND AROUND

■ BY AIR

Albuquerque International Sunport (ABQ) is the gateway to the state for most visitors. It is served by a number of major carriers as well as by two commuter airlines, Mesa Airlines (800-637-2247), which flies from Albuquerque to other cities in New Mexico, and Rio Grande Air (866-929-8646), which flies from Albuquerque to Alamogordo and Taos. The airport is 5 miles south of downtown Albuquerque. *Sunport Boulevard, off I-25; 505-244-7700; www.cabq.gov/airport.*

Santa Fe Municipal Airport (SAF) has commuter service (usually propeller planes) with connections from Albuquerque, Denver, and other Southwestern cities. The airport is 9 miles southwest of downtown. *Airport Road/U.S. 284 west of NM 14; 505-955-2908.*

■ BY BUS

Greyhound Bus Lines provides service to towns and cities throughout the state. *800-231-2222; www.greyhound.com.*

In addition, a number of shuttle services carry people between Albuquerque International Sunport and various hotel and non-hotel locations in Santa Fe. There are more than two dozen round trips daily, and the trip takes about 70 minutes. Two providers are **Sandia Shuttle Express** (505-243-3244 in Albuquerque, 505-474-5696 in Santa Fe, or 888-775-5696; www.sandiashuttle.com) and **Santa Fe Shuttle** (505-243-2300 or 888-833-2300; www.shuttlesantafe.com).

■ BY CAR

Two interstates provide nearly border-to-border access to New Mexico: I-25 runs north-south and I-40 runs east-west; they intersect in the middle of Albuquerque. Other major highways are U.S. 285, which connects the Santa Fe area to southeastern New Mexico, and U.S. 550, which slices through the sandstone mesas of the Jicarilla Apache Reservation, linking the Albuquerque area to the Four Corners.

■ BY TRAIN

Amtrak provides passenger train service along two routes through New Mexico. One route, traveling between Chicago and Los Angeles via Kansas City, Missouri, crosses the northern part of the state, stopping at Raton, Las Vegas (New Mexico), Lamy (15 miles southeast of Santa Fe, with a bus shuttle into the city), Albuquerque, and Gallup. The other route, crossing the country from Orlando, Florida, to Los Angeles, serves the extreme southwest of New Mexico, entering from El Paso, Texas, and stopping in Deming and Lordsburg before exiting the state. *800-872-7245; www.amtrak.com.*

■ FOOD

In one word, what sets New Mexico's cuisine apart is chile. Nowhere else in the country will you be asked to choose the color of the chile topping your food; but here, "Red or green?" is the official state question. In every pocket of the state, no matter how small, you will find restaurants serving all the variations of this ancestral New Mexican fare, from enchiladas to chile rellenos (chiles stuffed with cheese). In the fall, there's a good chance the chile will be fresh from the fields of southern New Mexico. Another specialty is sopaipillas (little pillows), deep-fried bread dough. These are served with a meal, but most New Mexicans save them for dessert, dribbling them with honey. If you're lucky, you might find *calabacitas* on the menu. This concoction of zucchini squash, onions, corn, and green chile is served as a burrito or just on its own. It's best in the fall, when the ingredients are fresh.

Outside the state's few urban areas, unimaginative American food reigns. Steaks, hamburgers, and salad bars are common. National food chains have made their way into the cities, but so have national food trends, which have made dining out much more exciting than it was 10 years ago. You'll find inventive Northern Italian dishes, wood-oven pizzas, tapas, all manner of Asian choices, sushi, and Greek gyros.

■ LODGING

Apart from the occasional "City Slicker" experience on a working cattle ranch, accommodations in New Mexico are basic: motels, a handful of hotels, and an increasing number of bed-and-breakfast inns. You'll find the greatest variety, and the greatest luxury, in the Santa Fe area—from a 1940s-era tourist court to a deluxe guest ranch and spa. Prices range from $60 to more than $500 per night.

Increasingly, B&Bs are providing a cozy alternative to hotels and chain motels in Albuquerque.

Reflecting New Mexico's penchant for individuality are a number of offbeat lodgings. Rustic cabins can be rented in mountain communities, and those in search of a meditative retreat can spend some time at one of the state's monasteries. Guests there must follow the rules, which tend to encourage silence. In Truth or Consequences, your motel might be built atop a natural hot springs. Stargazers will find telescopes at an isolated northern New Mexico inn.

Outside the cities, though, you'll find mostly that the chains rule, with an occasional locally owned motel.

■ RESERVATIONS SERVICES
New Mexico Bed & Breakfast Association. *505-766-5380 or 800-661-6649; www.nmbba.org.*
New Mexico Central Reservations. *800-466-7829; www.nmtravel.com.*
New Mexico Lodging Association. *505-983-4554; www.nmhotels.com.*

■ HOTEL AND MOTEL CHAINS
Best Western. *800-528-1234; www.bestwestern.com.*
Comfort Inn. *800-228-5150; www.comfortinn.com.*
Days Inn. *800-325-2525; www.daysinn.com.*
Doubletree. *800-222-8733; www.doubletree.com.*
Econo Lodge. *800-446-6900; www.econolodge.com.*
Hilton. *800-445-8667; www.hilton.com.*
Holiday Inn. *800-465-4329; www.6c.com.*
Hyatt. *800-233-1234; www.hyatt.com.*
La Quinta. *800-531-5900; www.lq.com.*
Marriott. *800-228-9290; www.marriott.com.*
Quality Inns. *800-228-5151; www.qualityinn.com.*
Radisson. *800-333-3333; www.radisson.com.*
Ramada Inns. *800-272-6232; www.ramada.com.*
Sheraton. *800-325-3535; www.sheraton.com.*
Travelodge. *800-255-3050; www.travelodge.com.*
Wyndham Hotels. *800-996-3426; www.wyndham.com.*

■ Ski Areas

When it comes to skiing, New Mexico is unmatched in its combination of fine powder and cloudless skies. The state receives more sun during the winter than Florida. Nine downhill ski areas, one Nordic center, and countless miles of national forest terrain await visitors wishing to take advantage of such gorgeous conditions. Following is a detailed list of the patrolled areas; for further information on skiing in the state, consult **Ski New Mexico** (505-982-5300; www.skinewmexico.com).

Daily adult lift ticket prices: $ = under $35 $$ = $35–$45 $$$ = over $45

■ Alpine Skiing

Angel Fire Resort

A full-service resort with comfortably wide slopes and panoramic views of the Moreno Valley. Families and beginners enjoy carpet-like, mostly intermediate slopes. There are 67 marked trails, two high-speed detachable quad chairlifts, and three double chairs. Slopeside lodging is available. *Drawer B, Angel Fire, 87710; 800-633-7463. www.angelfireresort.com. $$$*

Pajarito Mountain Ski Area

This day area in the Jemez Mountains is privately owned by the non profit Los Alamos Ski Club. To keep that status, the resort can't advertise its challenging mogul runs and smooth, wide-open beginner and intermediate slopes. It has 37 marked trails, one quad lift, a triple chair, three double chairs, and a surface lift. *Box 155, Los Alamos, 87544; 505-662-572. www.skipajarito.com. $$*

Red River Ski Area

This friendly, full-service resort rises from the center of town, providing runs for the expert, a ski-through "mining camp" for children, 57 marked trails, two triple chairlifts, four double chairs, and one surface lift. *Box 900, Red River, 87558; 505-754-2223. www.redriverskiarea.com. $$$*

Sandia Peak Ski Area

Just across the mountains from Albuquerque (about 45 minutes away), this small day area caters to intermediate skiers and snow-boarders. It can also be reached by the Sandia Peak Tramway, which takes skiers to the area's summit. The area has 25 marked trails, four double chairlifts, and two surface lifts. *10 Tramway Loop NE, Albuquerque, 87122; 505-242-9133. www.sandiapeak.com. $$*

Sipapu

A rustic family-run ski resort in the Carson National Forest, 22 miles south of Taos. This small ski area has recently expanded and now offers 31 trails, two triple chairlifts and two surface lifts. Dormitory-style lodging and cabins. *Route Box 29, Vadito, 87579; 505-587-2240. www.sipapunm.com. $*

Ski Apache

This sweeping day resort on the flanks of Sierra Blanca, about 16 miles northeast of Ruidoso, is owned and operated by the Mescalero Apache Tribe and boasts New Mexico's only gondola. Because of its proximity to Texas and Mexico, you'll hear many foreign accents here. The area has 55 marked trails, one four-passenger gondola, two quad chairlifts, five triple chairs, one double chair, and two surface lifts. *Box 220, Ruidoso, 88345; 505-336-4356. www.skiapache.com. $$$*

Ski Cloudcroft

The welcoming atmosphere of this small, village-owned day area makes it a great place to learn to ski. It caters to beginner and intermediate skiers, and even has a separate lift for inner-tubers. There are 21 marked trails, one double chairlift, and one surface lift. *Box 1290, Cloudcroft, 88317; 505-682-2333. $*

Ski Santa Fe

A day area that offers top-of-the-world views of the Jemez Mountains and the Santa Fe Basin, along with challenging tree skiing and confidence-building trail skiing. At 10,350 feet, its base elevation is the highest in the nation, promising excellent skiing conditions. About 16 miles east of Santa Fe, this area has 45 marked trails, one quad chairlift, one triple chair, two double chairs, and two surface lifts. *2209 Brothers Road, Suite 220, Santa Fe, 87505; 505-982-4429. www.skisantafe.com. $$$*

Taos Ski Valley

This full-service resort 19 miles northeast of Taos is New Mexico's contribution to world-class skiing. Conditions are consistently good, and the ski school is repeatedly ranked the best in the country. The area has 110 marked trails, including a series of legendary chutes; four quad chairlifts, one triple chair, five double chairs, and two surface lifts. Some lodging packages include ski school. *Box 90, Taos Ski Valley, 87525; 505-776-2291. www.skitaos.org. $$$*

■ Nordic Skiing

Enchanted Forest
Skiers and snowshoers alike can enjoy groomed trails that wind among tall pines and aspens and through sweeping meadows. On full-moon nights, tours are offered. Lessons and rentals; no lodging. About 3.5 miles west of Red River. *417 West Main Street, Red River, 87558; 505-754-2374 or 800-966-9381. www.enchantedforestxc.com.*

■ Spas and Hot Springs

Whole books have been dedicated to the naturally heated pockets of water that rise to the surface across New Mexico. These hot springs, where temperatures can reach 130 degrees Fahrenheit, are the result of a violent volcanic past. Most are in isolated locations, often on public lands, and clothing is usually considered optional. The soothing waters are harnessed at licensed public spas in three areas: Jemez Springs, Ojo Caliente, and Truth or Consequences. In the Santa Fe area, two spas offer a broad menu of soaks, but with no natural hot springs to tap into, they heat the water artificially.

■ Jemez Springs

Jemez Springs Bath House
One gurgling fountain serves this quaintly refurbished 19th-century bathhouse on the banks of the Jemez River. Water is piped into private tubs deep enough to submerge a basketball player. Men and women are separated and bathing suits are optional. Also offered are massages, herbal wraps, a fitness room, and an outdoor group hot tub area. Lodging is available in the village. *602 Jemez Springs Plaza, NM 4; 505-829-3303.*

■ Ojo Caliente

Ojo Caliente Mineral Springs
This turn-of-the-century spa may be the only place in the world where arsenic, iron, lithia, soda, and sodium are found in the same place; each bubbling to the surface from its own spring. Men and women have separate bathhouses where they can enjoy an arsenic soak and a wrap in wool blankets. Outside are soda and iron

pools and an Olympic-size swimming pool. A variety of massages and skin treatments are offered. Overnight lodging is available. *50 Los Baños Drive; 505-583-2233 or 800-222-9162. www.ojocalientespa.com.*

■ SANTA FE

SháNah Spa and Wellness Center
Enjoy a treatment designed to detoxify your lymph system or a massage that follows Ayurvedic principles at this top-of-the-line spa, located on the tranquil grounds of the Bishop's Lodge Resort north of Santa Fe. The spa opened in 2002, and treatments, including facials and clay wraps, are offered on their own or as part of a resort package. *1297 Bishop's Lodge Road; 505-819-4000. www.shanahspa.com.*

Ten Thousand Waves
The pools here are not fed by natural springs, but the spa is wonderful anyway. It resembles a Japanese bathhouse, with private and public hot tubs interspersed among the piñon pines and junipers in the foothills outside of town. Massages and a variety of skin treatments are available. *Hyde Park Road; 505-982-9304. www.tenthousandwaves.com.*

■ TRUTH OR CONSEQUENCES

Charles Motel and Bath House
Private tubs, men and women separated. Blanket wrap, massage, and alternative therapies are available. *601 Broadway; 505-894-7154 or 800-317-4518. www.charlesspa.com.*

Firewater Lodge
Soak in private tubs and choose from a variety of healing therapies. *313 Broadway; 505-894-5555.*

Indian Springs Apartments
Water seeps up from a gravel bottom in this continually flowing pool encased in volcanic rock. Motel attached. *218 Austin Street; 505-894-2018.*

Marshall Hot Springs Spa and Resort
Soak in a gravel-bottomed tub fed by natural flowing water, then indulge in a massage. Accommodations are available. *311 Marr Street; 877-894-9286. www.marshallhotsprings.com.*

Riverbend Hot Springs Hostel

Connecting open-air tubs once used as fish tanks overlook the Rio Grande and Turtle Mountain beyond. Motel attached. *100 Austin Street; 505-894-6183. www.nmhotsprings.com.*

Sierra Grande Lodge

The most deluxe spa and lodge in town, it has an extensive menu of treatment options. *501 McAdoo Street; 505-894-6976. www.sierragrandelodge.com.*

■ CAMPING

With more than half of the state's 121,666 square miles designated as public land, you can bet there's a campsite that will meet your needs. Most of the state park campgrounds are equipped with showers, electrical hookups and playgrounds. National Park campgrounds run the gamut, from those equipped with flush toilets to those with outhouses only and no drinkable water. Forest Service campgrounds tend to be more rustic: they have outhouses and you can't always count on finding drinking water. The Bureau of Land Management has a handful of campgrounds, equipped with pit toilets and drinking water. The U.S. Army Corps of Engineers also operates a few campgrounds that have toilets and drinking water. All have reservation systems, except the Bureau of Land Management.

Bureau of Land Management. *505-438-7542; www.nm.blm.gov.*

National Park Service. *800-365-2267; reservations.nps.gov.*

National Recreation Reservation Service (for sites managed by the U.S.D.A., the Forest Service, and the Army Corps of Engineers). *877-444-6777; www.reserveusa.com.*

New Mexico State Parks. 8*77-664-7787; www.nmparks.com for information, www.icampnm.com for reservations.*

Recreation.gov (for sites managed by federal agencies). *www.recreation.gov.*

■ OFFICIAL TOURISM INFORMATION

New Mexico. *800-733-6396; www.newmexico.org.*
Albuquerque. *800-284-2282; www.abqcvb.org.*
Gallup. *505-863-384 or 800-242-4282; www.gallupnm.org.*
Santa Fe. *505-955-6200 or 800-777-2489; www.santafe.org.*
Taos. *505-758-3873 or 800-732-8267; www.taoschamber.com.*

■ Useful Web Sites

Albuquerque Journal. The state's largest newspaper. *www.abqjournal.com.*

Alibi. Excellent source of weekly entertainment options in Albuquerque. *www.alibi.com.*

Collector's Guide to the Art of New Mexico. A virtual guide to galleries, openings and other special events in Taos, Santa Fe, and Albuquerque. *www.collectorsguide.com.*

Discover Navajo. Bills itself as the official guide to the Navajo Nation and includes information about events in Arizona, New Mexico, and Utah. *www.discovernavajo.com.*

Golf Media Group. Guide to golf courses in New Mexico. *www.golfmediagroup.com.*

Indian Pueblo Cultural Center. Gateway to New Mexico's 19 Pueblo Indian tribes. *www.indianpueblo.org.*

Jicarilla Apache Nation. Web site of this Apache tribe in northern New Mexico. *www.jicarillaonline.com.*

Mescalero Apache Reservation. Web site of the Apaches of south-central New Mexico. *www.mescaleronet.com.*

New Mexico Department of Cultural Affairs. About museums and monuments, historic preservation, and New Mexico arts. *www.newmexicoculture.org.*

New Mexico Magazine. Online version of the oldest state magazine in the United States. *www.nmmagazine.com.*

New Mexico State Government. The starting point for just about everything you'll need or want to know about the state. *www.state.nm.us.*

New Mexico State University. A comprehensive look at southern New Mexico's largest university. *www.nmsu.edu.*

New Mexico Wine Growers Association. Find out about the vineyards, the wineries, the festivals, and the award-winning wines. *www.nmwine.com.*

Public Lands Information Center. A good starting point for activities and facilities on public lands. *www.publiclands.org.*

Santa Fe Opera. World-class productions at this outdoor venue. *www.santafeopera.org.*

Santa Fe Reporter. Weekly newspaper carries news and culture coverage and has annual "Best of Santa Fe" guides. *www.sfreporter.com.*

University of New Mexico. Web site of the state's largest university, including its medical center. *www.unm.edu.*

■ Festivals and Events

Something is going on nearly every weekend throughout the year somewhere in New Mexico. Following is just a sampling. For a more complete listing, check the New Mexico Department of Tourism Web site: *www.newmexico.org.*

■ February

Mardi Gras in the Mountains, Red River. Weeklong Cajun-flavored celebration in the ski area and in town. *800-348-6444; www.redrivernewmex.com.*

Mount Taylor Winter Quadrathlon, Grants. Grueling 75-kilometer bike, foot, ski, and snowshoe race up Mount Taylor and back. *505-287-4802.*

World Championship Shovel Races, Angel Fire. Homemade contraptions built atop a snow shovel speed down a ski run. *800-446-8117; www.angelfireresort.com.*

■ March

Rockhound Roundup, Deming. Gemstone collectors gather for weekend of activities, including field trips. *505-546-0348.*

■ April

Trinity Site Tour, Alamogordo. Car caravan to the site of the world's first atomic bomb explosion, now on White Sands Missile Range. First Saturday of the month. *505-835-0424.*

■ May

Mescal Roast, Carlsbad. Traditional Mescalero Apache ceremonies include dancing and cooking and tasting of the mescal cactus. *505-887-5516; www.livingdesertfriends.org.*

Ralph Edwards Fiesta, Truth or Consequences. A parade, carnival, and live music mark this celebration of the television show host behind the town's name. *505-894-2946.*

Tour of the Gila, Silver City. Five days of professional bicycle racing on the roads around Silver City. *505-388-3222; www.tourofthegila.com.*

■ June

Festival Flamenco Internacional, Albuquerque. Two weeks of flamenco workshops and performances with world-class teachers at the University of New Mexico. *505-242-7600; www.feelflamenco.com.*

Old Fort Days, Fort Sumner. Billy the Kid Tombstone Race and Great American Cow Plop highlight this four-day community festival. *505-355-7705.*

■ JULY

Roswell UFO Festival, Roswell. A parade and odd-looking beings are featured at an out-of-this-world weekend festival. *505-623-5695; www.uforoswell.com.*

Santa Fe Chamber Music Festival, Santa Fe. Six weeks of concerts, open rehearsals, outreach presentations and roundtable discussions. *505-983-2075; www.santafechambermusic.org.*

Santa Fe Wine Festival, La Cienega. Sample New Mexico wines at this weekend festival at El Rancho de las Golondrinas. *www.nmwine.net.*

Spanish Market, Santa Fe. Prestigious juried show of traditional Hispanic artworks on Santa Fe Plaza. Last weekend of the month. *505-982-2226; www.spanishmarket.org.*

■ AUGUST

Bat Flight Breakfast, Carlsbad. Enjoy breakfast while watching the bats return to Carlsbad Caverns National Park after a night of foraging. Second Thursday of the month. *505-785-2232; www.nps.gov/cave/batprog.htm.*

Connie Mack World Series, Farmington. National finals for amateur baseball teams. *www.cmws.org.*

Fiesta de San Lorenzo, Bernalillo. Parade and Matachines dances celebrating the town's patron saint. Always held August 9–11. *505-867-3311.*

Great American Duck Race, Deming. Waddlers compete in races on a land course. Fourth weekend of the month. *505-544-0469 or 888-345-1125; www.demingduckrace.com.*

Santa Fe Indian Market, Santa Fe. Largest showing of traditional and contemporary Native American artwork in the country. Third weekend of the month. *505-983-5220; www.swaia.org.*

■ SEPTEMBER

All American Futurity, Ruidoso. World's richest quarter-horse race. *505-378-4431; www.aqha.com.*

Hatch Chile Festival, Hatch. Parade, fiddlers' contest, chile roasting, and cook-off, plus more chile products than you can imagine for sale. Labor Day weekend. *505-267-5050.*

New Mexico State Fair, Albuquerque. Two weeks of agricultural and livestock exhibits, competitions; food, midway, nightly rodeo. Starts the weekend after Labor Day. *505-265-1791; www.nmstatefair.com.*

Santa Fe Fiestas, Santa Fe. Longest-running community celebration in the nation, this weekend event honors the Spanish retaking of the city in 1692. Burning of Zozobra, pet parade, arts and crafts fair. Begins the Thursday after Labor Day. *800-777-2489; www.santafefiesta.org, www.zozobra.com.*

Whole Enchilada Fiesta, Las Cruces. Enjoy a bite of the world's largest enchilada, along with music and crafts booths. *505-541-2444, www.twefie.com.*

■ **OCTOBER**

Albuquerque International Balloon Fiesta, Albuquerque. World's largest gathering of hot-air balloons. For 10 days in early October, they take to the skies every morning in competition. *505-821-1000 or 888-422-7277; www.aibf.org.*

Harvest Festival, La Cienega. See how wheat used to be milled and grapes crushed at El Rancho de las Golondrinas, a living history museum south of Santa Fe. *505-471-2261; www.golondrinas.org.*

■ **NOVEMBER**

Festival of the Cranes, Socorro. Celebrating the return of sandhill cranes and snow geese to Bosque del Apache National Wildlife Refuge. *505-835-1828; www.friendsofthebosque.org/crane.*

■ **DECEMBER**

Santa Fe Film Festival, Santa Fe. Documentaries and independent American films and contemporary films from around the world are seen at this eclectic five-day gathering. *505-988-5225; www.santafefilmfestival.com.*

■ **INDIAN EVENTS**

Throughout the year, Native Americans celebrate the seasons, honor their patron saints, and give blessings through traditional dances. The public is invited to many of these events, but visitors should always remember that they are guests and act respectfully. During the Christmas holidays, dances take place daily at nearly every pueblo; many have Christmas Eve dances and processions. The following is a partial list of special events. For detailed information, including rules regarding photography, check with the tribe directly at the phone number or Web site below. (Information for pueblos without their own Web sites can be found on the individual pueblo pages of the Indian Pueblo Cultural Center.)

Powwow dancers at Taos Pueblo.

Indian Pueblo Cultural Center. *505-843-7270 or 800-766-4405; www.indianpueblo.org.*

Jicarilla Apache Nation. *505-759-3242; www.jicarillaonline.com.*

Mescalero Apache Reservation. *505-464-4494; www.mescaleronet.com.*

Navajo Nation. *520-871-6436; www.discovernavajo.com.*

Acoma Pueblo. *505-552-6604 or 800-747-0181.*

Cochiti Pueblo. *505-465-2244.*

Isleta Pueblo. *505-869-3111.*

Jemez Pueblo. *505-834-7235 or 877-733-5687; www.jemezpueblo.org.*

Laguna Pueblo. *505-552-6654.*

Nambé Pueblo. *505-455-2036.*

Picuris Pueblo. *505-587-2519.*

Pojoaque Pueblo. *505-455-2278.*

San Felipe Pueblo. *505-867-3381.*

San Ildefonso Pueblo. *505-455-2273.*

San Juan Pueblo. *505-852-4400.*

Sandia Pueblo. *505-867-3317; www.sandiapueblo.nsn.us.*

Santa Ana Pueblo. *505-771-6700 or 505-867-3301; www.santaana.org.*
Santa Clara Pueblo. *505-753-7326.*
Santo Domingo Pueblo. *505-462-2214.*
Taos Pueblo. *505-758-1028; www.taospueblo.com.*
Tesuque Pueblo. *505-983-2667.*
Zia Pueblo. *505-867-3304.*
Zuni Pueblo. *505-782-4481.*

■ JANUARY

Feast Day, San Ildefonso. January 23; buffalo, deer, and Comanche dances.
King's Day, most pueblos. January 6; installation of new governors followed by animal dances, including buffalo, deer, eagle, elk.
New Year's Day Dances, most pueblos.

■ FEBRUARY

Candelaria Day Dances, Picuris and San Felipe Pueblos. February 2.

■ MARCH

Easter Dances, most pueblos. The dances include spring corn and basket dances.
St. Joseph Feast Day, Laguna Pueblo. March 19; harvest dance.

■ APRIL

Gathering of Nations Powwow, Albuquerque. One of the largest powwows, with Native Americans from across the country competing in dance contests and the Miss Indian World contest. 505-836-2810; www.gatheringofnations.com.

■ MAY

Red Rocks Arts and Crafts Show, Jemez Pueblo. Pueblo pottery and jewelry for sale.
Santa Cruz Feast Day, Cochiti and Taos Pueblos. May 3; blessing of the fields and corn dance.

■ JUNE

Blessing of the Fields, Tesuque Pueblo. First Saturday of the month; corn dance.
San Antonio Feast Day, Sandia, Santa Clara, and Taos Pueblos. June 13; corn dances at Sandia and Taos Pueblos, Comanche dance at Santa Clara Pueblo.
San Juan Feast Day, San Juan and Taos Pueblos. June 24; buffalo and Comanche dances at San Juan Pueblo, corn dance at Taos Pueblo.
San Pedro Feast Day, Santa Ana Pueblo. June 29; corn dance.

■ July

Feast Day, Laguna, Santa Ana, Taos Pueblos. July 26; corn, harvest, and other dances.

Little Beaver Roundup, Jicarilla Apache Reservation. Second or third weekend; rodeo and powwow.

Mescalero Apache Maidens Puberty Rites and Mountain Spirits Dance, Mescalero. July 4.

Nambé Falls Ceremonial, Nambé Pueblo. July 4; bow and arrow, buffalo, snake, and corn harvest dances by visiting tribes.

San Buenaventura Feast Day, Cochiti Pueblo. July 14; corn dance.

■ August

Feast Day, Santa Clara Pueblo. August 12; buffalo, Comanche, corn dances.

Feast Day, Santo Domingo Pueblo. August 4; one of the biggest corn dances of the year.

Inter-Tribal Indian Ceremonial, Gallup. Early August. Tribes from across North America gather for five days of parades, rodeo, powwow, and arts and crafts fair.

■ September

San Augustine Feast Day, Isleta Pueblo. September 4; harvest dance.

San Geronimo Feast Day, Taos Pueblo. September 30; trade fair, ceremonial foot race, pole climb, and various dances.

■ October

Feast Day, Laguna Pueblo. October 17; harvest and social dances.

San Francisco Feast Day, Nambé Pueblo. October 4; corn or elk dance.

■ November

San Diego Feast Day, Jemez and Tesuque Pueblos. November 12; buffalo, Comanche, corn, and deer dances.

■ December

Nuestra Señora de Guadalupe Feast Day, Jemez, Pojoaque, Santa Clara, Tesuque Pueblos. December 12; bow and arrow, buffalo, and Comanche dances. Matachines dance at Jemez.

(following pages) Church of San Francisco de Asís, Ranchos de Taos.

G L O S S A R Y

acequia   Irrigation ditch.

arroyo   Usually dry, water-carved streambed.

bulto   Small carved wooden sculpture, usually of a saint.

carreta   Rudimentary two-wheeled wooden cart hauled by oxen. They were the only vehicles used in New Mexico in the 1700s and early 1800s.

chamisa   Shrub with slender, flexible branches that display small yellow blooms in the fall. Also known as rabbitbrush.

farolito   Lantern consisting of a small brown paper sack in which a votive candle is placed in sand or dirt. On Christmas Eve, *farolitos* line rooftops, doorways, and sidewalks.

frijoles   Beans.

horno   Beehive-shaped outdoor oven used by rural Hispanics and Pueblo and Navajo Indians, mostly for baking bread.

jacales   Rudimentary buildings in which vertical poles were lashed close together and covered with mud plaster. Roofs were made of dirt supported by vigas and *latillas.*

kachina   Anthropomorphic spirit guide that manifests itself in dancers at Pueblo ceremonies. Also, small wooden figurines that resemble the costumed dancers.

kiva   Circular or rectangular ceremonial chamber, usually subterranean, at a pueblo. Off limits to visitors.

latillas   Small, peeled poles used as ceiling beams. They are placed between larger vigas and sometimes arranged in herringbone patterns.

llano   Plain, as in Llano Estacado.

luminaria   In northern New Mexico, *luminarias* are small bonfires set ablaze on Christmas Eve to warm the hands of neighbors walking among the festive *farolito* displays. Elsewhere in the state, the votive candles placed in paper sacks are referred to as *luminarias.*

petroglyph   Figure carved into rock wall by ancient Indians.

pictograph   Figure painted on rock wall by ancient Indians.

pueblo   Community, village. Early Spanish explorers called the first Indians they encountered "Pueblo" Indians, because their towns resembled Spanish villages.

reredos   Altar screen.

retablo   Two-dimensional line painting of a saint or holy person on a flat board that is designed to hang on a wall.

ristra   String of red chiles, seen hanging outside homes throughout New Mexico.

santo   Image or statue of a holy person or saint, such as a *retablo* or *bulto*.

viga   Exposed roof beam, usually made of pine, that juts from the sides of an adobe building.

The writing on the walls at Petroglyph National Monument.

RECOMMENDED
R E A D I N G

■ FICTION

Abbey, Edward. *The Brave Cowboy* (1956) and *Fire on the Mountain* (1962). Both novels describe a stubborn man rooted to the state.

Anaya, Rudolfo. *Bless Me, Ultima* (1972) and *Heart of Aztlan* (1976). Mixes folklore with fiction in two books about growing up Hispanic in New Mexico.

Bradford, Richard. *Red Sky at Morning* (1968). A coming-of-age story about a young boy who is shipped off to relatives in rural New Mexico when his father is called to serve in World War II.

Hillerman, Tony. *Dance Hall of the Dead* (1973), *People of Darkness* (1980), *Dark Wind* (1982), *Ghostway* (1984), *Skinwalkers* (1986), *Thief of Time* (1988), and *Talking God* (1989). Takes readers along on the fictitious crime-solving paths of Jim Chee and Joe Leaphorn, officers with the Navajo Tribal Police. His series of murder mysteries are a wonderful introduction to Navajo culture.

Laughlin, Ruth. *The Wind Leaves No Shadow* (1948). Historical novel traces the spicy career of Doña Tules Barceló, influential owner of a gambling house in the 1830s, when New Mexico was still part of the Mexican frontier.

Nichols, John. *The Milagro Beanfield War* (1974), *The Magic Journey* (1978), and *Nirvana Blues* (1981). A Taos resident, Nichols shares his love and reverence for New Mexico in this trilogy.

Richter, Conrad. *Sea of Grass* (1936). A slice of life on the eastern New Mexico plains in the late 19th century.

■ **NONFICTION**

Bandelier, Adolf. *Delight Makers* (1971). Re-creates Indian life along Bandelier National Monument's Frijoles Creek.

Bunting, Bainbridge. *John Gaw Meem: Southwestern Architect* (1983). A look at the man behind some of the state's best examples of Spanish-Pueblo architecture.

Burdett, William H., ed. *Roads of New Mexico* (1990). Atlas with historical data, weather information, a list of movies filmed here, and incredible detail showing unnamed gravel roads, water tanks, and fence lines.

Chronic, Halka. *Roadside Geology of New Mexico* (1987). A good book to have handy when cruising the highways. It discusses the state's fascinating geology, route by route.

Church, Peggy Pond. *The House at Otowi Bridge* (1959). Tells the story of Edith Warner, who lived alongside the Rio Grande, maintaining friendships with the San Ildefonso Indians and the scientists who were developing the world's first atomic bomb at nearby Los Alamos.

Coleman, Jane Candia. *Stories from Mesa Country* (1991). Essays about women surviving among the West's rugged deserts and mountains. She writes from a ranch in New Mexico's boot heel.

Dutton, Bertha. *American Indians of the Southwest* (1983). An exhaustive study of the region's Native Americans.

Horgan, Paul. *Great River: The Rio Grande in North American History* (1968). Deep and beautifully descriptive, it gives wonderful insight into the region as it matured from a primitive hunting ground to statehood.

Lavender, David. *The Trail to Santa Fe* (1958). A compact book that traces the birth and death of the Santa Fe Trail.

Lisle, Laurie. *Portrait of an Artist: A Biography of Georgia O'Keeffe* (1980). A well-researched biography.

Looney, Ralph. *Haunted Highways* (1979). Ghost towns revisited.

O'Keeffe, Georgia. *Georgia O'Keeffe* (1976). A full-color collection of O'Keeffe's work, with accompanying text written by the artist.

Piper, Ti. *Fishing in New Mexico* (1989). Written for fishing fanatics, it details the state's stream and lake offerings, best bait, and best time to go.

Roberts, Susan and Calvin. *New Mexico* (1988). A comprehensive and readable history.

Schaafsma, Polly. *Indian Rock Art of the Southwest* (1980). The definitive book on Indian petroglyphs and pictographs.

Simmons, Marc. *New Mexico: An Interpretive History* (1977) and *Albuquerque, A Narrative History* (1982). Lively and easy to read.

Utley, Robert. *Billy the Kid: A Short and Violent Life* (1989). Among the more accurate texts on the subject.

Varney, Philip. *New Mexico's Best Ghost Towns* (1987). A comprehensive treatment.

I N D E X

COMPASS AMERICAN GUIDES

Alaska	Kentucky	Pennsylvania
American Southwest	Las Vegas	Santa Fe
Arizona	Maine	South Carolina
Boston	Manhattan	South Dakota
California Wine Country	Massachusetts	Tennessee
Cape Cod	Michigan	Texas
Chicago	Minnesota	Utah
Coastal California	Montana	Vermont
Colorado	New Hampshire	Virginia
Connecticut & Rhode Island	New Mexico	Washington
Florida	New Orleans	Washington Wine Country
Georgia	North Carolina	Wisconsin
Gulf South	Oregon	Wyoming
Hawaii	Oregon Wine Country	
Idaho	Pacific Northwest	

Compass American Guides are available at special discounts for bulk purchases for sales promotions or premiums. Special editions, including personalized covers, excerpts of existing guides, and corporate imprints, can be created in large quantities for special needs. For more information, contact your local bookseller or write to Special Markets/Premium Sales, Fodor's Travel Publications, 1745 Broadway, MD 6-2, New York, NY 10019, or e-mail specialmarkets@randomhouse.com

COMPASS AMERICAN GUIDES

Critics, booksellers, and travelers all agree: you're lost without a Compass.

"This splendid series provides exactly the sort of historical and cultural detail about North American destinations that curious-minded travelers need."
—*Washington Post*

"This is a series that constantly stuns us . . . no guide with photos this good should have writing this good. But it does." —*New York Daily News*

"Of the many guidebooks on the market, few are as visually stimulating, as thoroughly researched, or as lively written as the Compass American Guide series."
—*Chicago Tribune*

"Good to read ahead of time, then take along so you don't miss anything."
—*San Diego Magazine*

"Magnificent photography. First rate."—*Money*

"Written by longtime residents of each destination . . . these handsome and literate guides are strong on history and culture, and illustrated with gorgeous photos."
—*San Francisco Chronicle*

"The color photographs sparkle, the archival illustrations illuminate windows to the past, and the writing is usually of the utmost caliber." —*Michigan Tribune*

"Class acts, worth reading and shelving for keeps even if you're not a traveler. "
—*New Orleans Times-Picayune*

"Beautiful photographs and literate writing are the hallmarks of the Compass guides." —*Nashville Tennessean*

"History, geography, and wanderlust converge in these well-conceived books."
—*Raleigh News & Observer*

"Oh, my goodness! What a gorgeous series this is."—*Booklist*

ACKNOWLEDGMENTS

■ FROM THE AUTHOR

Grateful appreciation is due to Fritz Thompson, a Wagon Mound native son, for his editorial comments and boundless knowledge of New Mexico's hidden treasures shared over numerous green chile enchilada lunches. Thanks also go to Phoebe Spencer for her unwavering support and to Martin Frentzel for his professional guidance. Recognition also goes to Kit Duane, editor of the original edition of this book, for her patience and encouragement, and to my Fodor's editor, Kristin Moehlmann, whose fresh perspective brought new life to the current edition of the book.

■ FROM THE PUBLISHER

Compass American Guides would like to thank Rachel Elson for copyediting the manuscript, Ellen Klages for proofreading it, and Joan Stout for indexing it.

Compass American Guides is grateful to the following individuals and institutions for the use of their photographs or illustrations:
Albuquerque Museum/Center for Southwest Research, p. 41 top; Albuquerque Museum/University of New Mexico Architecture Department, p. 41 bottom; Paul Chesley, pp. 17, 173, 180, 192, 219, 255, 266; Michael Freeman, pp. 64, 73, 97, 100, 131, 156, 185, 238, 240; Eduardo Fuss, p. 57, 278–281; Kerrick James, pp. 12–13, 14, 20, 35, 44–45, 47, 48, 52, 54, 55, 58, 61, 62, 68–69, 77, 81, 89, 95, 98, 101, 105, 106, 110–111, 114–115, 119, 123, 137, 141, 142, 145, 149, 152–153, 165, 167, 169, 199, 200–201, 212, 217, 221, 226, 228–229, 242, 243, 246, 269, 272, 295, 298–299, 301; Museum of Fine Arts, Boston, p. 86 (Gift of the William H. Lane Foundation); Museum of New Mexico, pp. 25 (Neg. No. 20206), 31 (7152), 38 (11826), 71 (photo by Nathan Kendall; 21684), 75 (T. Harmon Parkhurst; 3895), 83 (Ben Wittick; 15588), 91 (11409), 92 (Wyatt Davis; 50086), 116 (99869), 118 (Charles E. Lord; 90663) 121 (9763), 127 (Robert H; Martin; 41984), 139 (Wesley Bradfield; 12986), 174 (44178), 179 (Ben Wittick; 16443), 189 (C.S. Fly; 2115), 191 (J.R. Riddle; 14523), 193 (11933), 203 (35871), 207 (28908), 209 (W.H. Horne Co.; 13785), 210

(90515), 215 (O.C. Hinman; 136499), 224 (Edwin Wilkinson; 90510), 250–251 (8987), 253 (Ralph H. Anderson; 129962), 257 (5324), 258 (45011); New Mexico Museum of Space History, p. 230 (Ron Keller); Northern Arizona University, Specal Collections and Archives Department, p. 171; Polly Mullen Photography/United World College, p. 262; U. S. Forest Service, p. 236.

The extract (pp. 72–73) from *Great River: The Rio Grande in North American History,* by Paul Horgan, is reprinted by permission of Wesleyan University Press. The extract (p. 232) from *Fire on the Mountain,* by Edward Abbey, is reprinted by permission of Don Congdon Associates, Inc. Copyright © 1962 by Edward Abbey, renewed 1990 by Clarke Abbey.

■ About the Author

Nancy Harbert has been a New Mexico resident since 1979. She moved to the state from Colorado to work for the *New Mexican,* Santa Fe's daily newspaper, and subsequently covered the state legislature for United Press International. She joined the *Albuquerque Journal* in its Las Cruces bureau in 1981, moving to the main office in Albuquerque in 1982, and eventually becoming assistant state editor. She has been a freelance writer for the past 18 years, contributing regularly to *Time* and *New Mexico* magazines. Her articles have also been published in the *New York Times* and regional newspapers.

■ About the Photographers

Paul Chesley has been a freelance photographer with the National Geographic Society since 1975. He has had exhibitions in museums in London, Tokyo, New York, and Honolulu, and his photographic essays have appeared in *Life, Fortune, Time, Newsweek, Stern/Geo,* and *Paris Match* magazines. He has participated in 14 Day in the Life projects around the world. Paul lives in Aspen, Colorado.

Kerrick James is well known for his photography of the Southwest. In addition to being featured in Compass American Guides' *Arizona, Las Vegas, New Mexico, San Francisco,* and *The American Southwest,* his work has provided the covers for two National Geographic books and appears frequently in *Arizona Highways, Outside,* and *Sunset* magazines. He lives with his wife and sons in Mesa, Arizona, and teaches photo workshops in Arizona and Utah.

Michael Freeman, based in London, England, has traveled the globe for both British and American publishers. He has photographed more than 40 articles for *Smithsonian Magazine.* In addition, he teaches photography and has written numerous books on the subject, including the best-selling *Complete Guide to Digital Photography* (2003) His photographs also appear in *Adobe: Building and Living with Earth* (1994).